I'M JUST DEAD, I'M NOT GONE

I'M JUST DEAD,
I'M NOT GONE

Jim Dickinson

Edited and with an Introduction by Ernest Suarez

University Press of Mississippi ★ Jackson

www.upress.state.ms.us

Designed by Peter D. Halverson

The University Press of Mississippi is a member of the
Association of American University Presses.

Portions of this work have previously appeared in *Oxford American*
(Issue 83, Winter 2013).

All photos courtesy of the Dickinson family unless otherwise stated.

First printing 2017
∞

Library of Congress Cataloging-in-Publication Data

Names: Dickinson, James Luther | Suarez, Ernest, editor.
Title: I'm just dead, I'm not gone / Jim Dickinson ; edited and with an
introduction by Ernest Suarez.
Description: Jackson : University Press of Mississippi, [2017] | Includes
index.
Identifiers: LCCN 2016036375 | ISBN 9781496810540 (cloth : alk. paper)
Subjects: LCSH: Dickinson, James Luther. | Sound recording executives and
producers—United States—Biography. | LCGFT: Biographies.
Classification: LCC ML429.D526 A3 2017 | DDC 781.64092 [B]—dc23 LC record available
at https://lccn.loc.gov/2016036375

British Library Cataloging-in-Publication Data available

About Jim Dickinson . . .

"Bob said to me, 'If you've got Dickinson, you don't need anybody else.'"
—DANIEL LANOIS, *Harp* magazine

"He's this . . . This genius from down around Memphis. The man's a damn resource. Jim Dickinson's always been a fabulous producer. It's just that most of what he's done has been invisible to the naked eye."
—RY COODER

"You see, Ladies and Gentlemen, I have always suspected that Jim has visited this planet several times before. How else could he be so intuitively creative and knowledgeable?"
—TOM DOWD, producer/engineer, Atlantic Records

"Jim Dickinson is an improbable recombinant—a demonic original Sun Records rocker who reads Faulkner and Robert Penn Warren. He can play the shit out of his National Steel and then jump on the piano and lay down the no doubt best key of C picking you're ever going to hear."
—JERRY WEXLER, Atlantic Records

"First time I met Jim Dickinson, he rented the studio. Man, he like to scare me to death. I'd just come off the road with Jerry Lee, and you know, he's kicking over piano stools. Jim, he was wilder'n Jerry Lee. But I loved his music."
—ROLAND JANES, engineer and session guitarist, Sun Records

"Dickinson had a very spontaneous approach to recording and showed me a lot about making truly untamed music."
—ALEX CHILTON, Box Tops/Big Star

"Dickinson is great. I tried to get him to play on my solo album but he had moved and nobody had his current phone number."
—BILL WYMAN, the Rolling Stones

"In his book, *Country*, Nick Tosches calls Jim Dickinson's debut album 'one of the most bizarrely powerful musics of this century.'"
—ROBERT PALMER, author of *Deep Blues*

"When I think of Jim, I can't help but think of the work he's done for my pictures with Ry Cooder. I certainly can't imagine anyone I'd rather sit down with and talk about the very brief era when rock 'n' roll was something other than pop music. His tastes agree with mine, which proves I must know something about music, because he knows more than anyone."
—WALTER HILL, director

"My father is a treasure. His presence inspires my respect, creativity, and love. I love playing his music and playing my music for him. He is a master . . ."
—LUTHER ANDREWS DICKINSON, North Mississippi Allstars

"When I think of my father, I think of a hard but sensitive man, youthful but wise. As a producer he shows me how to bring the best out of my music. As a father, he helps me to bring the best out of my person. Jim Dickinson will always be my greatest mentor and Jim Dickinson's music will always be my greatest influence. I'll always be proud when I think of my father."
—CODY TAYLOR DICKINSON, North Mississippi Allstars, producer of *Take Me to the River*

"I no longer think of Jim Dickinson as a guy who makes music like no one else, though that is sure enough true. I think of him and the music he makes as something a lot bigger. Sort of like the sky: dark one moment, full of light another, thundering and blowing you away awhile then sending breezes of ramshackle-rigged transcendent grace to raise and deliver you from it all."
—NICK TOSCHES, from the liner notes to "Dinosaurs Run In Circles."

ODE TO JIM D.

SHADES OF ANTICIPATION IS THE EVER PRESENT GLINT IN JIM D'S EYE.
HEARING STRANGE NOISES THAT OTHERS LET PASS BY.
MUSIC THAT MAKES YOU SHOUT WALK THE BACKS OF GOSPEL BENCHES,
MAKES YOU MOAN YES, EVEN CRY
IT COULD BE- IT MAY BE- IT IS
JIM D'S SOUL OF SOUND BOUNCING OFF THE SKY.

SAM PHILLIPS
ONWARD AND UPWARD

CONTENTS

PART II: EPILOGUE AND THE BIBLICAL CHAPTERS

ACKNOWLEDGMENTS

James Luther ("Jim") Dickinson described his handwriting as resembling that of a schizophrenic six-year-old boy or Beethoven. Dickinson's widow Mary Lindsay and his son Luther spent months transcribing Jim's handwritten manuscript of *I'm Just Dead, I'm Not Gone*. Son Cody was the go-to guy if there were any questions.

Before he passed, Jim chose Birdman Records' David Katznelson to work with Luther and Mary Lindsay on the manuscript. Thank you, David, for your brilliant contributions. *I'm Just Dead, I'm Not Gone* would not be the same book without you.

Our friend and colleague Robert Gordon introduced Mary Lindsay to Microsoft Word. "It's the industry standard," said Robert. "The manuscript must be in Microsoft Word before you can submit it." Thus began one of the worst years of Mary Lindsay's life. Word seemed crazy, headstrong, erratic, and uncontrollable. Many thanks to Andrew Paslay. With your patient tutoring, we did it!

Jim's working title for *I'm Just Dead, I'm Not Gone* was *The Search for Blind Lemon*. When Mary Lindsay decided to prepare a compilation of music, film, video, and text to present it to the public, John Fry made the full facilities of his Ardent Recording Studios, Memphis, Tennessee, available to her. John, you left us too soon and are sadly missed. You and Jim must be smiling down on us from Heaven. "Production *in absentia* is the highest art."

The efforts of Elizabeth Montgomery-Brown, Jody Stephens, Adam Hill, Chris Jackson, and others at Ardent were invaluable. Rachel Hurley put together the presentation and a gorgeous Facebook page, *Jim Dickinson's Legacy*. Thanks to you all. Your loving care for us is never-ending.

The Search for Blind Lemon program had a rousing start. With Dr. William Ferris's nod of approval, Mary Lindsay's intern Reed Turchi put together a fantastic day celebrating Jim Dickinson's genius, beginning with

Mary Lindsay's presentation of *The Search for Blind Lemon* in the Wilson Library at the University of North Carolina, Chapel Hill, and ending with a concert of live music from Big Star's *Third* album, originally produced by Jim Dickinson. Thank you, Reed. As Dr. Ferris put it, "Reed Turchi can move mountains."

When portions of *The Search for Blind Lemon* were being excerpted for publication in the *Oxford American* magazine, Laura Foreman and Bill Newport protected us from contractual problems. Thank you.

Former background singer and lawyer Saul Belz has been effective through countless legal complications during Jim's career and ever after. We sleep better at night due to your outstanding efforts on behalf of Jim and his estate. Thank you, dear friend.

One day the phone rang. When Mary Lindsay answered it, Sarah Lazin introduced herself. (Writer Holly George-Warren had mentioned her to Mary Lindsay as a top-notch literary agent.) Sarah said, "Mojo Nixon told me about Jim's book when we met at South by Southwest music conference in Austin. I'd like to read it." Thank you, Mojo. You couldn't have made a better connection for us.

Dr. David Evans invited Mary Lindsay to give a presentation of *The Search for Blind Lemon* to his History of Memphis Music class at the University of Memphis. Afterward, Dr. Evans said the manuscript was entertaining and educational and invited Mary Lindsay to submit it to the University Press of Mississippi, where it was not accepted for publication. "The manuscript needs to be cut, edited, and have an introduction written," judged Dr. Evans.

About this time Mary Lindsay read a comment by Ernest Suarez published in the *Washington Post*: "The music of the Dickinson family is a major thread in American Art." Mary Lindsay called Luther: "I like the way this man thinks. Maybe he could be our editor. Can you get in touch with him?" "Not a problem," said Luther. "He's a friend of mine. We're having lunch next week." Ernest Suarez has been angelic in his devotion to Jim and his book. He will always live large in our hearts. Thank you, Ernest. You have our gratitude. Your editing prowess and heartrending introduction tell readers who Jim was, what he did, and why they should care. Your work led to the manuscript's acceptance for publication.

Sarah Lazin and her assistant, Julia Conrad, shepherded Jim's manuscript through the process of making a deal with primo Editor-In-Chief Craig Gill of the University Press of Mississippi. Sarah, thank you for representing our interests with your much-appreciated tact and professionalism.

Craig, words cannot express our admiration for the expertise you gave the publication of Jim's book, now called *I'm Just Dead, I'm Not Gone*. Your devotion made us feel at home. Your assistants Katie Keene and McRae intern Emily Bandy were kind yet strict in insisting we meet our deadlines. Good job.

David Leonard donated his time and artistry to ready the photographs for publication. Thank you!

Many people have supported us over the years as we struggled to get *I'm Just Dead, I'm Not Gone* published. We wish we could mention every one of you. Please know that you are appreciated.

"I'm just dead, I'm not gone," is Jim's self-penned epitaph.

MARY LINDSAY DICKINSON
Zebra Ranch
Independence, Mississippi

A complete discography of Jim's work can be found at WangDangDula.com (http://wdd.mbnet.fi/jimdickinson.htm).

I'M JUST DEAD, I'M NOT GONE

INTRODUCTION

Jim Dickinson and his family's musical legacy form an important thread in the United States' cultural tapestry. Dickinson played with and produced performers as diverse as Aretha Franklin, the Rolling Stones, Ry Cooder, Duane Allman, Arlo Guthrie, and Albert King. Those experiences make for intriguing reading, but Jim didn't want to write a book that, as he put it, announced "Here's me with Ringo."

I'm Just Dead, I'm Not Gone is a deeply personal chronicle of the genesis and development of the Dickinson family's embrace of "primitive modernism," Jim's term for "a modernized history of American Roots music painted in broad strokes and basic colors." He felt his early experiences were the most crucial, and that honing his production chops at Sun, Ardent, American, and Criteria from Sam Phillips, John Fry, Chips Moman, and Jerry Wexler formed the underpinnings of his art. He wanted to explain how Alec (the family yardman), WDIA, Dewey Philips, Furry Lewis, Will Shade, and Howlin' Wolf shaped his personal taste and life.

Jim Dickinson was, above all, an artist. In addition to playing, producing, and composing music, he wrote, painted, made films, and directed and acted in plays. His touchstone works of art were Miles Davis's *Sketches of Spain*, Langston Hughes and Charles Mingus's collaboration of *The Weary Blues*, Jack Kerouac's *On the Road*, and William Faulkner's *Absalom, Absalom!* The pathos and depth of Davis's recording and of Hughes's verse inspired him, and Kerouac's celebration of spontaneity and romantic individualism spoke to his own iconoclastic nature. But Dickinson's embrace of Faulkner is perhaps the most telling. Faulkner modeled his fictional Mississippi county, Yoknapatawpha, on Lafayette and bordering counties, including parts of the Hill Country, the Dickinson family's longtime home. Nonetheless, as Ralph Ellison noted, "for all his concern with the South, Faulkner was actually seeking out the nature of man." Similarly, while Dickinson's connection to Memphis and the Hill

Country are the bedrock of his musical practices, he and his family have used that foundation to create art with global resonance.

Dickinson preached the miracle of Memphis music, a passion that began to stir in the summer of 1949, when as a seven-year-old he and his family moved from Chicago and bought a house east of the Memphis city limits on a three-acre lot surrounded by cotton fields and farms. Dickinson's relationship with the family's yardman—whom Jim calls "his greatest teacher"—changed his life. At lunchtime Alec would come in the house and listen to WDIA, the first radio station programmed by African Americans for an African American audience. Jim listened intently to country and electric blues, "wild music that seemed about to spin out of control." Later he accompanied his father to work downtown, and beheld "four black men dressed like hobos or field hands . . . singing and playing—a 4-string tenor guitar, a violin, a washboard with drumsticks, and a string tied to a broomstick and run through a washtub—the strangest music I had ever heard." Later he went to the library and checked out Samuel B. Charters's *The Country Blues*, and realized that he'd "seen the great Will Shade and the Memphis Jug Band in the alley, with Charlie Burse on guitar and his brother, Good Kid, on washboard."

Dickinson's experiences were extraordinary but not exceptional. Memphis was a reflection of what Greil Marcus famously dubbed "the old, weird America" when describing the provocative confluence of blues, country, and folk music on Harry Smith's idiosyncratic *Anthology of American Folk Music* (1952), a box set often credited with jumpstarting the folk and blues revival of the fifties and sixties. In the fifties Memphis had a growing population of roughly 500,000, almost equally divided between whites and blacks. Neighborhoods, schools, churches, and centers of entertainment were segregated. Dickinson points out that at the time, black and white musicians "did not mix musically or racially, except in the minds of Dewey Phillips and the generation of white boys who sought out blues, jazz, howling hillbillies on the Grand Ol' Opry, and moaning bluesmen from Randy's Record Mart."

The blues, Elvis, and early rock 'n' roll prompted Dickinson and many young whites to question the racial divide. In 1949 RCA had introduced the 45-rpm record, a perfect venue for a three-minute blues or rock 'n' roll song. Radio and a bevy of knowledgeable and innovative disk jockeys, including Phillips and Rufus Thomas, turned Dickinson and other teenagers on to Howlin' Wolf, Muddy Waters, John Lee Hooker, and other greats who hailed from Mississippi and played the clubs on Beale Street, a locale Dickinson calls the "magic, Harlem of the South," a wonderland that pulsed with sounds that changed music all over the world and where Dickinson procured his first guitar—a white, gold-flecked Stratoline—at a pawn shop on the corner of Beale and Pontotoc.

Memphis also endowed Dickinson with a sense of theatricality, a gift he cultivated as a student at Baylor University and Memphis State University. He recalls that "Memphis was strange and wonderful in the 1950s," a city many of his boyhood and teenage heroes regularly graced. Lash LaRue, a rebellious caped movie-star cowboy, brought his rodeo revue to town and got busted for pilfering three typewriters and an adding machine. Sputnik Monroe, a 220-pound white professional wrestler, became a hero to many local African Americans for consistently acknowledging their presence in the remote regions of segregated Ellis Auditorium (where Dickinson would also see Elvis perform). When police arrested Sputnik for vagrancy on Beale Street—a trumped-up charge for hanging out with blacks—he hired a black attorney to defend him in court. Sputnik later enlisted the twelve-year-old son of record executive Sam Phillips—the man who launched Elvis—to pose and perform as the "World's Most Perfectly Formed Midget Wrestler." During teenage dance concerts, Bullet, a "legless, armless torso and head of a bald black man," would be carried on stage, where he "bellowed like a banshee for two or three excruciating minutes" before being carried off. With typical insight and compassion, Dickinson observes that Bullet must have "hated the audience that called his phantom name. He blew them away with screams from hell, like a dragon breathing fire. His howl's burning sound seared the audience's soul in a moment of ultimate release."

I'm Just Dead, I'm Not Gone makes apparent another part of Dickinson's consciousness, a belief in the mysterious that at times took the form of prophecy, karma, serendipity, and most importantly, a heartfelt conviction in the enigmatic connection between place and creativity. After visiting Blind Lemon's grave on the Texas flatlands, Dickinson, then a college student at Baylor, wondered "What was it in the eternal darkness of his world that had caused him to sing out?" and plotted his return to Memphis, where he "searched for traces of musicians in Sam Charters's book." He looked up Gus Cannon and Furry Lewis, began staging plays, founded what would become the annual Memphis Country Blues Festival, started recording, and met his bride-to-be, Mary Lindsay Andrews, a beautiful equestrian whose intelligence, devotion, and talents are the heart of the Dickinson family's triumphs.

During the fifties and early sixties, Dickinson helped cultivate the Beat, jazz poetry, and experimental art scenes that budded in Memphis. Steve Cropper, Duck Dunn, and Al Jackson Jr., who would form the house band at Stax, and a host of other musicians whose music had national impact were youngsters playing around town. Jimmy Crosthwait, a washboard player and future puppeteer, beat on bongos and read poetry in coffeehouses. He would go on to become part of the Electric Circus in the New York City's East Village and to play with Dickinson in Mud Boy and the Neutrons, a performance art electric blues band. Dickinson and Stanley Booth—who would become an important music critic, best known for his authoritative *The True Adventure of the Rolling Stones*—met at Memphis State University, delved into the city's musical history, and went on to share experiences at Muscle Shoals and Criteria studios.

Dickinson composed *I'm Just Dead, I'm Not Gone* over several decades. He tended to write in longhand in the mornings; Mary Lindsay transcribed. His last wishes at his home in rural Coldwater, Mississippi (where Mary Lindsay still runs Zebra Ranch Recording Studio), concerned his memoir, particularly its haunting and poetic conclusion. As an ambulance raced toward him for the last ride away from his beloved home, he instructed his son Luther to "find the Memphis music/biblical chapters. They are in the zebra notebook in the record crate, under the stack of ordered chaos," and remarked, "I told the story I wanted to tell."

The tale he wanted to tell is a full account of his early career, and sets the stage for a narrative that ranges beyond the period covered by *I'm Just Dead, I'm Not Gone*; it provides the framework for the ways the Dickinson family has continued to help shape and amplify the musical heritage of Memphis, the surrounding Mississippi Hill Country, the United States, and even the world. Jim Dickinson's legacy remains alive in his sons Luther and Cody's music and films. It remains alive in the work of his "victims," the many artists he produced and inspired, including Ry Cooder, John Hiatt, Albert King, Amy LaVere, the Replacements, Toots and the Maytals, Big Star, and Luther and Cody's band, North Mississippi Allstars. It remains alive at Zebra Ranch, where music continues to be created in and by the spirit reflected in Dickinson's characteristically philosophic "production manifesto":

The unretainable nature of the present creates in Man a desire to capture the moment. Our fears of extinction compel us to record—to re-create—the ritual ceremony. From the first hand-print cave painting to the most modern computer art, it is the human condition to seek immortality. Life is fleeting. Art is long. A record is a "totem," a document of a unique, unrepeatable event worthy of preservation and able to sustain historic life. The essence of the event is its soul.

In 1998 Bob Dylan called Dickinson his "brother" during his televised acceptance of the Grammy Award for Album of the Year for *Time Out of Mind*, on which Jim played keyboards. In 2007 Jim received the Lifetime Achievement Award for Engineering and Production from the Americana Music Association. In 2011 he received a Brass Note on the Beale Street Walk of Fame in Memphis, and was inducted into the Mississippi Music Hall of Fame alongside "Big Joe" Williams and Elmore James. In 2012 he joined W. C. Handy, Howlin' Wolf, Elvis, B.B. King, Otis Redding, Dewey Phillips, Jerry Lee Lewis, Sam Phillips, Al Green, Isaac Hayes, ZZ Top, and others as one of twenty-five inaugural inductees into the Memphis Music Hall of Fame. *I'm Just Dead, I'm Not Gone* tells us where it all began through Dickinson's distinctive blend of intelligence, humor, wit, and candor.

William Faulkner observed, "The past isn't dead. It isn't even past." Dickinson's spirit lives in the music he created and inspired, in his art, and in his immediate and extended family's achievements. It resides in Luther's description of the emotional intelligence that he and Cody inherited from their father and that informs the power and integrity of the Dickinson family's creative practice: "You have to reach down in your gut and pull out your art in a way that connects the past to this day and age." *I'm Just Dead, I'm Not Gone* digs deeply, and excavates the settings, people, and passions that inspired Dickinson's last words: "I have given my life to Memphis music and it has given me back a hundredfold."

ERNEST SUAREZ
Washington, DC

Part I

THE SEARCH FOR BLIND LEMON
(1941–1971)

Chapter 1

WENT TO SEE THE GYPSY
(1961)

BE STILL AND KNOW THAT THERE IS GOD read the sign in the old woman's yard. There were cages crowded with chickens and rabbits and a pen with goats. It looked like a gypsy camp. Locals believed she held ritual sacrifices and read the still warm entrails to foretell the future. The sign on the trailer read, OPHELIA HARWOOD—CONSULTANT PSYCHOLOGIST. Framed certificates and diplomas filled the walls inside, every available surface covered with stacks of books and magazines. She sat across from me studying a lunar chart and muttering, "Boy, you don't know what you want, do ya?"

"No, ma'am," I said, truthfully.

Spring 1961, Waco, Texas: my failed freshman year of college. Ophelia Harwood's trailer camp lay at the mouth of Cameron Park, sprawling acres of trees, bushes, and vines, some completely wild and some sculpted into otherworldly grottoes with monolithic stones and strange statues. The meandering Brazos River's prehistoric canyons and cliffs had been carved with Indian legends of Lovers' Leap. It was easy to get lost in Cameron Park. Students were warned to stay away after dark with stories of murderous "chain gangs" and the Hook Man. We spent many drunken nights driving the dark tree-tunneled narrow winding roads. I had seen Ophelia Harwood's camp and read the sign many times that year. So there I sat:

> Flunking out of school
> In dread fear of being drafted
> Crazed by drink and drugs
> Struggling to finish my so-called
> novel begun in Memphis long ago

I told her I wanted to be a writer.

She grunted, "You might do some writing later on but you better stick to the music. It comes naturally to you."

I hadn't told her I played music!

"You're in the middle of a fourteen-year slump. Nothin' you can do about it. Just ride it out. I got Scorpios coming to me worse off than you. One committed suicide. Stick with the music. You might write a couple of books later, but now you're too confused."

She told me things about my past and my future. She told me my father was sick and that was the source of our conflict. She told me my grandmother was going to die; my family was going to move. She told me not to get married because I didn't know what I wanted. She wished me luck. "You're going to need it," she said.

I left the gypsy and started drinking. The gypsy had done little to alleviate my anxiety. Ghosts from home called me in the Texas night. What had brought me to the cliff's edge? Who, where, and what were the people, places, and chain of events that brought me face to face with the terror that comes in the night?

Set the controls on the way-back machine for once upon a time, to the beginning. Out of the primordial ooze comes the Swamp Beast, dripping slime and tadpoles. Sharpen up your razor; pour gin in your glass. Play me some blues, my man, and take it back one night at a time. Run it by again and let me shoot at it.

Chapter 2

"MY FATHER WAS A TRAVELIN' MAN . . ."
(1787–1949)

My family tree includes John Dickinson, a signer of the Constitution of the United States; Almeron Dickinson, a defender of the Alamo; and Charles Dickinson, who ended up on the losing end of a duel with Andrew Jackson (a family villain). My Great Uncle Tom, a one-armed railroad lawyer who rolled cigarettes on his starched dress shirt's empty sleeve, kept the family history. He told it to me in a cracked old voice through tobacco-yellowed snaggleteeth.

My father, Big Jim, liked things in order: columns of numbers, parallel lines, cotton rows, and stacks of cartons in a warehouse. His father was a wholesale grocer in Little Rock. Big Jim ran away from home at age fourteen to escape a cruel, controlling, schoolteaching mother. He went to the Smackover oil fields. The boom was on. He got a job in a grocery store. The store owner knew my grandfather, and contacted him about my runaway dad. My father told my grandfather that if he were taken home, he would run away again. So he was sent to military school. My father loved marching in lines. But he had already developed a problem with authority and was in trouble much of the time. He was caught bootlegging moonshine in his car's radiator. He said he graduated. I was never sure he did.

He wanted to build bridges. He managed to get into Georgia Tech's engineering program, which entailed one semester in class and one working on a road gang. He liked the roadwork, but was impatient with school classes. In the spring of '29, he quit school, and went with a group of friends to get construction jobs on the Grand Coulee Dam. His friends dropped off one by one, leaving my father stranded in Oklahoma. My father liked working and having a job. As a result of seeing his father, "Jimmy Dick," lose the family money on the Cuban sugar market, financial security was important to him. He liked for his columns of figures to add up.

He got a job as a traveling salesman selling specialty items, wholesale to retail. A career was born. The company teamed him with a crusty old salesman to break him in and show my father the territory. The first day the old man got in the driver's seat of his Model T Ford, with a pint whiskey bottle and a Colt .44 revolver next to him. They drove dry river beds and gullies as often as roads, going from town to town, through the bleakest part of the Oklahoma territory, jobbing General Foods products to local grocery stores. The old man said nothing to my father all day. The next day my father bought a pint of whiskey and a gun, and laid them down on the seat next to the old man's. Every time the old man took a drink, my old man took a drink. They got along fine after that. They would stop and shoot their pistols at jackrabbits in the shadows behind the telephone poles along the road.

After his first week my old man was on his own. He opened up the Oklahoma Territory for Jell-O and Sanka coffee (imagine explaining to some half-wit Okie what Jell-O was). My father carried a small test tube full of quinine, and told his customers it was "deadly caffeine, enough to wipe out Oklahoma City"; that's what Sanka took out of coffee. My old man was a hell of a salesman. He peddled a million dollars of penny matches a year, but that comes later.

Big Jim worked his way up even as the stock market crashed. My father had a good job when most men were struggling. Businesses closed; people lost their jobs. Men who had never considered unemployment looked for work desperately. My father hired men with Master's degrees to sell Jell-O door to door. He was "cooking with gas," as he liked to say. He came home to Little Rock a success. He had a job, big city clothes, and a new car with the first car radio in central Arkansas.

He was driving his new car on a snowy winter afternoon by the school where his mother taught when he saw a girl with her head down, walking in the snow. He stopped and offered her a ride. She was Martha Huddleston and became his wife and my mother. A conservatory-trained accompanist, she taught and played piano in the Baptist Church most of her life and never took a nickel for it.

The Traveling Salesman and the Music Teacher were an unlikely couple: my father, a backsliding Methodist who drank and gambled; my mother, a Hard-shell Baptist. They married in Little Rock, went to Memphis for their honeymoon, and headed back to the Oklahoma dust bowl.

My mother must have felt lonely, spending days in hotel rooms while my father earned a living. She learned to put up with his drinking and his rowdy "brothers of the road" salesmen. She heard sordid stories of Big Jim's checkered past, stories involving monkeys in hotel rooms and card games with Baby Face Nelson. But she "made the adjustment," as she used to say.

My father went to work for the Diamond Match Company, and was transferred to Memphis, which was not quite home but good enough. I was conceived in a rooming house by the zoo and carried to term. My mother wanted to have her baby in Little Rock, where I was born on November 15, 1941. My mother was not quite five feet tall, so small I put her in danger. Like Caesar I was ripped from the womb. We went home from the Baptist Hospital on December 7, "a date that will live in infamy."

The company transferred my father to Los Angeles. In Hollywood we lived in an apartment house down the hill from Griffith Observatory, later immortalized by James Dean in *Rebel Without a Cause*. My maternal grandmother, Huddie, came to help my mother take care of me. No small task even then. She took me for long walks in a four-wheel walker stroller. One afternoon, so the story goes, she rolled me down Hollywood Boulevard, and we encountered Mae West, star of stage, screen, and radio, the Dolly Parton of her day. Mae West looked in my stroller and said, "My, what a handsome boy." My grandmother asked how she knew I was a boy. Mae West replied, "Honey, I have a way with men."

We had shiny, oilcloth blackout curtains that my parents put over the windows at night. There was talk of Japanese submarines off the California coast, speculation that years later proved to be true. My father hated L.A. He was uncomfortable in the West Coast market. His way of doing business didn't work there. After six months we moved to Chicago and everything changed.

My parents loved Chicago. No blackouts and submarine paranoia like on the West Coast. We lived on the North Shore, just a few doors from Lake Michigan. My mother liked the stores and the conveniences of the big city. She walked me on a leash attached to a brown leather harness that strapped under my arms. My father had a job with government priority so he wasn't drafted. We had an extra car and gas rations all through World War II. We sat in the front room of our lakeside apartment, and listened to news of WWII over the big brown radio. The war was far away.

The stories and music of the radio came from far away, but every afternoon there was a show from Chicago. *Two Ton Baker, the Music Maker* played piano and sang, presented news, weather, and a sort of running commentary. He never stopped playing the piano under the dialogue. He played differently from my mother. My father said he played jazz. He had a theme song—"There's just one place for me, near you"—which he played at the beginning and end of his show. My father liked Two Ton Baker. So did my mother. It was something we shared. But the stories on the radio were mine: *Bomba the Elephant Boy*, *The Green Hornet*, *Sergeant Preston of the Northwest Mounted Police*, *King the Wonder Dog of the Yukon*, *Tom Mix*, and *Captain Midnight*. "Pluck your magic Twanger, Froggie!" said Smiling Ed McConnell with his Buster Brown gang. Midnight the Cat would mew "Nice" and Squeaky the Mouse would start the music box. Over the tinkling background, Froggy the Gremlin would sing, "Every time I go to town, the boys start kicking my dog around." The metallic melody ground to a slow halt, like my grandfather's record player in Little Rock. Squeaky would say, "Little music box is running down. Kerplunk!" Smilin' Ed would segue into a commercial for Buster Brown Shoes: "That's my dog Tige. He lives in a shoe. I'm Buster Brown. Look for me in there, too."

Next came *Captain Midnight*, the most artistic and futuristic super hero. He lived in an observatory overlooking the city, and flew a rocket plane armed with high-caliber machine guns. At the end of each episode, before the last commercial break, the announcer would say, "And when we return, Captain Midnight will give you his secret coded message for the day." In order to understand the secret message, you had to cut out the waxed paper covering your jar of chocolate-flavored Ovaltine, enclose fifty cents, and wait forever for a Captain Midnight secret decoder badge to come in the mail. The gold-colored tin badge had two rows of alphabet letters, one inside the other, on a turning disc. The initials CM (for Captain Midnight) and the current year in relief lettering were at the top. You needed a new one every year.

Gene Autry, "the Singing Cowboy," was best of all, featuring cowboy music and comic book–style adventure stories. The show came from Melody Ranch. The cowboys were his band. Gene was the boss, and always won, no matter what villain or Nazi agent tried to do him in. He had a horse, a gun, a guitar, a cowboy suit, and a hat—everything I could want. My father—a harsh vocal critic—held his nose and sang "Back in the Saddle Again," making fun of Gene's song.

My mother rocked me in her brown wicker chair and sang "Froggie Went a-Courtin' and he did ride / sword and pistol by his side."

> I had a pistol
> Big Jim had a sword in the closet in his room
> He wore it when he was in military school
> I would wear a sword when I went to school
> My father's sword was too big
> I would be big when I went to school

My father's office was downtown. We went there sometimes and listened to the radio driving home. A liquor store my father liked was off the outer drive that ran along the lakeshore. A larger-than-life man's head and shoulders were in the window. The face was a concave sculptured mask with eyes that followed you as you passed. I watched it as we drove by. My mother told me God was always watching and could see all, like the eyes in the liquor store window.

Our street ran from Lake Michigan to Sheraton Road. Our area was unkindly known as Kikes' Peak. We were one of three Protestant families on the street. There were lots of kids my age. We played war; it seemed natural with all the war talk. We divided into sides and pretended to fight. The rivalries were heated, exciting, and lingered in the air after we went inside to our families.

Bobby Zwick, the king of the kids, had a skull and crossbones finger ring. He and his redheaded sister, Brenda, ruled the neighborhood. He had a three-wheel bike, faster than anything else around. I had a red Radio Flyer wagon that I dragged up and down the sidewalk, picking up junk from the gutter: wire, bottle caps, the occasional automobile part, a five-dollar bill. Neighbors told my mother, "Little Jimmy is gonna grow up to be a junkman."

A black man, also named Jimmy, swept at the neighborhood barbershop. My friend Billy once called him "colored boy." He replied, "You know my name."

My mother said the grocery store/Chinese laundry was a bookie joint. Edward's toy store was my first conception of heaven. My father got black-market electric heaters and other appliances restricted by World War II regulations at Jack's Fix-It Shop. I saw *Snow White, Duel in the Sun,* and other films projecting the myths and legends of my youth at the 400 Movie Theater. On Halloween the kids dressed in costumes, gathered under the 400's marquee, and trick-or-treated passers-by rather than going door to door.

A seawall at the end of the street cut off the beach. Wooden steps went down to the cold, empty lake where I was not supposed to go. My mother and I stood at the wall and watched the waves. Once we saw a flying saucer. I've told the story so many times over the years that the pictures in my actual memory have been erased. My vision was so bad—still unaided by glasses—God only knows what I actually saw, but my mother remembered it until the day she died. The saucer was reported in the *Chicago Herald-Tribune* and on the radio news the next day. There had been similar sightings out west.

My mother said it was probably one of the government's secret weapons left over from World War II. She said it looked like a garbage can lid, flying over Lake Michigan toward the Navy Pier. Truthfully, I don't remember, but have told the story to friends and strangers alike for years. I did a report with a big picture I drew on poster board at school. It seemed normal since my own sane and sober God-fearing mother had seen it. That was the first time people thought I was crazy.

We took a family trip to Dearborn, Michigan, across the lake from Chicago. We visited Dearborn Village, which houses Thomas Edison's laboratory, re-created as a tourist attraction. I was fascinated by the gadgetry, especially recording equipment with big horns that recorded sound and the silent movie pictures that were so different from the movies I saw at the 400.

> Black and white images flickered and jerked
> Moving not like people moved in life
> But like cartoons
> This was where these films and records were made
> The magic voice inside the box

Marshall Field's department store had a giant Christmas tree, rising high through the huge store. Mr. and Mrs. Santa Claus, with real white hair, whiskers, and red velvet suits with white fur trim, marked the North Pole Village's entrance. A first-rate operation. Each child talked to Santa and was asked to sing a song. Midget elves recorded the song onto a disc of white cardboard that looked like a smaller version of my grandmother's old 78 records. Every child sang "Jingle Bells" or "Silent Night," but I sang "I'm a Ramblin' Wreck from Georgia Tech and a Heck of an Engineer." Santa and Mrs. Santa were surprised. "Like all the jolly good fellows, I drink my whiskey clear."

Santa laughed. My mother was embarrassed. I played the record over and over until it wore out, fascinated by my own voice coming out of the box, singing "Ramblin' Wreck" and talking to Santa Claus. I could remember the feeling of the moment and hear it re-created on the white cardboard record.

We rode the train back and forth from Chicago to Little Rock. The Texas Eagle steam engine locomotive had shiny silver Pullman cars. We rode in a private compartment with seats that folded down into bunk beds. I took my first baby steps on that train. I had a pet box turtle with the American flag painted on its shell. My father got it for me at the circus. The turtle traveled in a white cardboard container with air holes in it. I kept the container on the windowsill so I could see it while I looked out the train's window.

Chicago was full of big-city dangers. When we visited my maternal grandmother, Huddie, I was off the leash. My first memories of freedom are from Little Rock. I roamed the neighborhood and eventually prowled the downtown area. I still recall my first solo trip to the neighborhood drug store to buy a comic book and a cherry phosphate.

Huddie is a mystery. She was French, had studied to be a nun, and would not speak of her family or past. She provided shelter during my stormy childhood.

My only memory of Grandpa Dick is a fishing trip to his cabin at Lakewood. We fished off a wooden pier. I was catching fish and he wasn't. He talked me into changing places with him. I continued to catch fish and he continued not to. Later that day he tried to teach me to skip flat rocks on the water's surface. It delighted him that I couldn't do it. His stones skipped three or four times. Mine plopped. I guess it made up for the fish. He died in the Veterans' Hospital in Hot Springs.

I remember my maternal grandfather, Pappy, wearing a terry cloth robe and sitting in his old slingback lawn chair upstairs in his office. He would get up before dawn, go to the kitchen, scrape the thick grease off the turnip greens in the icebox, spread it on stale cornbread, and eat it. He told me stories about making "slumgullion" (hunter's stew) with squirrels, rabbits, and wild onions. He told me, "Don't stand around with your hands in your pockets, Jimmy. People will think there's nothing else in them."

Pappy was a jack of all trades. He sold cars for the local Nash dealer. He worked for a wholesale hardware warehouse, and was the timekeeper/bell ringer for wrestling matches at the old Shrine Auditorium. The promoter,

Tony Cabooch, was a colorful character. Whenever I tried to wear a black shirt and a white tie or a purple shirt with a yellow tie, my mother shook her head and said, "You look like Tony Cabooch." I took it as a compliment.

Pappy died in his sleep, sitting in that old lawn chair. They said it was a blessing; that I was too young to understand. I am sitting in that old chair as I write these words. When I remember, I take my hands out of my pockets.

Both my grandfathers died while we were still living in Chicago. They were buried in the same graveyard in Little Rock. On Sunday afternoons we went to the cemetery after church, and Huddie changed the flowers on Pappy's grave, up the hill overlooking railroad men buried by train tracks. One tombstone had a locomotive engine carved on it. Years later in *Boomer's Story* Ry Cooder sang, "Dig my grave by the railroad, so I can hear the trains go by."

I don't know when I first heard the music in my head. I can't remember not hearing it. Sometimes in the morning it would be the first thing I heard, shutting out reality—traffic outside the window and people moving around:

> In the apartment by the lake
> My mother's voice
> My father coughing
> Or running his electric razor
>
> Before I turned on the radio
> To hear Don McNeill's Breakfast Club
> I would hear music in my head:
> Far away and out of focus
> like a radio station not quite tuned in.
> Not the sound of any particular instrument or vocal
> just music,
> melody and rhythm modulating behind my eyes.
> A solo performance just for me,
> an unseen companion,
> the very sound of my living,
> inside me,
> my own personal broadcast
> that the radio in my head played at its own will.
> I had no control over it.

My mother sat at the upright piano, playing and singing song after song off old pieces of sheet music from her past. I searched those songs for meaning. Like Gene Autry and Red River Dave's cowboy songs, each told a story of a place and time far away.

My mother gave me the gift of music. Her father played piano and his father before. Her mother played banjo and violin. My mother wanted me to take piano lessons before I started school. My mother had been a semi-pro in childhood. Not a prodigy, she was quick to explain, just a good young player. She accompanied an older girl violinist. They played classical competitions statewide. My mother's drive and competitive spirit pushed her over the edge, causing an emotional breakdown at age fourteen. Afterward, she continued to play in church but never professionally. She wanted me to play and I wanted to play, like Two Ton Baker. My piano teacher, whose name I don't remember, had snow white hair like my grandfather's and "ghost fingers" with transparent, almost blue skin, like those I would see on many great piano players, including Charlie Rich and Jerry Lee Lewis. My teacher's expression was blank and emotionless. One day one of his children ran into the room screaming and crying with a bloody nose. He looked up emotionlessly and continued the lesson as his child ran crying from the room. A cold fish.

He told me about the lines, spaces, and dots that symbolized notes on the keyboard. Due to my poor vision, I could not see dots. I saw a blur; the lines and spaces seemed to move on the music sheet as I tried to focus on them. The keyboard's shape made more sense to me, the white keys on the bottom, the black keys divided into twos and threes on top. This pattern seemed significant. I thought he was kidding about the dots on the paper, the way adults obscure truths by telling children one thing when there's also a "grown-up explanation." Song lessons began with "Motor Boat," which consisted of playing middle C in repeated eighth notes, an irony that would be revealed years later.

I started school at the National College of Education in Evanston, and did not get to wear my father's sword to school. My art teacher was from India. She wore brightly colored robes and had a jewel on her forehead. We painted rocks. I gave the art objects to my father, who kept them all his life. I still have them.

Once lost, innocence is forever gone. The line between real and make-believe separates childhood from the grown-up world, a lesson I learned too soon.

A carelessly thrown rock changed everything one day on the playground. I put out a kid's eye during our recess war game. He was a big, curly-haired Italian boy in my class. By chance or fate, I saw him years later when I returned to Chicago for the Playboy Jazz Festival (he was the friend of a friend). I could not tell if he recognized me. I had no trouble recognizing him. His left eye was blank, the color of milk. I don't remember what I was thinking when I threw the rock. Clouded by guilt and regret, I remember the moment visually as if watching a bad movie. Seeing my victim years later went a long way toward making me nonviolent.

I will carry his mother's curse to my grave.

Chapter 3

MEMPHIS
(1949–54)

As they say in professional wrestling, business was about to pick up. In the late summer of 1949 we moved to Memphis, Tennessee, into a big old house on three acres east of the city limits with a cotton field in front and farms behind. A railroad track ran less than a mile north of the property. When we drove up the long gravel driveway the first thing I saw was a small black man standing with a big sickle, like the one Death holds to mow down the condemned. This strange little man wore a hat that seemed too big for him, not formed or fitted like the hat my father wore to work, but round on top and crushed in the back. Later I learned this was worn to create the illusion of being taller. I learned many things from this man; he became my greatest teacher.

Everyone called him Alec, short for "Smart Alec," although that wasn't his real name. Alec was our yardman. My father hired him to clean up the property, which had been tied up in a divorce case and grown wild.

I spent a lot of time in the trees, bushes, and drainage ditches of our new yard, but Alec did all of the work, mowing grass and trimming hedges. I followed him. Slowly he taught me many things: how to tell the time of day by my shadow, when it would rain by the leaves on the trees, how to throw a pocket knife underhanded, how to shoot craps, and play Pitty Pat, Smut, and Red Dog. He told me of his weekend adventures with moonshine, dice games, and Car 44 (the local police car). At noon he came into the house to eat lunch. He tuned the kitchen radio to WDIA, "the black spot on the dial," and listened to Honeyboy and "Bless My Bones" Brother Theo Wade play music I had never heard on white radio.

I had heard boogie-woogie piano, and one day over the car radio I had heard a loose, horn-driven instrumental with a rhythm section like the band at the circus. My father told me it was Dixieland. But I had never heard music like what they played on WDIA. The beat was heavy and repetitive. The notes were long and mournful, like songs in church. The piano didn't sound like my mother or Two Ton Baker. It was wild music that seemed about to spin out of control. Alec sang while he worked; sometimes songs without words, just long vowels that sounded like an animal howling or a tortured soul moaning in the lonesome night. He sang to pass the time and make work go faster, smoother.

Alec couldn't read or write. He could sign his name and read the ball scores in the newspaper. He believed the sun revolved around the Earth. He quit school in the fifth or sixth grade. Sometimes he went back on Friday because they had "ice squeem." He was wise with instinct and natural intelligence, and was kinder to me than any person outside of my family ever was. I think he thought it was part of his job to teach me to be something besides a smart-aleck Yankee kid.

Alec taught me to be cool, to hold my cards close to my chest, not reveal myself to strangers, and how to put somebody on when they were trying to get one over on me. He taught me the importance of loyalty, to protect that which and those whom I loved, and not show weakness in defeat. He was a great teacher and a truly wise man.

I lay in bed each night and waited to hear the train pass at 10:10 on the N.C. & Saint L. tracks north of our place. I imagined stories centered on the train. The passing train carried me into the night, into a dream world of patriotic conflict and heroic deeds. I was a freedom fighter in a postwar society controlled by a military dictator. Hiding beneath the covers from enemy storm troopers, I listened for the night whistle and forgot to say my prayers. Our yard was like a park or the forest preserve where we picnicked. There were birds, squirrels, and twenty trees that two men could not reach around. Occasional coons, possums, and wild things rustled in the trees at night. I played outside, listened to green flies' daytime drone, and at sundown, to bugs, frogs, the unknown something in the grass that called my name, "Jimmy-Jimmy-Jimmy," the nighttime cry of crickets, locusts, katydids, tree frogs, and the hoots of owls circling.

My parents liked to dine on the Peabody Hotel roof and dance to big bands from out of town. From time to time they took me, "as part of my education."

Starched white table cloths
and hotel silverware
like the City of New Orleans dining car.

Spit and polished black waiters
dressed to the teeth,
who were all "Yah, Suh," and "Yes, Ma'm."

They called my father "Captain"
and grinned gold toothed smiles,
bowing at the waist.

He called them "Pancho."
I liked the ice water and the butterfly dinner rolls.
Most of all I liked the drummers.

My mother told me playing the drums made you crazy. Her distrust of professional musicians sprang from a bad experience dating a clarinet player. She told me over and over, "Jimmy, you can be anything in life you want to be. But don't be a musician."

She might as well have told me not to put beans in my ears.

Our lives took on a slower rhythm in Memphis. People talked slower, holding on to their words, almost singing. I played in a drainage ditch that ran through our yard of big, old trees and bushes, over an acre of jonquils, yellow in winter's last feeble snow, instead of Chicago's grimy concrete alleys. At first it seemed pitiful in comparison to the frozen world by the lake. I hated it. The first few nights I fell asleep to the whine of the window fan on the sleeping porch and prayed I would wake up back in Chicago. Slowly the place sank into my soul.

The school was old, weird, and boring. They let us out at cotton-picking time and for the Mid-South Fair. I guessed it was a school for farmers. I did not belong. I was suspected of being a Yankee and was not to be trusted.

I had finished the second grade at the National College in Chicago, but still couldn't read. They put glasses on me and kept me in the second grade. The glasses cleared up the fuzzy edges, but didn't correct the multiple vision I'd had all my life. I learned to read by words' shapes and memorizing what I heard.

The country school's social structure was important. Of course, the students were all white, but some were from farm families and others were from new suburban, postwar-boomer families. The lines were drawn clearly.

No lines were stronger than the racial barriers. In Chicago neighbor-hoods separated races and even nationalities. Interaction was rare. In Memphis, black people were everywhere, but confined within segrega-tion's invisible walls. It was black or white. No third-world tan or yellow. Jesus loves the little children, but there were rules: drinking fountains, restrooms, movie theatres, waiting rooms, public transportation, schools, and churches were all rigidly and absolutely divided along racial lines. Culture was exclusive to skin color. Strangest of all were the lines between black and white music.

My father's new office was in downtown Memphis on Front Street, close to Cotton Row, where the international cotton empire conducted business. King Cotton. The Diamond Match office encompassed the Falls Building's seventh floor. You could see the Mississippi River from the west windows. The Falls Building was old and historic. Legend has it W. C. Handy and his band had played on the rooftop Oriental Gardens. The south side of the Falls Building opened onto Park Lane, or Whiskey Chute, as the locals called it, an alley between Front Street and Main Street that bootleggers used during Prohibition to roll whiskey barrels from the river to Main Street taverns and speakeasies. Park Lane was a great place for kids, a little world unto itself: a barber shop, a store that sold model airplane kits, and best of all, the Fun Shop Magic Land, a dark and mysterious corner shop that sold amateur magic tricks.

Most Saturday mornings, I went to the office with my father. After he went through the mail and finished the bookkeeping, we headed to Pete and Sam's, an Italian restaurant with a screen door and checkered tablecloths. On weekends the Falls Building's front was locked, so we exited the side door that opened onto Whiskey Chute.

> I was used to playing in the alleys in Chicago
> But I soon found my way around Whiskey "Shoot"
> You never know when it was going to reach out and grab you
> when the ground would open and pull you down the rabbit hole
> It's a one-way wolf ticket with no return trip
> on the other side of the secret door
> it's Technicolor.

Outside the door to the alleyway four black men, dressed like hobos or field hands, were singing and playing—a four-string tenor guitar, a violin, a washboard with drumsticks, and a string tied to a broomstick and run through a washtub—the strangest music I had ever heard. A white couple, acting drunk, jitterbugged in the alley. The tall thin man with the washtub bass sang, "Come on down to my house, honey, there's nobody home but me."

He laughed, went down low on the broomstick, shouted "Yeah, yeah, yeah," and laughed some more. I was hypnotized. It was like being hit over the head. Never in my short life had I heard anything so moving. It was music from heaven, yet these men were clearly not the angels described to me in my mother's church.

After one song, my father put a dollar bill in the coffee can and made me leave. But I carried the words and music with me. I hear it now, more than fifty years later. After that experience, other things in life did not seem as important as finding that magic music.

Such musicians were just blocks away in the Beale Street community, but were utterly inaccessible to me, a white boy. How would I discover more about them?

Later I went to the library. There was only one book. Samuel Charters's *The Country Blues* had a chapter called "Memphis Jug Bands." I had seen the great Will Shade and the Memphis Jug Band in the alley, with Charlie Burse on guitar and his brother, Good Kid, on washboard. I didn't find out who the fiddler player was until years later when Charlie Musselwhite told me his name, Red Robie.

Summer is day heavy
The light moves more slowly east to west
The light holds on
Divisions fall down
They get hot and melt and the night comes on thick and deep

It seems like it was always summer in Sunday School
In the days before air conditioning
the noisy window fan and the piano music
made the heat bounce around the room in 4/4 time
"In the highways, in the hedges,
I'll be somewhere working for my Lord . . ."
"Oh, do Lord, oh, do Lord, Oh do remember me,
Look away beyond the blue."

In Memphis my father joined Colonial Country Club. He loved to play golf and poker. There was a golf course, a swimming pool, and a big old Southern mansion-looking clubhouse where occasional dances were held for members only. I saw several big bands there. Not the touring bands we saw at Peabody Skyway, but local versions like Berl Olswanger, Sy Rose, and Bill Justis, sit-down musicians wearing tuxedos and reading sheet music with singers.

My father played golf on Saturday afternoon and cards on Saturday night. He liked gin rummy. He remembered every card drawn face up. A friendly game of gin could degenerate into cutthroat five-card draw, or even to shooting dice, which my father viewed as low gambling. (Alec loved to shoot craps.) As I got older I noticed my father played cards later and later.

My father, a Methodist, didn't attend what he called the "damn Baptist" church. Sometimes he would be out all night, and not come home until after my mother and I had gone to church. I sat in the Amen corner down front of the congregation while my mother played piano. I was proud of my mother's playing, which brought life to the old familiar tunes in the Broadman Hymnal.

Only a couple of kids in our church went to White Station School with me. Ronnie Stoots, who sang in my first band and toured with the Mar-Keys, was in my Sunday school class. The preacher had been my mother's student in Little Rock. She was always partial to folks from her hometown.

On Sunday afternoons, after church service and lunch, we went downtown to a matinee at one of the big, old first-run movie houses. My mother liked musicals, especially those starring Gene Kelly. Musicians in the movies fascinated me. The piano players—Jimmy Durante, Oscar Levant, Hoagy Carmichael—were never the main character or hero. They were like the comic sidekick in the "B" westerns, the Gabby Hayes character.

We drove to Little Rock to visit grandmother Huddie many weekends. My parents picked me up at school Friday afternoons, and we crossed the river into Arkansas. West Memphis was notoriously wild and wide open. There was a dog track and a stock-car dirt track. Nightclubs lined the highway: Danny's Club, the Cotton Club, Uncle Ben's Jungle Inn, and most alluring of all, with its huge neon sign of a couple dancing in full evening dress, the Plantation Inn. Downtown, the Sunset Drive-In showed movies—*Reefer Madness, The Miracle of Birth, Black Like Me*—the Censor Board in Memphis banned. Beyond West Memphis was farmland, cotton fields, and tenant cabins in rows. Forrest City, Brinkley, DeValls Bluff. We would stop in Carlisle and have dinner at the K.C. Steak House, which served the best steak I ever had. My last meal there was on my honeymoon.

Outside Little Rock was a stretch of highway by the old river backwash, which looked like a swamp. Green moss clung to the bank. Dried out cypress trees and stumps stuck up out of dark, stagnant water coated with thick slime. I looked forward to that strange stretch of road.

We would get to my grandmother's house about eight o'clock on Friday night. My parents would go out with old friends in Little Rock, leaving me with my grandmother and the radio. I was strongly attracted to Rochester's gruff, growling voice on *The Jack Benny Program*. "Mr. Benny, Mr. Benny," he would croak and the audience laughed. "What is it, Rochester?" Benny replied, and the show was on. Phil Harris, the bandleader, told stories about Frank Remley, his drunken guitar player. It was a radio show about a radio show; the characters played fictional versions of themselves, like twin mirrors in the barbershop where the reflection repeats into infinity. I waited for the story to unwind every Saturday night.

One Saturday night my grandmother and I were at her next-door neighbor's house, listening to "Rhapsody in Blue" from the Hollywood Bowl on their big console radio. Clarinets lead to a long piano movement that builds and builds to violins playing the melodic theme's final release. Even now, when I hear that moment of final release, I journey back to Little Rock and the living room radio.

Huddie's house was full of what I guessed were memories. I listened to rain against old windows in the long afternoons, trying to hold on to those memories. Late at night, the old house made noises I could never figure out. Recalling it now, I recognize the sound of time passing and age encroaching.

The sun went down
over the cemetery
across the railroad tracks.
When the trains passed,
they whistled
until they were gone.
The trains passed

and the whistle hung in the air
trying to stay
and finally fading up into the night.
Night birds and crickets ran together into one song.
The night croaked like a tree frog
and the curtains rustled across the foot of the bed.
The breeze blowing in through the window
was not black like the night outside.
It was clear,
colorless,
almost silent.
It was filled
with ghosts from the graveyard
hanging on like the train whistle
somewhere out and down
the two lonely tracks
to somewhere.

Wisteria vines covered one side of Huddie's screened-in porch. Sometimes I spent the whole day in the space behind the wisteria. Stones were in the gutter where rain ran when it dropped off the roof. The dirt was sandy and cool when I dug my fingers into it. I found big-headed roof nails, different from big wood nails. A bullet hole was in the windowsill; the police had shot at the Dog Town Ripper, a villain from North Little Rock, whom they had cornered under the house. He was wearing a woman's flower-print dress and a sunbonnet. The Ripper's girlfriend, my grandmother's housemaid, was hiding him. Huddie painted over the bullet hole, but never replaced the windowsill. It added to the wisteria cloaked old house's mystery.

Saturdays in Little Rock we went downtown to my aunt and uncle's jewelry store. One of the best comic book shops I ever saw was next door. Main Street had it all: a dime store, a bookstore, and around the corner, a music store selling records. I could walk down Main Street to the Capitol Movie Theater. Further down, toward the Arkansas River, was an army surplus store with push-button switchblade knives in the window.

One summer day I saw something I never forgot. On the corner across the street from my grandparents' house, I saw an organ grinder with a monkey. The man turned a crank that stuck out of a one-legged black box that made a clanking, tinny music. The monkey was tied by a leather leash and a harness, like the one my mother used to walk me in Chicago. Neighborhood children gathered around the old man and the monkey, listening to the strange, almost frantic sound of the music box and laughing at the monkey as he seemed to dance on his leather restraint. Every few minutes the man stopped turning the musical crank and passed around a metal cup, soliciting coins from the children. Eventually, the audience tired of the spectacle and wandered away. The organ grinder and the monkey disappeared into the afternoon. The music, the monkey dance, and the laughing children seemed sad to me.

In May, Cotton Carnival brought parades and the Royal Barge landing on the riverbank at the foot of Union Avenue. Fireworks flared from Mud Island. Sparkling skyrockets exploded as we watched from my father's office window. The Royal American Midway Show set up next to the Falls Building for Cotton Carnival. The Midway had rides, games of chance, and sideshows with freaks and hoochie coochie dancers. Harlem in Havana interested me most. A pitchman with a microphone told the audience about wonders they could witness. A black saxophone player droned and a drummer thumped as the pitchman brought out a dancing girl to showcase the exotic pleasure inside. When I went to the Midway with my parents, I stayed at the outdoor stage in front of that tent as long as possible. My father had little patience with my interest and my mother had no sympathy at all. I didn't get into the tent for the Big Show until I was a teenager and skipped school.

Chapter 4

THE WOLF
(1954–58)

I was with my father at a warehouse in West Memphis, Arkansas. My father and the warehouse manager were counting cartons of clothespins. It was summertime. Big fans built into the walls hummed, but I heard what sounded like jungle drums from a Tarzan movie. I followed the pounding up wooden stairs to an office. Painted on the glass door was a lightning bolt and red letters, K-WEM RADIO. The door was open. Four Negro men in sun-bleached work clothes played music. One man, bigger than the others, growled words I could not understand into a silver microphone. I watched until my father found me. Outside in the parking lot, I snapped on the car radio and searched until I found the strange music I had heard in the warehouse. The announcer said, "You have been listening to the Howlin' Wolf."

The music stuck in my head. I had an older friend with a 78 rpm copy of Wolf's "I Got a Woman" on Chess Records. I listened to it over and over. Then one day in Ruben Cherry's Home of the Blues record shop on Beale Street I found a Chess record with a grey album cover with the drawing of a lone wolf howling at the moon. I took it to the checkout counter and Ruben said, "Boy, you got the blues there."

> Heed the call of the wolf
> The haunted cry of an animal
> Alone in the night
> His voice makes the room rumble
> With echo that seems to hang in the air
> His singing so strong
> that between the vocal
> lives the sound of the drums
> and the French harp sucked up into the mix.

Notes blend together
And merge into a melody line
Not being played by one instrument alone

He is a primitive-modernist
Using chords and modal harmonies
Of a dark ritual past
Brought up from mother Africa
And slavery
Through
An electric amplifier.

Howlin' Wolf led me to Muddy Waters, John Lee Hooker, and then Jimmy Reed. I started to discover lines and patterns repeating within their songs, a chord progression. It seemed learnable in ways my mother's piano sheet music did not.

The disc jockeys—Rufus Thomas, Martha Jean the Queen, and Honeyboy—on WDIA and WLOK were my new teachers.

Chapter 5

BUTTERFLY AND DISHRAG
(1955-67)

Alec saw I wanted to play music, and wanted to help. He was a great singer and always sang while he worked, but could play no instrument. On Saturday mornings, when he came to wash my father's company car and get paid for the week, he brought me piano teachers.

Butterfly was the first guy. He was the stepson of the man who owned the George Washington Broad Street Cafe, where Alec hung out and Frankie Lane tipped a cop car over by hand. Butterfly had just gotten off the penal farm; his heavily processed hair was shaved clean an inch above his ears. Alec explained he had to pay off the barber to save the top of his rooster-tail hairdo. I watched as his huge hands danced over my mother's piano keys. He played "Three O'clock in the Morning," one of Alec's favorites, and tried to show me the "blues scale," with the flat third and seventh. I didn't get it.

The second teacher Alec brought me was better. Alec called him "Piano Red," which seemed to make him mad. He was not Piano Red. I knew that and tried to look sympathetic. He was older, hunched over, and wore an old gray overcoat and snap brim. He was obviously drunk. He sat at the piano and coughed deep in his chest.

"What chew wants to hear, boss?" he grumbled.

I asked if he knew "Come On Down to My House," the song I had heard the Jug Band play in Whiskey Chute.

He laughed and said, "How does you know that song? Man, that song's older than yo' Daddy." He played through the melody once and spoke to me solemnly. "I'm gonna show you somethin'. Pay attention to this," he said. "Everything in music is made up out of codes. . . ." I thought, "Codes. . . . Secret codes!!! Like Captain Midnight. No wonder I couldn't understand it. It's in codes!! Why didn't my mother tell me that??!!"

"This is how you makes a code. You take one note, any note. Then you goes three up and four down, just like in poker. Three up and four down and you gots a code."

Of course he meant chord. It works anywhere on the piano. Not steps and half steps like the music teacher told me, but keys on the keyboard. Three notes up and four notes down and you have a major triad, tonic root note on the bottom, first inversion. Say you start on an E note, the pattern leads you to notes C, E, and G which make a C major chord. Using the new "code" I could teach myself major triads up and down the piano. That was what I needed to know. A triad on top and an octave on the bottom could open into a boogie-woogie pattern in the blues scale. Apply to that appropriate rhythm and syncopation, and you are playing rock 'n' roll piano, pal!

So I learned the music's secret from the Phantom, unknown to me by any other name until a rainy afternoon years later. I was hanging out in Melody Music store on Poplar Avenue by the viaduct when the Phantom stepped out of the storm.

He took off ragged work gloves, shoved them in his overcoat pocket, and ran his hands over one of the keyboards in the showroom floor stock. I was afraid the owner would run him off. He played "Sophisticated Lady" without sitting down. He saw me watching and stopped. He looked up. "Come on down to my house . . ." he rumbled in recognition.

"Thanks for what you showed me," I said, trying to think of something better to say.

He shrugged, waved his hand goodbye, and shuffled back into the rain. Ferguson, the old black guy who did the maintenance on band instruments back in the workshop, came over to me and said, "Man, how does you know that ol' man? That was Dishrag. He used to be somebody. That was Dishrag."

Chapter 6

PRETTY BROWNS IN BEAUTIFUL GOWNS
(1949-55)

Beale Street was magic, the Harlem of the South. When the black slaves were freed after the Civil War, those who came to Memphis from plantations in the Mississippi/Arkansas Delta, settled in downtown, east of the Union fort on the bluff. Beale Street. A series of big shots like Big Jim Kinnane allowed the district to run wide open. Bars and gambling halls, whorehouses, and trim joints flourished. It was a world within a world where few whites ventured.

By the fifties—after reform mayor E. H. "Boss" Crump, Prohibition, and a string of mayors Crump backed—Beale Street became a four-block-long string of pawn shops, pool halls, a couple of movie theatres, a hotel for blacks, and barrooms that never closed. Replete with colorful characters and urban myths, it was a place of wonder to a teenage white boy. Music was everywhere. Speakers pumped jive out on the sidewalks. Street musicians sat huddled on the corners with tin cups full of shiny new unsharpened pencils, begging for change from passers-by.

An old man with both legs amputated to the knees and pieces of rubber tire strapped onto the stumps scooted along, ever busy, always up to something. Down by the old train tracks a wild man in an old Memphis Red Sox uniform shouted at traffic and seemed to play baseball with passing automobiles.

Pimps and hustlers bought gaudy clothing at Lansky Brothers on Second and Beale. Old Man Schwab, owner of the old-fashioned dry goods store A. Schwab's, was one of my father's best customers. He called my father "match-a man" in a phony Italian accent, which was odd since he was an old-country Jew and my father was clearly not Italian.

Beale Street was another world. Alec told me wild stories of bad men like Frankie Lane who held his pocket knife between his gold-capped teeth and strutted down the middle of the street, daring all comers to take him on. I loved going to Beale Street with my father. He was known by merchants and bookies alike. He took me there to get my first zoot suit, my first guitar, and my first real understanding of our segregated world.

From Main Street to Pontotoc Avenue white folks were tolerated, if not welcomed. Below Pontotoc, it was no man's land. The north side of Beale and Main was occupied by Tony's Fruit Stand, where my mother shopped for nectarines when she was pregnant with me. The south side was the Blue Light photography studio and Home of the Blues record store. On the corner of Beale and Pontotoc was Nathan Novick's Pawnshop with the notorious "Lou the Jew" Rayfield. When Big Jim took me to Beale Street to buy my first electric guitar, we went to half a dozen stores before Nathan's. There were pawnshops on the north side of the street with racks of guitars—old, new, worn out, and shiny—on the sidewalk. Silver metal National guitars like nothing I had ever seen. Loudmouthed Hebrew hucksters fast-talked their pitch and my old man back-talked with the best of them. He loved to wheel and deal. It reminded him of Chicago.

Finally, we ended up at Nathan's. My father knew it was the payoff. An ancient, high-yellow shill in a loud three-piece suit, a painted silk tie with a flowery pocket handkerchief, and a suede fedora stood in the doorway. It was late summer. He was dressed for midwinter but did not sweat as he worked passers-by like a carnival pitchman.

Inside was Lou Rayfield's domain. He wore a white shirt, bow tie, and suspenders, had a thin trimmed mustache like Groucho Marx, and clenched a smoldering cigar stump in his teeth. He cursed and grumbled, "How much money you got? You don't have any money. Get the hell out."

Police badges, handguns, brass knuckles, and flashy jewelry filled rows of glass showcases. Lou stood at the back of the store with the guitars. He and my father dickered back and forth. My old man was really enjoying himself. Finally Lou brought out a white guitar with gold-flecked membranes running through it. I loved it. He threw in a green and black cord to sling over my shoulder.

At home I stood in front of the full-length mirror wearing my white and gold-flecked Stratoline and dreamed of the future.

Chapter 7

DADDY-O DEWEY
(1949-58)

It's hard if not impossible to describe Dewey Phillips. If he's known at all, it's as the Memphis disc jockey who played Elvis Presley on the radio first. He is little known as the man who brought to life the IDEA that was Elvis. The same year we moved to Memphis (1949), Sam Phillips came to town from Florence, Alabama, and Dewey Phillips (a brother of the soul, not the flesh) lost his job selling sheet music in a dime store and started broadcasting a nighttime music program on WHBQ radio.

I would like to say I was hip to Dewey from the start. Sadly, I was not. I was hooked on WDIA and Rufus Thomas, and was late coming to Dewey. Memphis loved him. He was loose, sloppy, and incoherent. Everything else on radio was tight and scripted with a formal tone. Dewey joked and talked in multiple voices to people who weren't there. He "interviewed" baseball legend Dizzy Dean and actress Kim Novak. Doing all the voices he would ask, "How you doin', Diz?" He would turn off mic and say, "All right, pardner," in his Dizzy Dean voice; then he would say, "Come on in here, Kim Novak," and reply, "Hello boys," in a forced *basso profundo.*

He made up commercials. "Good ol' Falstaff beer. If you can't drink it, freeze it and eat it. Open up a rib and pour it in."

But the music was the thing. He'd play Hank Williams's "Your Cheatin' Heart," Sister Rosetta Tharpe's "Strange Things Happening Every Day," or the Reliable Jubilee Singers' "Tell Me Why You Like Roosevelt." No rules or restrictions. Yet there was a consistency, a texture to the songs he chose, a "place" to the sounds and voices; the black/white crossover that defined the Memphis Sound was the real deal, the motherlode, the golden age.

I got to know Dewey later in life, after his fall from grace. The deterioration of Dewey and Elvis's relationship symbolizes the corporate sellout of rock 'n' roll culture.

Memphis was strange and wonderful in the 1950s, with colorful local heroes like stock-car outlaw Hooker Hood, Sputnik Monroe "The World's Greatest Wrestler," and Daddy-o Dewey, who blasted the airwaves with "Red Hot and Blue." Elvis represented a lifestyle that already existed in Memphis.

Hoods

Rogues

Teenage rebels

Greasers with sculptured baroque pompadoured dragon tail hair cuts

Pegged

Draped

Pimp pink zoot suits

Direct from Beale Street

Silk on silk

Lace front tux shirts

With collars turned up

Were an open invitation

To rumble.

Two cultures, divided for centuries by race and property rights, reached for each other musically, and inevitably embraced and collided.

The threat of communism and nuclear holocaust put the big squeeze on the American Dream. TV simultaneously made the global village smaller and bigger. The fifties held the promise of prosperity. The new music represented the individual human spirit's triumphs and grew to symbolize freedom to the world. The idea came into focus like a camera lens, properly aligned, clarifies the image.

Dewey Phillips was the emcee, the stage manager, and the ringmaster of the music that changed the world.

Chapter 8

BIG JIM AND ELVIS
(1949–1956)

I don't remember when trouble started between my father and me. When I was born, he stopped gambling and drinking heavily. After we moved to Memphis, he started to slip. Part of the problem was his job. In Chicago he had been executive vice-president of the Diamond Match Company. When they closed the Chicago office, the company wanted him to move to New York. Like L.A., it was big-city business, and he didn't want to raise a family in that environment. Thank God.

In Memphis, Big Jim was demoted to regional manager. After a few years, Diamond Match closed its Memphis office, and again wanted my father to move to New York. Instead he took another demotion, and ended up a regular wholesale traveling salesman, i.e., where he had started.

He no longer wore the custom-tailored three-piece business suits from Chicago with a beaver fedora. He changed to corduroy sport coats, flannel shirts, and a gray Stetson. He started calling himself "Old Man Dickinson." He was doing business with people he'd known all his life, people who knew his father. He drove from town to town, through the Mississippi and Arkansas delta, peddling matches, toothpicks, and clothespins at wholesale warehouses to tough country merchants in shirtsleeves. It was a far cry from commanding an office of clerks and pretty young secretaries. Colonial Country Club where he played golf was another world from the Chicago Athletic Club, where he had taken steam baths.

Maybe that was it, but it could also have been the rebellions of a teenage son in love with black music. Big Jim blamed it on "that damned movie," as he called *Rebel Without a Cause*, which we saw as a family (if you can imagine that). My mother didn't take it as personally as he did.

We started to argue at dinnertime. He would come home from what my mother called the "Jute Mill," a day of selling to customers he didn't necessarily like. How exciting could counting clothespins be? He would have a couple of drinks to unwind. By dinnertime he was looking for a fight—and there I was. We argued about my schoolwork, my friends (most of whom he thought were worthless), not cleaning up my room, little things that would suddenly become important issues. We argued about the length of my hair and eventually about politics. He was a hard-line Dixiecrat. He blamed the world's woes on FDR and hated Eleanor more than you could imagine. I was always half a Commie. I had a magazine picture of Castro on my bedroom wall.

He started to gamble again. On Saturday afternoons he played golf at the country club. He stayed at the club and played cards all night sometimes. My mother said nothing, but things had changed.

My grandmother Huddie was the peacemaker. When she visited, she sat between father and me at the dinner table. When we rode in his car, she sat in the back with me, and kept me from hanging over the front seat and starting trouble. She pulled my shirttail and shook her head "no" when I was on dangerous ground. My mother acted like it wasn't happening.

My old man and I shared many character traits, which made the conflict more intense. I never fought back physically, but I didn't back down when he got mad. Sometimes it was bad. Playing catch as a kid made me feel uncomfortable and frustrated my dad. Due to my screwed-up vision, I have never been able to play sports. I could usually judge pretty well between multiple images, but if I looked into the sky to catch a ball, I was lost.

He took me fishing and duck hunting a couple of times. Once we went deer hunting with my mother's uncle, Dave Huddleston, up in Minneola, Missouri, at my great-grandparents' old home. (The railroad and the highway had bypassed Minneola, and the town had dried up and blown away, except for the Huddlestons and a couple of hound dogs.)

Great Uncle Dave, the youngest of three children, stayed home to take care of his parents. His brother and sister had gone off to school. There was Indian blood in the family and it showed up in Dave. An old Indian burial ground and a cave were on the family property. Great Uncle Dave married late to a younger woman. She died in childbirth and he went wild. Neighbors heard him crying and howling in the night like an animal. The child, a girl, was taken away from him and raised in an orphanage. Great Uncle Dave took up living in the Indian cave.

When my father and I went to Uncle Dave's, ostensibly on our deer hunting expedition, Uncle Dave produced a big pickle bottle of clear white moonshine. That night I discovered the reason my father drank.

Typically, my father was a mean drunk, but on this moonshine he turned into a teddy bear. I saw him drink white corn whiskey twice and the same thing happened both times. He smiled and chuckled like a happy child. He sang college songs I had never heard him sing, and he tried to perform an odd dance, the "Cootie Crawl," he claimed to have mastered in Oklahoma. He was a new and different person without a care in the world. I think my father had an allergy to something in store-bought whiskey; it could have been the source of the sinus cough that plagued him all his life and turned into emphysema.

My best friend was Bill Madison. We met in Boy Scouts and our families were close. My mother knew his mother from the P.T.A., and my father knew his father from the Methodist church he sometimes attended. Bill's family lived close to school. He had two sisters and a brother, who was building a hot rod out of a '32 Ford in their backyard. They had a beat-up old upright piano they let me pound on and some good records, my favorite being "St. James Infirmary Blues" by Phil Harris (Jack Benny's bandleader).

We hung out together in school, and on Friday or Saturday night we met our girlfriends at the movies. Many weekends Bill and I went into the country to run his father's coon dogs.

One spring afternoon we talked about our future as we walked through a thicket of sweetgum trees somewhere east of town.

"What do you want to do when you grow up, Jimmy?" Bill asked out of nowhere.

"Have adventures," I said.

"Isn't this an adventure?" he replied.

"No. This is fun, but I mean real adventures far away with famous people."

"This adventure is good enough for me," he said.

I hoped I had not hurt his feelings, but I wanted intrigue and danger, like the adventures in *Captain Midnight, Sky King,* and *Gene Autry and the Phantom Empire.*

The summer before junior high school, my family went on a vacation to Kentucky Lake-Paris Landing. Bill went to Scout camp. We planned to meet our girlfriends at the Park Theatre when we returned home on Saturday. But my family stayed at the fishing camp over the weekend. When we got home notes were tied to the doors of our house: "Don't let Jimmy call Bill Madison."

I knew it was bad.

Lightning had struck and killed Bill while he was walking the dogs out in the country. Newspapers reported it as a "Freak accident—killed instantly—one bolt of lightning in the brief storm—standing under tree."

The funeral was over. They had tried to contact us at Paris Landing, and had the Highway Patrol looking for us. I missed the whole thing. I'm just as glad I did. My world closed around me. My girlfriend attended the funeral like it was a social event. I never felt the same way about her.

I don't know where the darkness came from. My mother said it was the Dickinson black-Irish mood. Like the music in my head, it was always there. After Bill Madison was killed, I lost my bearings.

First day of class in the seventh grade I saw a kid sitting in the back of geography class drawing cartoons like a madman. Gauger could draw a whole cartoon frame with one or two super clean lines but his cartoons were wordless pantomime. He saw my drawings with word balloons and went nuts. It had never crossed his mind to add dialogue. We cartooned back and forth all year.

Gauger was an army brat. His family moved to Hawaii after that year. I knew from drawing with Gauger I would never be a cartoonist. My hand wasn't steady enough. My vision was too weird; my line wasn't clean. I would always be frustrated.

The next year, with Gauger gone, I took my first art class at White Station. Ronnie Stoots from Sunday school was in the class. The teacher, Dorothy McGinnis, was the first person to encourage me in the arts. She became my champion and protector through high school.

My limitations led me away from realism. She encouraged me to reach, to push the visual perception of the object beyond its two-dimensional boundaries. I took extra art classes in high school instead of study hall. During other classes, I worked on my art projects and assignments.

In art class Ray Fitts, an accordion player, told me about Elvis. He had seen Elvis on the Dorsey show and said I had to see him. The second time Elvis was on the show, I tuned in. He sang "Tutti Frutti" and "Blue Suede Shoes," then came back and did "Baby, Let's Play House." The world and the future changed. It was like seeing Will Shade and the Memphis Jug Band, only turned up and rocking.

Black shirt, white tie, just like Tony Cabooch. His hair was long, black, and anointed with grease. It was beautiful. He was beautiful. He smiled a sneering smile and stuttered, "Thank you, ladies and gentlemen." The trio behind him was simple, solid, and rocking like no white country singer's ever. They might have looked like Hank Williams's Drifting Cowboys, but they sounded more like the stage band for the Harlem in Havana dancing girl show at the Cotton Carnival Midway. They had the Jug Band's same almost-out-of-control-power, but these were white people on network TV.

I was there when Elvis played his first gig in Memphis after the Dorsey TV shows. He had just released "I Was the One"/"Heartbreak Hotel" and bombed playing Vegas for the first time; it was too much for middle-aged mobsters. Nationally, he was breaking out bigger than anyone since Frank Sinatra.

Ellis Auditorium consisted of the North Hall and the Music Hall. Elvis would perform to both sides at once. My father got me a ticket from a friend at WHBQ. I sat, surrounded by strangers, waiting to see the truck driver from Tupelo. My seat was second from the aisle, maybe twenty rows back. To my right sat a teenaged girl who looked sixteen. She sat quietly, not moving a muscle. The opening act was Hank Snow, the Singing Ranger. He performed alone. He was a very small man with a big country and western guitar, a spangled Nudie suit, and cowboy boots. His big song was "I'm Movin' On." "When you hear my wheels hit the tracks, you'll know your true lovin' Daddy ain't comin' back," he sang. The girl beside me didn't respond to his performance in any way, though others applauded and screamed.

After a brief intermission, Elvis's band took the stage alone. For the first time in Memphis, they had a drummer. After one instrumental number, they brought out the Jordanaires quartet. Still nothing from the girl on my right.

Finally, I asked, "Are you all right?"

She looked at me blankly and said, "I'm saving myself for Elvis."

When Elvis walked on stage, she went nuts. I did, too. So did every human being in Ellis Auditorium North and Music Halls. He walked slowly onto the stage, grinning to the crowd. He wore blue slacks and a bright green sport coat with a white shirt and no tie. He carried his guitar behind him loosely, almost dragging it. An electric charge ran through the audience; every molecule of air seemed to vibrate.

He worked the crowd, which responded to his every move. With one audience in front and another behind, he wheeled around, holding himself up with the microphone stand or falling to his knees like a tent revival preacher, pointing his finger at the audience and pleading. He seemed to be simultaneously playing to each individual and posing for a thousand photographs. Every move was perfect. He prowled the stage like a big jungle cat. He teased and joked with the crowd like a long-lost friend. He introduced his mother and father, seated in the audience to my left. They stood as a spotlight swung to pick them out.

After what seemed like only a few minutes, he said, "Well, ladies and gentlemen, this is our last song. It's a new one we learned in Las Vegas. Me and the boys are going into the studio and record it next week. Hope you like it. This has been real nice playing for the home folks and all and now I only got one thing to say. YOU AIN'T NOTHIN' BUT A HOUND DOG," he sang, "cryin' all the time." The tempo was up with the rumba pattern bass line, common to early rock 'n' roll, syncopated to the top eighth-note beat. Elvis let his guitar swing down almost behind him, as he gripped the microphone and sang "You ain't never caught a rabbit and you ain't no friend of mine."

He sang the same verse over and over, but it didn't matter. No one cared. It was the most exciting thing I had ever seen. He was like a preacher at the end of his sermon, inviting lost souls to follow the profession of faith and join the body of Christ. People ran down front on the sides of both stages, filling the aisles as Elvis stalked like a striptease dancer, and fell to his knees as the tempo cut to a slow drag. Elvis sang the last chorus, half again as slow as the rest of the song, like Muddy Waters at the end of "Got My Mojo Workin'." I talked about the show for months. I described it in detail to friends and family whenever I got a chance, spreading the new religion of the King of Rock 'n' Roll, or as George Klein would say, "Elvis Himselvis."

In seventh grade I had an English teacher who turned me onto Edgar Allan Poe and Samuel Taylor Coleridge, the first a drunk and the other a drug addict. There was something compelling about the darkness and mystery surrounding them. Their words were thick and deep. "Kubla Khan" held me in its power. I discovered the *Rubaiyat of Omar Khayyam*, which took my imagination beyond the Western world to Oriental spiritualism and antiquity. It was like discovering another Bible, a history of man seeking another world, a world of soul.

On Wednesday nights, my father worked Arkansas, Mississippi, or Missouri. Wednesday was also the night my mother played piano at the church for choir practice. I enjoyed having the house to myself. One night I dug below the nightclothes in the bottom drawer and pulled my father's bourbon out of his chiffon robe. It tasted bitter and strong, but warm in my belly. I was safe in bed by the time my mother got home, so she was none the wiser. It became a weekly ritual.

I started stealing a little liquor here and there from spots around the house where my father stashed bottles. Bourbon, gin, vodka, rum, even white wine. I poured it all together into a fruit jar. Friday nights, I put the fruit jar in my car coat's oversized pocket, and snuck it into the picture show at the Normal or the Ritz, "B" movie second-run houses beneath the Plaza's social level. A couple of my troublemaking friends and I would purchase large grape or orange sodas with lots of ice and empty the fruit jar. That's how it started.

Later, I made screwdrivers with orange juice and terpin hydrate with codeine cough syrup and sat on the floor of my room, listening to jazz 45s. My favorites were "I Hear a Rhapsody," the flip side of Earl Bostic's "Harlem Nocturne," and a Moondog EP I found in a Little Rock dime store. Moondog, a blind street musician, made remote recordings of his strange, percussive rhythm band. On the record, I could hear whistles of steamships in New York Harbor, bells of passing trolley cars, and zoo animals' roars, all part of the normal city soundscape. (Years later the Moondog record inspired my keyboard part on the *Paris, Texas* motion picture score.)

I accidentally discovered the Memphis underground art community. The Guild featured foreign movies and art films not shown in commercial family theatres. There was no popcorn or soft drinks, but free coffee and lemonade. I saw the Bergman and Fellini films, but most importantly, *Jazz on a Summer Day* and *Orfeu Negro* (*Black Orpheus*), which had a long-lasting and recurrent effect on my life.

The Book Shelf bookstore had a selection of *Evergreen Reviews* and Folkways Records; the Adult Education Center on the Southwestern (now Rhodes) campus had a bookstore in the basement and a resident theatre troupe, where I first trod the boards.

In the fifties Memphis's artistic underground was sparse and spread out. A pseudo art colony was by the river and the railroad yard where author/historian Shelby Foote lived. Other artists lived near the Academy of Art, next to the Overton Park Shell in Midtown. The Shell, an amphitheater/performance venue the WPA built during the Depression, was the Memphis Symphony's home.

Musicians actors painters
Sculptors and dancers
Separated into camps with little crossover or mingling
This was the bitter

end
of the Beatniks
The Beat Generation
of Hip and Cool
Jazz Poetry
The beginning of the folk music revival
Guiltless drunkenness
Exploratory sex
The first curiosity about drugs and Eastern religions
A generation destined to consume
Itself
Searching for answers
To poorly defined questions
Old
Before its time
Beat

I did pretty well in school before junior high. I liked math and science, but then came spelling and a cursed writing class in seventh grade. I couldn't spell due to my screwed-up vision and couldn't write clearly due to the tremor in my hands. My hands didn't shake badly; they shook like A. P. Carter from the Carter Family. The first time you "fail" is traumatic. Then you get used to it. You realize the world does not end. I still can't spell and I write like a trained monkey. In junior high I started having headaches. These days it would be seen as a symptom of dyslexia. After an EEG, during which they failed to put me to sleep with a triple dose of sodium pentathol, "enough to knock out a horse," as the doctor said, they sent me to a head shrinker, a hypnotherapist who taught me self-hypnosis as a remedy to what he diagnosed as "nervous tension headaches." He also provided my first tranquilizer.

Chapter 9

ON A TRAIN THAT IS PASSING THROUGH (1955)

The end of the Memphis summer is a pressure cooker.
The lush green of spring has long since faded
Through the sun-bleached ripeness
of the dog days. Hot, dry, long afternoons drag
Toward the slow down of fall
and harvest.
Time starts to lean
Forward toward the countdown
Before school starts again
and the repetition of routine.
There is always
The anticipation of the unexpected
The possibilities of whatever
The new girl at school

Her name was Vera. She had dark red, almost black hair pulled back in a
ponytail. She wore horn-rimmed, cat-eyed glasses like the sexy secretaries on pulp detective dime novels' covers. She wore cashmere sweaters
with buttons down the back. That did a lot for her figure, which needed
no help. When she strutted down the hall, books clutched to her chest,
the waters parted. She had transferred from Kingsbury, a school full of
hoodlums and jukebox babies. She rode in a carpool with a friend of mine
from homeroom. He stuttered, barely managing an awkward introduction
on the school parking lot. She smiled. That Friday night at a school sock
hop in the cafeteria, she walked up to me during the last dance. I was
standing around, trying to keep my collar up.

"Well," she said, sarcastically. "Since it looks like you're not going to
ask me to dance, I guess I'll have to ask you." She was a great dancer. She

told me to call her. We talked on the phone for hours, days, weeks during that school year. Her father, an ex-newspaperman from a small Alabama town, played chromatic harmonica and had the first real record collection I saw. Her mother liked me. We spent hours drinking coffee and smoking Pall Malls in the kitchen.

Vera was soft and feline. She didn't know anybody at White Station, but had her eye on society, hell-bent on being a sorority girl and moving up the food chain. Even then, I was a little left of center. We dated off and on through high school but she always had her eye on some pre–Ivy League slick with a mama's-boy haircut and a high-end future. We went to horror movies at the Normal Theatre by the university: *Curse of the Cat People, Return of the Wolfman*, and best of all, *Creature from the Black Lagoon*. The white bathing suit scene with the scaly Lizard Man swimming secretly beneath the unaware bathing beauty was an unforgettable vignette in my early pursuit of happiness.

Vera had no use for Elvis. She was a pupil at Jane Bishoff's dance studio, studying modern dance and jazz dancing. There was no professional dance troupe in Memphis in the 1950s. From time to time, Jane took her most talented dancers to perform at a supper club, Silver Slipper, out on the highway. One night, Vera encountered a young, unknown Elvis. He was clowning backstage, flirting with girls and flashing a shiny, tin badge inside his pink sport coat that read, "Chicken Inspector." She was unimpressed, to put it mildly. To further her point, Vera played me a 78 record of "Big Mama" Willie Mae Thornton singing the original recording of "Hound Dog." I made her play it over and over, fascinated by the loose groove and the sarcastic lyrics glossed over in Elvis's simplified white-boy version.

This was one gem of arcane knowledge I drew from her father's record collection, which was mostly vintage Dixieland. "Big Mama" Thornton's "Hound Dog" featured Kansas City Bill and Orchestra, which sounded like no more than a trio. It was the same song Elvis sang, but with more lyrics, more story, and an incredible groove. The drums turned the beat over and over. There were extra beats in the chord progression and irregular word phrasing in the vocal delivery. The band howled and barked like dogs as the song faded out. I loved it, my favorite thing since Will Shade and the Jug Band in Whiskey Chute. I made Vera play the intro on that worn-out 78 over and over, trying to discover this primitive-story-in-song's secrets: "You told me you was high class / But I could see through that / and Daddy I know you ain't no real cool cat."

I think Vera saw where my life was headed before I did. To me, she represented my only chance at a so-called "normal" life, which included graduate school and a day job in a world where I would have been miserable. The more I got into an artistic lifestyle, the further I grew away from her value system and her father's right-wing politics. The mainstream establishment I had been taught to accept slipped further away. Music opened the door to a life that pulled me into something only my grandmother had seen coming.

Chapter 10

THE REGENTS
(1957-60)

I can't remember why I went to Blue Ridge, a training camp for potential leaders in the Hi-Y, the YMCA/YWCA youth organization, late in the summer before I turned sixteen. I wasn't a member, much less a potential leader. It happened fast. Suddenly, I was on my way.

The bus ride from Memphis to Black Mountain, North Carolina, was long. Some girls from East High caught my attention right away. Somebody brought an old Stella guitar but couldn't play, so I played "Just a Closer Walk with Thee," and was a hit with the females before we left Tennessee.

Blue Ridge was held at Black Mountain College, where old Beatnik artists of the late forties and early fifties matriculated. It was almost too picturesque, remote and closed off like a hunting lodge, in North Carolina's beautiful green hills. The "leadership" classes were boring and worthless. But every night there was a sock hop dance in the old gym. Friday night, the next to last night in camp, was a talent show.

Four guys from Memphis put together a vocal group and I played piano. My old man had sung on the radio with a quartet when he was military school. I figured, "What the hell?" We performed Johnny and Joe's "Over the Mountain, Across the Sea" and Clyde McPhatter's "Money Honey." I played piano standing up, with my back to the audience. The place went nuts. We were a hit. The next night at the final sock hop farewell party, we were gods among men, the "Boys from Memphis." I thought about it all the way home on the long bus ride. Something was taking form around me.

Every year White Station High School put on a talent show. Students from all grades were eligible for tryouts and almost everybody made it. After our triumph at Blue Ridge, I started to make plans. The year before, a group of seniors had performed as a four-piece band with a five-man vocal group, a sort of Dixieland band with trumpets, baritone sax, bass, piano, and drums. The drummer, Bill Roland, was a friend from the country club. The notorious and mysterious Al Stamps had transferred from East High and played piano. The band and singers (who performed in white tuxedo jackets, black shirts, and white ties) won the talent show, and were big in East Memphis. Later that year they won the Battle of the Bands at the Casino Youth Building on the Mid-South Fairgrounds.

A kid a year ahead of me, Rick Ireland, played guitar, and fixed the school's P.A. system at the sock hops and other functions. He introduced me to another guitar player, Stanley Neil. My band's nucleus was born.

We had a friend who sort of played drums, and signed up for the school talent show. We were going to play the instrumentals "Flip Flop and Bop" and "Rockin' with Red," and tried to work up our act at Ricky's house. Rehearsal was the day before the talent show in the school cafeteria. Another band—two guitars, a girl piano player, and a drummer a year behind us in school—had signed up to play. A vocal group with Ronnie Stoots from my Sunday school class and pretty-boy Charles Heinz, who had a trained voice, performed "Ave Maria" in the show. A singer from my Blue Ridge group performed with them.

I was suspicious and with good reason: they did my arrangement of "Money Honey," which featured the scream before every chorus. But the big problem was that our drummer could barely hold on to the drum sticks and their drummer kicked ass! Eddie Tauber, a short little Jewish kid from Vera's homeroom, soon became the infamous "Steady Eddie."

We did okay. They played my arrangement of "Money Honey" with Charles Heinz spraddle-legged, flipping his long greasy hair, and won the show. But by the end of the night I had enlisted the drummer and the pretty boy singers, and the other band had no future.

We called ourselves the Regents after the telephone exchange in West Memphis, but everybody called us the Jim Dickinson Combo. Charles and Ronnie sang ballads and I did the rough stuff. We started out playing house parties and worked our way up to the fraternity circuit. That summer we played the CYO (Catholic Youth Organization) at St. Louis Church in East Memphis. I was sixteen and had a '48 Buick big enough for the whole rhythm section.

We never had a regular bass player. Once we played in the psycho ward at Kennedy Veterans' Hospital. Inexplicably, they had an upright bass in their recreation room. We got Jimbo Hale, who played with Stanley in Roy Cash's country trio, to do the gig with us. During that set a nurse asked us if a patient could sing a song. We were thrilled to back up a black singer. He sang something that was almost "Three O'clock in the Morning." Afterward, the nurse thanked us, "Oh, that did Lester so much good. We can barely get him to talk."

"He was good," I said. "What is he in here for?"

"Lester killed his family," she replied.

That was one of the only shows with a bass. Jimbo played the Mid-South Fair with us, too. I was sick as a dog and pumped full of codeine cough syrup. I was more of less used to playing half drunk, but the cough syrup added a dreamlike, underwater quality. Some country girls down front swooned over Charles Heinz. That was something new. They followed us after the set, and mooned and giggled until they had to get on their school bus and return to Munford.

One Saturday, Ricky, Stanley, Eddie, and I went downtown to an old Quonset hut, Meteor Recording Studio, in the South Memphis ghetto. Les, the least of the Bihari Brothers, ran the record label and the crude and sparsely furnished studio. It was midwinter, and colder inside than outside. Les, middle-aged and dressed like a nondescript businessman, saw us looking around.

"Getting the heater fixed," he said.

I couldn't help notice the guy at the piano was wearing his overcoat and a pair of gloves with fingertips cut out. It looked like the cold was a permanent situation. But I loved it right away. The mics, the control room, the tape recorder! I forgot the cold. We played "Flying Saucers Rock 'n' Roll." Les was knocked out. Stanley hit him up for five dollars. I was down for whatever. I would have come back and tried to get the fingerless gloved piano player's job, but Ricky had a better idea.

Another studio (in Brunswick, Tennessee, northeast of town) was in a big old barn behind a Dairy Queen Drive-In with a big flashing neon sign that looked like a space satellite. We had Charles and Ronnie with us, and had specially rehearsed our best rock ballads. I had a pretty good triplet feel for a white guy and Charles was really good.

That night I met someone who would be very important in my musical education. He was engineering in the studio and cooking burgers in the Dairy Queen. Packy Axton had a Robert Mitchum haircut and a slow, humorous style that made him appear almost retarded. He was one of the coolest people I ever met. His mother and uncle owned the studio.

We played, but mysteriously, the sound would not stick to the tape. It showed up on the meters and they could hear it going down, but it would not play back on the tape. Ricky was disgusted. "Hillbillies," he complained.

Packy's uncle, Jim Stewart, who was trying to start a record label, liked Heinz a lot. Charles ended up with a recording deal. I had taught him to play enough piano—octaves and triplets—to write his own songs. The result, "Prove Your Love," was the second recording released on Satellite Records (soon to be Stax).

Charles "Prove Your Love" Heinz quit the Regents to tour behind the record. On the road, he had a car wreck somewhere in Missouri. Charles went through the windshield and broke all his newly capped teeth, putting an end to his budding career. Years later, Charles became a very successful minister of music.

THE MAN IN BLACK

Stanley Neil played rock 'n' roll with sheer contempt; that's what made it so good. He loved country music and played with Roy Cash and Jimbo Hale for the love of the art. Roy, Johnny Cash's nephew, had a radio show on KWEM called the Roy Raymond Show. I don't think Stanley made any money playing with Roy but it was his passion. They wore black and gold cowboy shirts and pants with gold lamé military stripes down each leg's seam. Stanley insisted on wearing this outfit on our rock gigs, which delighted me but irked Ricky no end.

One night in 1957, Stanley took me to Johnny Cash's home, a ranch house in East Memphis, off of Shady Grove Road. The mailbox was shaped like a guitar. Cash was warm and friendly, joking with us, showing us a home movie of Elvis in Vegas with a couple of showgirls. Elvis wore his famous gold Nudie suit, had a champagne bottle in each hand, a costumed showgirl under each arm, and a foot-long cigar in his mouth. He was obviously drunk. Cash laughed and laughed, and told us Elvis had tried to buy the film for big bucks. He didn't want his mother to know he smoked. The second time Stanley took me to the House of Cash, my idol Jerry Lee Lewis was passed out on the couch. Cash said Jerry Lee's wife had put him out.

Steady Eddie built his drum kit one piece at a time. He found his kick drum in a pawnshop, his snare in some music store, and painted them red. He had big black letters, ET, on his kick drumhead with silver glitter outlines. I told people it stood for Early Times. He didn't have a floor tom-tom until my senior year and he never had a hi-hat. He had a 26"

Zildjian ride that's the reason I have high-frequency loss in my left ear to this day. Before Eddie got the 26" ride, we would break into the school band annex on Friday night and "borrow" a cymbal and bring it back Sunday afternoon or Monday morning. (We almost got caught a couple of times.) That 26" ride was a killer. Terry Johnson from the Royal Spades had one like it; they could peel paint off the bandstand. We got a reputation for being wild and loud. We played the Sun catalogue. Ricky was the first Memphis guitarist who could play a Chuck Berry solo. Microphones were hard to get. We started with a handheld tape recorder mic plugged into a guitar amp. A high school fraternity paid us with a professional mic they had probably stolen from a church. We lifted a mic stand from one of the party rooms we played, and put the tape recorder mic on the back of the piano.

Our reputation grew. We worked college fraternity parties at Memphis State and Ole Miss. The college parties got a little rougher—beer kegs, sorority girls dancing on the tables, and fights and drama over whether or not they were going to pay us. They liked Jimmy Reed and Muddy Waters material better than the high school kids did. But they also liked to mess with the band. They would grab the mic, sing "Fuck, Suck," jump on the stage, dance like Elvis, or do a drunken duck walk. Some nights as we loaded our meager equipment after the party, frat boys would pour beer on our heads from the upstairs windows of the frat house.

When a fraternity had a special party, it was cool to hire a black band. The Mad Lads and The Thomas Pinkston Trio (actually a quartet) specialized in these parties. Pinkston had been the child protégé violinist in the W. C. Handy Band. His business card read, "Thomas Pinkston World's Greatest Negro Hawaiian Guitar Player."

Many of these parties, some of the best I ever attended, were held on a sandbar on the Arkansas side of the Mississippi River. Thomas was a great singer with a rough whiskey voice, like Rochester's on the Jack Benny show. He had an ancient (to me) drummer, L. T. Lewis, who had played with Count Basie. I copied Pinkston when I sang, but paled by comparison.

During Cotton Carnival we played hotel ballrooms in downtown Memphis. I thought we had really arrived when we played the Peabody Hotel. Some of these parties were for adults, who usually acted worse than the kids.

We made good money. We were nonunion, but usually played for more than union scale. My father couldn't understand why I didn't want a summer job. The money I made playing with my band didn't count. He wouldn't see it. For all our similarities in mood and character, the big difference between us was he didn't possess the artistic temperament that kept rearing its head in my life. He had a good voice, but it meant nothing to him. He had sung in a quartet when he was in military school. They performed on the radio in Chattanooga. He saw no possibility of a future or career in the arts.

In '57, before guitar players were a dime a dozen and you could learn how to play like Chuck Berry at your local music store, there were three guitar teachers in town: old man Tanquerey, who taught only classical and Spanish (flamenco) guitar; Len Vernon who taught basic jazz and was very good; and Lieutenant Forrest O'Kelly, who taught at Berl Olswanger's, but was a cop, which ruled him out even then.

So you taught yourself. I still maintain rock 'n' roll should be self-taught. Guitar players usually fell into two categories: jazz players who could maybe read music and played arrangements, and hillbillies, cowboy players who could not read music and played instinctively.

Black musicians, relegated to play either white, roadhouse honky tonks like the Plantation Inn or their own establishments, also fell into two categories. Schooled musicians played big band holdover jazz standards at sit-down, reading gigs in the theatres on Beale Street, with more sophisticated music than what was played at any of the white clubs except the Peabody Rooftop. The second type played black juke joints in the heavy 'hood or out on the highway, with a mixture of aspiring locals and traveling acts left over from the medicine shows who played blues from town to town on the "Chitlin' Circuit."

These worlds and groups did not mix musically or racially, except in the minds of Dewey Phillips and the generation of white boys who sought out blues, jazz, howling hillbillies on the Grand Ole Opry, and moaning bluesmen from Randy's Record Mart. Amid the commercials for Hair Care ("for Kinky Hair") and ads for an "autographed picture of the Lord Jesus Christ standing in the garden," we heard Sonny Boy Williamson and Howlin' Wolf. We heard Smilin' Eddie Hill and his Country Cowboys in the morning and Dewey Phillips in the afternoon, playing everything from Hank Snow to "the late, great Johnny Ace." We soaked it up. When we met a brother follower of the new faith, we at least checked each other out.

Charlie Freeman came out of nowhere. Meeting Charlie was like meeting Packy Axton or Stanley Neal. At sixteen I could tell this guy was a pro. Somebody brought him and Steve Cropper over to my house because they played guitar. They both went to Messick in midtown Memphis, a social barrier between us, since everything in Memphis was a matter of race and where you went to high school.

We jammed in my basement that afternoon. I had bought a Silvertone Duo Jet from Steady Eddie. Cropper had a Telecaster. Charlie took lessons from Len Vernon and passed what he learned on to Cropper. Charlie leaned toward jazz but had a funky tone, a feel more like Lowman Pauling, who played with the Five Royales. We exchanged phone numbers. Charlie Freeman never met another musician without exchanging phone numbers, a ritual I watched over and over. Cropper kept getting shocked from stepping off the rubber mat that covered the concrete floor (he never did figure it out). Charlie never got shocked.

Charlie and Steve played with Packy Axton, Duck Dunn, Don Nix, Terry Johnson, and Wayne Jackson (who was from West Memphis and grew up listening to the music from the Plantation Inn). They called themselves the Royal Spades, named after a pinky ring with a diamond inside an Ace of Spades that singer Ronnie Stoots wore. Stoots sang with both my band and Charlie's.

I played a couple of gigs with them at Neil's Hideaway, a chicken wire joint on South Memphis's outskirts. On my first gig there I naively asked Packy, "What's the deal with the chicken wire?" It stretched around the front of the stage like a baseball backstop.

"Wait 'til eleven o'clock," was all he offered.

The gig was pretty smooth. The piano was a piece of crap but that was par for the course. I liked playing with horns, Terry Johnson swinging like a rusty gate. Eleven o'clock came and the hillbillies hit the chicken wire with anything not nailed down. Ashtrays, beer bottles, hi-ball glasses, shoes, pocket books, everything. We kept on playing the "T-Bone Shuffle" like nothing was going on. Pieces of debris came at us through the chicken wire. Then it was over as quickly as it started. Packy looked over at me and rolled his half-shut eyes. I never questioned him again.

Charlie asked me to join the Spades, but I told him I had my own band. It seemed like a loyalty issue. Long ago Alec taught me the concept of gang loyalty, protecting your cohorts. I really enjoyed playing with the Royal Spades, but couldn't walk away from the Regents.

In my high school art class was a girl from Colonial Acres. Carol Jensen was friends with Charles Heinz and from the same neck of the woods, the wrong side of the tracks from school and Poplar Avenue (a great dividing line that runs west to east through Memphis). Carol said her ambition was to marry Charlie Freeman. I wished her good luck.

The next year, when I was a junior, the talent show was a different story. We were stars. We had been gigging as backup for Kimball Coburn, a local Memphis-area celebrity of sorts. He had a regional hit called "Cute." He was clean-cut with a mama's boy haircut and a dark Italian suit. He would drop down and do a very embarrassing fruity little dance. But he had Portia Swain, a hot-looking blonde jazz dancer, as a side act. She danced while we played "Caravan." We got Kimball to guest star for the talent show.

We did our act and backed a girl group doing "Mediterranean Moon." In that group was Mary Unobsky, little sister of the notorious Mark "Butch" Unobsky, and Donna Weiss, who would later co-author "Betty Davis Eyes." After Kimball sang the ever-present "Cute," I came back and encored with "Hey Bo Diddley," with the audience singing the call and response.

The forbidden, fascinated youth culture was thriving. We went to West Memphis to see movies the infamous Lloyd T. Binford and the Memphis Censor Board banned in Memphis. We sought literature from *Evergreen Review* and City Lights. I got my copy of *Howl* from a friend of my mother who had a bookstore in Texas. After my mother discovered what it was, she only gave it to me after she had read it to me aloud. Due to my poor vision, my mother always read to me—the Bible, Pogo comics, *Treasure Island*. *Howl* was the last thing my mother read to me, an unforgettable experience for us both.

Paramount amongst the forbidden were records banned from radio. In the teenage underground copies circulated from big sister to younger sibling, like a secret traditional rite of passage. "Drunk," "Sixty Minute Man," and most significant of all, were Hank Ballard and the Midnighters' songs, forbidden magic with a hypnotic shuffle rhythm patter impossible to forget. "Sexy Ways," "Work with Me, Annie," "Annie Had a Baby," and the key to it all, "The Twist." If a teenage band could play these songs, success was assured.

Jimmy Reed started a guitar pattern that became a recurrent theme throughout his entire repertoire. It's played by two, sometimes three guitars, a lead and a rhythm. Chuck Berry takes the same three notes from a basic boogie-woogie bass line and makes them the rhythm guitar part that was the hard-drive of rock 'n' roll (and led to the eighth-note frenzy of punk rock). This same riff, with yet another slightly different groove and back beat, is present over and over in Hank Ballard and the Midnighters, unquestionably one of the best group names in rock 'n' roll history.

> The Midnighters.
> Dark and mysterious.
> The wee wee hours.
> The rising of the moon.
> A time when all good people
> were fast asleep.
> Surely not dancing
> to the forbidden
> Negro Be Bop!

My band played them all. We had a killer "Twist" groove in '59, at least two years before public acceptance and the fad. I still get that old feeling when I hear the three-chord turnaround and the shuffle of the eighth note pattern, the intro to "The Twist" itself. The pattern took on the name "Shifting" locally, as opposed to "Chuckabilly," which was slightly different from the Jimmy Reed pattern (none of which are played correctly today). The Stones call it "grinding."

The golden era was brief. Elvis went to Hollywood and then the army. Dewey Phillips was kicked off the air. Jerry Lee Lewis married his cousin. Chuck Berry went to prison. The bottom dropped out of the rock 'n' roll dream.

I cut my ducktails and joined a high school fraternity, thinking it would help get jobs for my band. It did. There was also social pressure. "Why don't you get a haircut? You look like a hood. Do you have to wear that motorcycle jacket? Sit up straight. Turn your collar down. I'm not going to be seen with a hoodlum." Girls, parents, teachers, preachers! Everybody wanted me to change. I tried. I got an Ivy League haircut, and started to wear a suede jacket and penny loafers instead of my beloved motorcycle boots with silver studs and horseshoe taps.

I made good friends in the fraternity, T. J. Oden, Lewis Young, Tom Winston. Vera applauded my change. She had joined DBS, the best high school sorority, and was busy moving up the social ladder, eye on the prize. I enjoyed belonging to something. Fraternity meetings gave me a purposeful ritual for Sunday afternoon.

It wasn't destined to last. I don't believe people really change. Despite Ebenezer Scrooge's transformation in *A Christmas Carol,* in real life you have to play the cards you are dealt. Cleaning up my image made it easier to think about college, and probably kept me out of juvenile court and reform school or worse. I created a Bruce Wayne alter ego as a disguise. But I missed my ducktails.

Chapter 11

THE POINT AND THE SETTING SUN
(1957–60)

The Arkansas side of the Mississippi River is lowlands, flat to Crowley's Ridge. The Memphis side of the Mississippi River is a tall bluff. Driving around downtown one Sunday afternoon I discovered an old deserted truck parking lot, on the south side of the bluff across from the warehouse district (where they later built the Rivermont). The Point was a great place to park, drink, or take a girl. The band and I would go to The Point after a bad gig or before a party, with a sack of ice, a bottle of vodka, a can of grapefruit juice, and be off to the races. After a couple of drinks, I liked to get in the back seat of my old Buick and stick my head in the bag of ice.

I spent many a Sunday evening at The Point watching the sun go down across the river. From the river bluff the setting sun appears to bounce in the last split seconds before it sinks into the Arkansas delta's horizon line, an optical illusion I have seen nowhere else. It usually bounces three times, like an orange ball in slow motion; then it's gone. Sometimes I watched the sunset with Vera or with drunken friends but more often by myself. It became a ritual.

Chapter 12

DIRE FEMALES
(1955-63)

The band was really hot that summer. Sometimes the Shifters' Billy Dover would play rhythm, so I could work my mic stand routine and stagger around drunkenly. I met Anne Moss at a Sigma sorority dance. "Sigma girls put out" was the line at the Smoking Tree at school. Anne wasn't in Sigma. She was still at Colonial and everybody knew Colonial was bad. It hardly got worse than at the Colonial Canteen, where the dance was held.

Anne came in late. The band was loud and cooking. Anne had blond ducktails, sharp pointed jukebox baby knockers, and pouty bedroom eyes. She wore a tight black skirt, an equally tight black cashmere sweater, suede penny loafers, and white bobbysocks. She stood with her head down so she could cut her eyes up through her lashes, what Raymond Chandler called "the old up from under." She turned Stoots and me on like a faucet. Stoots knew her by name, moved over easily, started grinning, and doing his Charles Heinz poses, but she was staring at me.

Stoots stole away, pissed off. He only did two songs the last set, and left me to do the singing. As usual we closed with "Hey Bo Diddley," playing it for fifteen or twenty minutes. The crowd stopped dancing and circled the band screaming "Hey, Bo Diddley," like a church chorus call and response. I picked up the mic stand and hit my knees, sticking the mic in my mouth and growling. I opened my eyes to get up. Who should be standing in front of me, cool as a Cuba Libre, her arms under two sharp steel-tipped titties, just barely under black cashmere pulled down as tight as her crossed arms could pull it down? Anne cold blue-eyed me up through dark lashes, looking up at me even though I was kneeling in front of her. She smiled a crooked orange smile, not moving a muscle. The crowd screamed. She never blinked. She only squeezed her arms tighter under her titties and shot me clean out of the sky. Nailed like the outlaw.

I called her the next day and we started going out. She wiggled when we made out. She rubbed me crazy with those tits of hers, moving back and forth across my chest, moaning low in her throat, teasing and twisting all over my Buick's back seat. I gave her the *Rubaiyat*, a new way to approach a chick with ducktails from Colonial Acres. I also gave Vera the *Rubaiyat*. She said her father had owned a copy since he was young. Vera and Anne got to be friends. They were a good match, Vera the inimitable mistress.

Anne never wore the black and black outfit again—must have been hunting clothes. If she had worn it again, I might have ruined her future plans. We got caught backstage during study hall. We were supposed to be working on the set for *The Glass Menagerie*. I was on the floor. She unbuttoned my shirt and dragged her nails across my skin slowly, blinking, looking up, smiling, and talking the whole time: "How do you like that, hum? Feel good? I'll bet it does. Ummmmmm!!!! Feel me diggin' in, daddy? Ooooh, yeah!!!"

In walked Coach Ralston, the short-stuff shop teacher, madder than a fucking hornet and hot to see this tough-looking young chick crawling all over me (he figured I was some sort of pervert weirdo). She got suspended from school for three days. I went back to art class.

There were other "Dire Females," as my mother called them. I was attracted to a type, a late-1950s thing. Many girls seemed to lead a life of selected fiction. The Brontë sisters and Ayn Rand had a death grip on the teenage temptresses who crossed my path, and like *Gone with the Wind*, swept through several generations of Southern females.

These girls fueled the fires of my frustration. In the '50s the "good girls don't do it" myth still prevailed. Popular fiction and movies furthered the myth. Saturday night at drive-in movies fostered a conflict between our parents' morality and the mobile sex machine the back seat of the family car provided.

Through the zoo parade of jukebox babies and high school princesses, Vera returned repeatedly like the theme song in a Hollywood movie. She haunted me with the promise of the normal life I would never have. I started working on a novel, *Rain Summer*, a thinly disguised biography of a James Dean character, very *Catcher in the Rye* and *Steppenwolf*, set in fifties Memphis. My writing owed a lot to the teenage classic *Street Rod* and William Goldman's *The Temple of Gold*. Vera read it and corrected the spelling. I wrote so she would read it. It foretold our relationship's doom, but also gave me a link to her and that fantasy life I could never have.

The original story ended in suicide on New Year's Eve, after the main character failed to go to college. I couldn't imagine life beyond high school. I wrote by hand in big black bound notebooks from my father's office supplies. I carried them everywhere. I worked feverishly, harder than I worked on anything during high school. I wrote about drinking and the heavy ever-present pre-sex from teenage wasteland. No music. I figured nobody would be interested.

My English teacher picked up on my interest in writing and told me I should sign up for speech and drama class.

Chapter 13

VASSAPOO, OPEN D GUITAR TUNING
(FALL 1959)

High school football season was over; winter cold was in the air. My band was opening for Bo Diddley. Jimbo Hale was playing electric bass. I had a date with Vera for the big fall party, a fraternity-sponsored dance. All her people would be there. Hell, everybody would be there. I picked her up. We rode to Willie King's Drive-In to score liquor. We pulled around back. I blinked my lights and waited. Dizzy walked out of the shadows, smiling his great gold-toothed grin, "Heat's on, Boss. The heat's on."

"What's up Diz?" I played along.

"The roaches are crawlin'. Come around last week and put up a spotlight. Said, 'We been watchin' you, Boy.' Well, they wasn't watching when I shot out the bulb." Dizzy kept a BB gun in his little shack where he waited for the food carryout. He was the outdoor waiter for the Drive-In trade. "Naw, sir, they wasn't watchin' ol' Dizzy close enough," he chuckled down in his throat. "What you need tonight?"

"Fifth of Dark Eyes." I slipped him $10.

"Oooo-eeee, got to watch out for that vodkum! Las' time I got a head full of vodkum, I stabbed my ol' lady and Dizzy ended up on the farm," he laughed out loud. He pocketed the ten-spot and returned to the shadows. In a few minutes he returned with the familiar brown paper sack. "You folks goin' to see Bo Diddley?"

"Yeah, Diz. Me and my band are opening."

"You take it easy then." He nodded to Vera and tipped his old black chauffeur's cap. We were off. We had time to kill and drove to the river. The lights on Riverside Drive were blue and lit the night in a strange still-black way. Cars went by. Telephone poles of the colored slum towered behind us, ghostlike, blinking in the night. Something far away screamed, "THIS IS IT." This is the night. Summer's great wake. The big beast coming to rest. Tonight.

The National Guard Armory was lit like a circus. The Memphis Belle, a B-17 bomber from World War II, sat in front, like a guardian angel. The parking lot was already full. I squeezed my old Buick in between the east Memphis Chevys and Pontiacs. We walked through the red mud to the back door, the musicians' entrance. Once inside Vera headed into the crowd, the tail of her cashmere coat flaring out behind her. She smiled at me over her shoulder and was gone for the evening. She would find me after the show and pour me into the car.

I stepped cold into a full-blown drama. Bo Diddley had caused a riot the night before in Nashville. A white girl had jumped on stage and started to dance. The story had run in the Memphis paper and the frat-boy promoters were sweating. Bo hadn't shown up. My band was contracted to play one set. We agreed to keep playing. We sounded good with Jimbo Hale on electric bass. Ronnie Stoots was singing alone. Charles "Prove Your Love" Heinz was history. I was jazzed to see Bo Diddley, and had little use for Stoots singing "Summertime."

It got later and later. We stretched out. The audience was getting crazy. Finally, we got word Bo had arrived. We stopped playing and went out the back door. Two Chrysler stations wagons had pulled up and parked on the sidewalk. They were covered with randomly placed pinstriped hot rod decals and a hand-lettered sign that read BO DIDDLEY BAND. Two giant black men in thick fur coats were driving. The three-piece band unloaded their drum kit. Bo argued with the frat-boy promoter. Ricky, Stanley, and I walked up. The frat boy, irate and overly agitated, shook a performance contract and screamed, "It says right here you are playing two hour sets and taking one break." Bo Diddley slowly reached in his pants pocket and pulled out a wadded up greasy piece of paper and unfolded it. Sure enough, it is the contract.

"Yeah," he says. "It say that in my contract, too." He wads it up and puts it back in his pants. He points at me. "He could have been Bo Diddley." He points at Stanley, who is in true racist near frenzy. "Or he could have been Bo Diddley," he continued. "But I is Bo Diddley and Bo Diddley is taking three breaks."

That was it. I agreed to play the breaks for an extra $150; the proceedings commenced. The hour struck and the witch man, great raiser of the dead, had arrived with an amplifier that looked like an icebox lying down and an orange guitar shaped like a Ford Fairlane. The trio wore knee-length red coats. Bo turned on the amp and tuned his guitar at full volume. The crowd screamed. Bo laughed and laughed, and kept tuning.

Then he started, drums laying a repeated pounding rhythm, maracas filling up the holes. Jungle sound filled the armory. The world stood on its head and screamed. No one was dancing exactly; the crowd moved like one great sheet. On a pedestal ten feet over the crowd's heads, mad men were rain dancing. The night stopped being pink and became flaming green. Everything was orange, like methylate spilled in a bathtub. Football disciples down front had six-pack beer cartons on their heads and whooped the Indian dance, hearing the organ grinder, hearing the mating call.

> Watching the great god with the orange scepter
> Screaming, ". . . sugar . . . sugar . . . ,"
> He jumped down my throat
> And started running around inside me
> The drums screamed
> The great swelling guitar tore the night
> Into little nights
> And blew them away
> To the red stars
> This was the dying time
> The end of the beginning
> Air alive with calls and moans
> Never
> Ending sun
> Orange and green
> Monolithic star of the day

Watching his hands was a mystery. The chords weren't recognizable. He seemed to play a pattern, first open and then closing his hand for the four chord. His hand zoomed up the neck, making the low bass string scream and rumble. I looked around. Ricky watched him, too, trying to figure it out. After the dance, I took Vera home and went to Ricky's. We worked in his music room until dawn, by which time we had figured out "open" D tuning. We broke the code. Bo Diddley's guitar was tuned to a chord. We were the new white disciples of the black man's magic powerful technique; it opened a new world of soul funk. Wild-eyed, still possessed by the witch man, I was in bed and away on a gray sleeping cloud.

Chapter 14

THE CASINO WITH SCOTTY AND BILL (1960)

In the 1950s, Wink Martindale was a Memphis TV personality with a kids' show on WHBQ—*Mars Patrol*, set inside a rocket ship with the audience facing a control panel. Each afternoon Wink and his crew of kids blasted off to a Flash Gordon serial adventure. He also co-hosted *Dance Party*, a Saturday afternoon teenage show featuring couples from local high schools and local musical guests. Anita Wood, Elvis Presley's girlfriend, co-hosted. That's where I first saw Jerry Lee Lewis playing with a trio (no guitar). At first the kids laughed at the long-haired piano player, but by the end of the first song they weren't laughing.

Martindale did a live, show-stopping interview with Elvis early in '56. Wink asked, "Elvis, when you got out of Humes High School, did you think all this was going to happen to you?"

"I didn't think I was gonna get out of Humes High School," Elvis snarled, leaning on a jukebox.

Wink moved to L.A. and the big time. WHBQ threw a farewell party concert at the old Casino Youth Pavilion on the fairgrounds. The lineup featured Thomas Wayne, starring behind his current hit "Tragedy," and Warren Smith, the "Ubangi Stomper," one of my favorite Sun artists. Scotty Moore and Bill Black had just quit Elvis, and were the backup band most of the evening. My band backed Kimball Coburn. We played two sets of four songs. Ronnie Stoots and I each sang one song a set. Kimball Coburn did two. Anita Wood, now Elvis's ex-girlfriend, was backstage. Bill Black always liked me. He thought I was funny. Backstage he asked me, "Dickinson, you got a bass player yet?"

"No," I answered.

"Well, by God, you got one tonight!" Bill had just gotten a Fender electric bass; it sounded great. We did our first set. I sang Little Richard's "Send Me Some Lovin'." It went over real well.

Second set, Ricky encouraged me to do "Hey Bo Diddley," but I hadn't brought my guitar. Bill said, "Why not use Scotty's?" Ricky asked Scotty's permission, since I was pretty drunk. I could tell he was reluctant, but nodded his approval. We did Stoots's song. Kimball did "Cute," his local hit. Bill looked over halfway through and asked me, "What's the name of this song?"

I told him, "Cute."

"Never heard it," he said, without missing a note.

I strapped on Scotty Moore's high-end Gibson guitar, and started to tune down to open D for "Hey Bo Diddley." I saw Scotty off stage, freaking out. It was too late to stop. I was too far gone. The crowd went nuts. They hollered back, "Hey, Bo Diddley," and hooted and hollered when it was done. I staggered off stage past Scotty frowning his disapproval, as Bill howled with laughter. Anita stood there, goggle-eyed. "That was fantastic," she gushed. "Could I have your autograph?"

I signed her arm with a ballpoint pen. Warren Smith slapped me on the back. Scotty doesn't trust me to this day.

After the Casino Wink Martindale Farewell Show, my band's shape changed radically. Ronnie Stoots quit and joined the Royal Spades full time. What hurt worst was when Stanley Neil joined the army. He was a great musician, and put an edge on the band we never regained. However, this meant I now played guitar all night. Playing guitar drunk and playing piano drunk are different things. On piano all you have to do is avoid the cracks. Our gigs suffered. I would do one Jimmy Reed song after another, which was not yet popular with the crowd. "Hey Bo Diddley" turned into a medley that sometimes lasted twenty or thirty minutes, causing fights and trouble. We developed a bad reputation. "We're not paying for a band. We're paying to watch Dickinson get drunk," one sorority complained. I could neither argue nor deny.

We still had no steady bass player; that made us a trio. I got a good friend of mine, Saul Belz, to sing background and play maracas. He was a good showman and had a better voice than mine. He came from a prominent, powerful Jewish family, big supporters of Israel. Somewhere I have a handbill in Hebrew for a bond rally that reads "The Regents—Guns for Israel." Saul had a really cool older brother. He turned me onto a Big Bill Broonzy record that introduced me to country blues. Big Bill played solo acoustic guitar. The songs didn't have the rigid twelve-bar structure of electric urban blues, like Jimmy Reed's or Muddy Waters's. It was black, primitive folk music, the motherlode where black music on radio came from. Saul's brother knew the older musicians. One night when I went to pick up Saul for a gig, Jerry McGill and his bodyguard, Norwood Carter, were at his house. Norwood was sitting on the refrigerator.

"Norwood," I asked, "How did you get up there?"

He flapped his arms and replied, "I'm an eagle. I flew up here."

"I didn't know you could fly, man," I said.

"You can fly, too," he said, holding out a black and red capsule in his hand. That was my first hit of speed. The gig that night was really hot, even if the tempos were a little quick. I didn't sleep until Sunday night.

Ricky got word Brenda Lee was auditioning guitar players for her road band. We went over the river to Danny's club in West Memphis for the tryout. The club was afternoon empty, and smelled like cigarette smoke, stale beer, and industrial-strength disinfectant. Amps were set up on the dance floor in front of the bandstand. A few local ringers had shown up, sheepishly sitting around the tables in front of the kitchen door. Ricky did okay. He was the only one who could read the chart. But the standout guitarist was a curly-blond-haired country boy a few years older than Ricky and me. Chips Moman talked fast and had a million-dollar grin. He took over, like he was in charge and ran the show. He had a conspicuous jailhouse homemade tattoo on his right forearm: a pair of dice showing snake eyes and the slogan, "Born to Lose."

Gene "Be-Bop-A-Lula" Vincent was also there, in the same tour package as Brenda. He was crippled and dressed in black. In the road case for his Stratocaster I saw a snub-nosed .38 Special and a bag of what I assumed was marijuana. This is the big time, I thought.

Chapter 15

BRING ON THE BULLET
(1960)

Barbara Teal looked like a fallen angel. She had platinum blond hair, huge green eyes that turned purple in the dark, and a smile that showed all her teeth. She was famous in the high school culture of 1950s Memphis. She went to Immaculate Conception Catholic girls' school, and dated a series of hoods, thugs, and football monsters. The first time I saw her was at a New Year's party at the National Guard Armory, a month after our gig there with Bo Diddley. Piano Red played and Jimmy Reed's son, Alvin, led the band. Red had long been one of my favorites. My band had played "Rockin' with Red" and "Red's Boogie" as part of our set since the beginning. Red was a pink-eyed albino with gold teeth. His show was an old-school R&B revue with a girl singer and vocal group. During his entire set members of the audience shouted, "Bring on the Bullet. Bring on the Bullet."

The Bullet was a quadriplegic. While the band played a one-chord vamp, crew members placed center stage what looked like a cross between a baby's high chair and a barstool. Next, a man dressed like a valet brought out a stuffed sofa pillow, carefully placed it on the stool/high chair, and brushed it off with a whiskbroom. The crowd chanted, louder and louder, "Bring on the Bullet, Bring on the Bullet!" Finally the stage crew and the valet carried on the legless, armless torso and head of a bald black man. The crowd went nuts. Stagehands carefully placed the figure on the sofa pillow, atop the stool-chair. The valet put a microphone in front of the motionless body. You had to wonder what he would do. The Bullet opened his mouth and screamed. That was his act. He bellowed like a banshee for two or three excruciating minutes; then the stage hands reversed the process and carried him off, stool, pillow, and all. That was it. What else could he do? The Bullet screamed, not words but pure emotion. The frustration and anger of a half a man, trapped in an immobile shell,

was released in the only way he knew. I tried to imagine his life on the
road, the endless time between performances. Was there an Anvil case
backstage with a sign reading, THE BULLET—THIS END UP? What did he
feel in those moments on stage that were all his own? What emotions
came to him as the crowd of white strangers called out, "Bring on the Bullet?" Was this all he had? This time on stage, screaming? He reminded me
of the organ grinder and the monkey. Who was he? What was his name?
What was his life other than the golden moments in the spotlight, when
he became the ultimate rock 'n' roll singer, the supreme protest beyond
Elvis, Jagger, Johnny Rotten, or Axl Rose, raging against life itself in an
incoherent scream of agony, hate, and frustration?

Surely, he hated the audience that called his phantom name. He blew
them away with screams from hell, like a dragon breathing fire. His
howl's burning sound seared the audience's soul in a moment of ultimate
release.

No one knows
Where the wild goose goes
After the show
It's back in the cage
For the geek
No more chickens today

Anyway, that was the first time I saw Barbara Teal. She was maybe
five feet tall. Her long platinum hair glowed like a halo. She danced and
laughed, showing all her teeth, and seemed to be having the time of her
life. At midnight, they lined up to kiss her. Thinking "what the hell," I got
in line and took my turn. It was electric. She tasted like strawberry soda.

Three weeks later, Barbara Teal was the new girl at school, starched
and shiny in a Catholic girl's school uniform. News spread like the plague.
By lunchtime every girl in school wanted to kill her and every boy wanted
to get into her pants. She showed up in my American History class last
period. She smiled. "Remember me?" she purred.

"How could I forget?" I was her comrade in a sea of enemies.

Dating Barbara was dangerous, almost a dare. North Memphis greasers and football behemoths from Christian Brothers College stalked her
like obsessed serial killers. We fought our way out of a party at Clearpool.
One afternoon at the Toddle House Drive-In she saw some hard-dicked
Harry she was trying to avoid, got down on the car floor, and told me to

get out of there. It put an edge on the possibility of a long-term relationship.

Vera hated it. She and Barbara had been in a dance class together as little girls. Jealousy ran deep. "Anybody but her," Vera told me. "You could have taken up with anybody but her, and I wouldn't care."

Barbara was there the night I graduated. She had one year of high school left. She looked spectacular. My grandmother liked her. They talked a long time about what a fine fellow I was. "She's very theatrical looking," Huddie told me. "Life is sometimes hard for a girl who looks like that." I didn't know what she meant, but it proved true.

When I was a senior, we played the talent show again. My parents were in Chicago visiting friends, so I had been drunk for a week. Vera and I had broken up. Barbara had come to White Station. I had a homemade stereo amp setup with a Harmony Monterey guitar with two DeArmond pickups, like Muddy Waters played on At Newport. We played "Bo Diddley"; then I dedicated "Sexy Ways" to the young, good-looking Spanish teacher, the faculty sponsor of the talent show event. Nobody noticed until Monday morning back at school. I got suspended for three days.

I had become somewhat of a celebrity in art class, especially after my first Merit Art Scholarship finalist award. Mrs. McGuiness allowed me to work unsupervised in the back area of whatever class was in session. I ignored whatever was going on in class completely.

After I saw a Jackson Pollock documentary at the Guild Art Theatre, I expanded my approach. I abandoned brushes and painted with the ends of paint tubes and a pallet knife. Sometimes while painting at home in the basement, I dragged an old towel across the wet paint, to create the idea of motion. Sometimes I beat the painting violently to change the subject and foreground's texture and motion. One day during a freshman class, I took a painting in progress into the parking lot and beat it with a towel. Students at the window watched and laughed. I heard Mrs. McGuiness say to her class, "When you paint like Jim Dickinson, then you can laugh." I struck the canvas again with newfound pride.

During senior finals I got a big surprise. In art class, which I figured on sleeping through, there would be a written exam. Okay. I faked my way through a section about materials and art history. But then I came to a discussion question concerning our own ideas about the creative process. I'm not sure I had ever thought about it. Art was something in which I always had an interest. It was associated with books I saw in my grandmother's library and the museum in Chicago.

Music and painting,
Coleridge, Poe
And Mickey Spillane.
Elvis on the Dorsey Show and
Rhapsody in Blue on the old brown radio.
My mother's piano in Baptist Church,
Froggie the Gremlin
And the organ grinder
With the monkey.

Without thinking about what kind of sense it made, I wrote a story about an Indian:

> An isolated Indian is carving a totem pole. He is unobserved, work-ing by himself, away from any family or tribe. As he labors away on the task it starts to rain, harder and harder. A storm sweeps over the Indian artist. He struggles on through torrents of rain and flashes of lightning until he is satisfied and goes home.
>
> Time passes. The artist returns, bringing with him a friend to whom he wishes to show his work of art. But he discovers his to-tem pole disappoints him. He realizes that what he wants to share is not the totem pole, but the rainstorm.

The story of the Indian and the Rain Storm demonstrates the frustration contained in the very nature of the artistic experience, and asks "Where is the art? Is the object the art or is the creation the art and the art object a shell?" This dilemma still troubles me.

Hidden in a corner of a Burke-Hall paint store in an anonymous shop-ping center in northeast Memphis was the Shop of John Simmons, a home-decorating curio shop. John was the son of a friend of my mother's. He was older than me and openly gay, which took a lot of guts in the late 1950s, in a city once described as the buckle on the Bible Belt. I put my oil paintings in John Simmons's shop, and to our mutual surprise, he sold them. The same person bought them all: "A Little Rain for Early Sooks Maxwell," "Rex Hotel," and "Spanish John." They were pretty good. I often wonder what strange individual collected my paintings. I gave the rest away: "Yellow Man" to Tex Campbell; "For the Body of John McCrosky" to Newport; "Balloon Man, My Love" long ago to John Logan in Texas; "Self Portrait" to others.

In the late sixties my most successful paintings melted into the mud and decomposed in the backyard of our old house across the street from the graveyard. I have sketches now, which I fear I can no longer execute. It is my "Biblical History of Creation and Eden." Maybe I could do it Gully Jimson style with interns or students. It may remain undone. . . .

Other than art my only interest in school was Gene Crain's course in speech and drama. He stimulated my interest in theatre. He got me to design sets for one-act plays, student productions. I drew up a set for *The Case of the Crushed Petunias*. I worked with the crew that built the flats and did the rigging. I was hooked.

The next year I drew the design for *The Glass Menagerie*, starring my friend, Andy Eudaly as Tom, and George Tidwell, the trumpet player for Al Stamps's band, as the Gentleman Caller. (Andy became my partner in the Market Theatre and introduced me to my future wife, but that's a little later.) Andy also took me to the Southwestern College Adult Education Center and introduced me to Ray Hill, the director of the Center Players. Ray had been Happy the Clown on the TV show *Bozo*. He was a short, fat man who looked like one of Santa's elves.

The summer before my senior year I did drum music backstage for Sartre's *The Flies*, drumming away like Olatunji while Electra did her Dance of Seduction. I got my first newspaper review: "Jim Dickinson's drums were a goo defect." Probably a misprint, but I have never known for sure. After my first outing on the boards at the center that summer, I did Tennessee Williams's *Talk to Me Like the Rain*, acting with Barbara Anderson when she was Miss Memphis.

I met Leon Russom working at the Center Players at Southwestern College in Memphis. Orphaned and living with relatives, he had started college a year early on a full scholarship. We did *Tartuffe* and Sartre's *The Flies*, with Leon always the male lead. He was the first person to show interest in recording my folk song repertoire. Home tape recorders were few and far between in the fifties. Leon had a nice one. He recorded my guitar and vocal version of folk songs and blues material for no specific purpose. We talked about the performance, referencing other artists and recordings. It seems like a small thing; yet it was a clear beginning of what I would do later.

The second summer at the Center Players we did a play by a local newspaperman. *Strange Flowers* had a beatnik scenario, set in the future. Again, Leon was the lead. I was the onstage piano player in the pit band, which included Rick Ireland on guitar and Metcalf Crump, grandson of "Boss" E. H. Crump, on drums. We were on stage providing music throughout the whole play.

The female lead, Jan Bradford, was a tiny girl with a killer deadpan Dumb Dora act. We became friends. Also in the play was John Lovelady, a Memphian who had worked in New York theatre and who went on to work with the Muppets. Leon became a pro. He was in the Broadway cast of *Oh, Calcutta!* bareass naked, and is still showing up as a corrupt CIA agent or crooked cop on various TV action dramas. Through Leon Russom I found Gus Cannon, but that was later, after Baylor.

I was never very interested in acting, but in my senior year Mr. Crain encouraged me to try out for *The Rainmaker*. I won the lead role with my pal, Andy, as the little brother in comic relief. Billy Hall was female lead. She later married Roy Cash, and has a daughter who became Miss America. I worked on my lines with Ann Moss and carried a script with me up until dress rehearsal. Crain was worried. He said, "I went out on a limb casting you as Starbuck. Did I make a mistake? Don't let me down." His concern was well founded. I had to flip a silver dollar fifty-two times during the play. All I concentrated on was not missing that damn silver coin.

The big night came. I dressed for the part. I had grown my ducktails back. I had a black turtleneck under my white-on-white Italian silk tux shirt, the trademark of Joe Banks, White Station's ranking hoodlum. I wore a black leather wristband like Ricardo Montalban. I was too cool.

Starbuck doesn't enter until halfway through the first act. Once onstage he never exits until the final scene. That night I had one of the crippling headaches that had started to plague me. I lay backstage on a couch left over from my *Glass Menagerie* set, and tried to relax and concentrate. I told myself, if I step on stage through the screen door into the farmhouse set, and I am still me, it's not going to work. But if I can become Starbuck, the con man Rainmaker, the master of the flipping coin, it's going to be okay.

The moment came. I flung open the screen door, stepped into the spotlight, and delivered my first line, "Wind? There's not a breath of wind anywhere on this Earth."

I heard an audible inhaling sound from the audience. A girl on the front row said, "He looks just like Kookie!!!," the super cool character on *77 Sunset Strip*, played by Ed Burns, who had the pop hit record "Kookie, Kookie, Lend Me Your Comb," and was the source of such classic pickup lines as "Baby, you're the gingiest!"

I was a smash. I never dropped the silver dollar. A girl I had been trying to date for months came backstage after the show and picked me up.
She took my striped Dr. Who scarf as a memento of the night. I never
asked for it back. I took it as a major compliment. I won Best Actor in
the Drama Department competition and was voted "Most Talented" of
my Senior Class Hall of Fame.

Chapter 16

THE VERY FIRST TIME
(1956-60)

I had it made in high school. Memphis, Tennessee in the late 1950s was a teenager's paradise. We were Lords of East Memphis. Emerging youth culture was all around us, creating the perfect environment for young rebels. In the immortal words of Brando in *The Wild One*, when asked, "What are you rebelling against?" Marlon mumbles, "What have you got?"

If the world wasn't ours, it would be soon. In front of us: college, draft, marriage, jobs, kids, debt, and maturity, but all of that was over the mountain. Not yet. Tomorrow night we'd buy booze and cruise territory we owned, controlled, and shared dominion over. From haircut to horseshoe-heel taps, we walked the halls of White Station High School with the confidence that comes from being The Man. "Bull of the woods. He's the boss."

Parties at girls' houses. Turn out the lights!
Room full of cigarette smoke and empty coke bottles
Yearning boys and eager girls. Hungry. Wondering.
From far away came late at night over the radio—
"Tell all the sand, and every blade of grass.
Please tell the wind to let my love pass.
Over the mountains a girl waits for me."

Prophecy. A song to time. We flew through the streets of East Memphis, crept downtown with a tan goddess with dark deep Sunday eyes as the night turned pink around the edges. The road became a jet-propelled elevator with old black cars and white Ivy League shirts. Drinking coffee late at night with a girl with lavender eyes and "cherry blossom lips."

Whatever secret nighttime held, you could escape to your home and retreat into the family order. Sleep in your bed and wake to the familiar where you were known and loved, a structure in which you were safe. There was freedom in the mandatory structure and comfort, the flow of predictable school days and events that defined existence. When you were where you were supposed to be, you were safe. You knew where to go and what you were expected to do; you could excel if you slipped by unobserved.

College would be different.

Chapter 17

VAMPUS OF THE CAMPUS
(1960)

Baylor University might seem an unlikely choice for my education. It is the world's largest Baptist institution, a fact that appealed to my mother, who spent countless hours searching *Lovejoy's College Guide* for anything that might spark my interest. Ole Miss and the University of Tennessee—party schools—were out. Baylor was the only school in the Southwest Conference without nationally affiliated fraternities or compulsory ROTC, which delighted me. Baylor had a famous Theatre and Drama Department. I had seen a Baylor production on an arts/current affairs show. The abstract set design impressed me. Paul Baker's Baylor Theatre was notorious. His tri-character *Hamlet* production was famous and controversial. The set for *Hamlet*, which literally hung over the audience, was developed by Virgil Beavers, with whom I was anxious to study. It was not to be.

Texas makes you feel small and exposed. Texans call it the Big Sky. Peripheral vision is expanded, like you're seeing too much. The horizon is open and naked; things stand out; nothing behind them, nothing around them, an over-awareness. The air is different. The Baylor campus was walking distance from downtown Waco, surrounded by multiracial slums, black on one side, Mexican on another. All the Baylor buildings were different, with no unifying architecture: buildings of different styles and materials too close together around a quadrangle of walkways, sculptured hedges, and landscaped decorative trees and bushes; a huge statue of Judge Baylor, seated and regal, and another of Judge Burleson with his top hat in hand. In front of the Armstrong Browning Library was a bas-relief of Pippa Passes, a young woman in mid-stride, based on a verse drama by Robert Browning. Two brown mascots were kept in the Bear Pit, a caged natural rock cave-like compound, when not attending football games.

On the first day of registration, my hands full of IBM cards, I stood in lines stretching as far as the eye could see. Several well-scrubbed crew-cut cadets in uniforms were seated at a table near the end of the card center. I felt cold thinking of my all-important 2S draft deferment.

My faculty adviser, Bob Flynn, was a resident playwright. For reasons unknown to me, he signed me up for a new drama class rather than the customary Drama 106, Professor Baker's much-respected Integration of Ability class that held the secrets of his creative process. I was registered in Drama 105, taught by Ivan Rider, an actor from Jackson, Mississippi. This simple substitution made all the difference.

The dormitory was insane: pre–World War II architecture with plenty of steel and brick, like the third little pig's house. The big bad wolf wasn't going to blow away Korkernutt Hall. I was in 123, the first room on the first floor. All freshman drama majors were in that wing.

Imagine a building of sexually frustrated teenage males, including obviously gay drama and music students, business school jocks, and religious fanatics. One guy, fortunately on the floor above, saw visions and ran up and down the halls screaming, "Holy Mary, Mother of God." It was a little much.

I figured my brief musical career was over, but the first people I met were musicians. At the end of the hall was Willie Kasarus, an upright bass player. If I had only had Willie in the Regents! He was full-on crazy. One night he lumbered down the hallway, wrapped head to toe in toilet paper, hollering, "The Mummy Walks! The Mummy Walks!" His roommate, Kenneth, was a jazz drummer. He hated everybody and had the habit of coming in drunk and pissing in the closet. Neither of them returned after Christmas break. You could tell some people just weren't going to make it. Me, for instance.

The first day of class was a blur of outlines and text requirements. By the time I got to Drama 105 I was confused, infuriated, and looking for the exit. Once inside the theatre, I cooled out. Ivan Rider, the drama teacher, was a big, strapping dark man resembling a gay Spanish matador. He had played Jim Bowie in Ramsey Yelvington's *Drama of the Alamo*. He had Tourette Syndrome and hooted an abstract percussion to his lectures. He was very compelling, his delivery deep with emotion and childlike excitement. He wore dark glasses in class, had a Balboa haircut with ducktails on the side, and a dragontail in the center. I had not seen one since '57, and never on an artist or adult. Most class time was spent studying contemporary drama. Ivan loved Tennessee Williams. I was right at home.

Somebody told us setting fire to the old wooden bridge on campus was a freshman tradition. They failed to inform us it was also a tradition to expel the culprits. So, one Friday night with nothing better to do, I found myself in the company of two carloads of fellow freshmen from the dorm, most of whom I did not know. We drove downtown to a service station and purchased a wastebasket full of red gasoline. Nothing suspicious about that!

We soaked the wooden plank bridge with gas, marking a big '64 for our class graduation year. When it was time to light the fire, I found myself alone. I guess I was the only smoker, at least with any matches. I struck a match and dropped it in the gas. It went out. I struck three matches at once, and let them burn for a couple of seconds before I let them fall. Flames shot fifteen feet in the air. I heard a siren scream. The campus fire department was just around the corner. I ran. I slid under a car parked in the dormitory lot and held my breath as firemen and cursing campus cops searched the area with flashlights.

My escape became the stuff of legend. The tone was set for my college career.

The following Sunday there was an open house at the theatre for all classes, including incoming freshmen. I dressed carefully. My oldest blue jeans, my once-white sneakers, a paperback book strategically placed in my back pocket, black T-shirt, horn rimmed prescription sunglasses. I was ready to rock. The theatre was behind the drugstore on the first block off campus. It was a thing of beauty: fifties architecture with a hint of Berlin Bauhaus. There were two performance spaces and a number of classrooms and offices. Art and photographs hung in the lobby. The building had its own aroma: part wet paint and lumber, part brewing coffee and cigarette smoke. It was one of the only places on campus where you were allowed to smoke.

This was more like it. Students looked like artists. Men with beards, girls in leotards and ballet slippers, overly made up and theatrical. Every one talked and wandered around. I was fascinated. As the crowd thinned out, I could not help but notice a girl sitting in the lobby, playing guitar.

She was strikingly beautiful with fire engine red hair and cat green eyes. I made eye contact; she did not look away. I followed her gaze from across the room until I stood in front of her.

"Nice guitar," I said. It was a 3/4-size lady's Martin.

"Thanks," she said in a low Texas whiskey voice. "It was my grandmother's. Do you play?" she asked, smiling.

I nodded.

"I always fall in love with the guitar players," she said.

Her name was Maree Cheatham. She was a senior. She filled me in on the theatre and Mr. Baker. We talked about music and she asked me to play. Her guitar was nice. I played a little Lightnin' Hopkins pattern. She smiled and bounced in her seat. "Oh, Blues Man," she moaned. "I love bluesmen."

In the milling crowd a boy about my age looked even more like James Dean than I did. He was dressed just like me, down to the paperback book, but he had me beat: he had a white tennis sweater knotted around his neck. Maree introduced us. "Here's somebody you need to meet. You two need to know each other. This is Merrell Williams."

He mumbled. I mumbled. It was enough.

Maree introduced me to other upperclassmen and a couple of teachers. She took me in the front office where we saw another "Somebody you just have to meet," a grizzly-looking old cowboy-hat-wearing character, much older than the rest. He was the only one who didn't look like he belonged. "This is Ramsey Yelvington. He wrote the Texas Trilogy, *The Drama of the Alamo.*" He smiled.

"This is Jim from Memphis. He plays guitar."

"'Dickinson. Jim Dickinson. Glad to meet you."

I wanted to mention my ancestral connection to the Alamo but figured I had time. His handshake was firm and sincere. We talked only a few minutes, but afterwards I had the feeling of old friendship. Maree took my hand and pulled me out of the theatre. She wanted to show me something. We entered a small workshop-looking building behind the theatre. I sensed we were not supposed to be there. As we ducked into what looked like a dance workout room, Marie hid behind a curtain and peeked out.

"I'm Ondine," she said.

I was supposed to laugh but I didn't. I'd missed some hidden reference. She smiled. "You don't play games, do you?" she asked.

I shook my head.

"What do you like to do?"

"I like to drink."

"Do you like to make love?" Her question hung in the air.

Pathetically, I missed the point, and she led me back to the theatre. It thinned to what looked like hardcore players. Girls had to be back to their dorms by 10 p.m. on Sunday night, somehow establishing the sanctity of the Sabbath (as if one needed further reminder). Some off-campus folks were going for coffee and offered me a ride. I was led off with a crowd of drama majors that I did not know. "Watch out whom you associate with," Maree said, ominously. "It can be fatal."

Again missing the point, I went for coffee and met James Lee Browning, who became my best friend and mentor in Baylor Theatre. Jimmy was no taller than my mother. West Texas came out of him like an exhaled breath. By nature he was a comedian with a sort of Bob Hope meets Mickey Rooney act. He had a car and a really cool off-campus apartment at an infamous antebellum mansion, the Catacombs.

The necessity for off-campus accommodations was painfully obvious. The dorm was nuts. To buy liquor, you had to drive almost twenty miles to the outskirts of town to a charming community, Elm Mott. No one but me would go to the Green Tree Lounge, a black beer joint near campus.

One Saturday night, I attended *Show Boat* at the Baptist student union. A Baylor football game was in progress, and some students in the audience were listening to it on transistor radios during the movie. When Baylor scored a touchdown, the audience cheered. I wasn't thinking about anything, half watching the old familiar story of racial barriers in the post–Civil War South, remembering songs my mother played to me umpteen times in childhood. Then the noble black paddlewheel boatman started to sing "Old Man River": "Here we all work on the Mississippi . . ." Suddenly I was very homesick. Thoughts of Memphis and childhood flooded my mind. "Here we all work while the white folks play . . ." Hot tears filled my eyes and ran down my cheeks. "Don't look up and don't look down. Don't you dare make the white boss frown . . ." I wept as he hit the lowest note that began the title refrain.

As the Technicolor troubadour sang the bridge, "You and me, we sweat and strain," the team must have scored. Students roared. I realized I was out of place. How foolish to care about things far away and forgotten. I hated the audience. I hated their damned football game. Philistines surrounded me! I got up, walked out, retreated to the dorm, and pulled the covers over my head.

Auditioning for the Theatre's first major production of the season, *Where's Charley?*, was compulsory for all freshmen. I had no interest in trying out, but I shoved a copy of *The Way of Zen* in my back pocket and headed for the audition. Each hopeful did a reading, a scene or a poem, and a musical number.

I got called back the next day. My 105 class teacher, Ivan, was directing *Where's Charley?*; he and Ray Allen wanted to meet with me in the green room before rehearsal. "You made quite a list of instruments on your tryout card. Can you really play all that stuff?"

I nodded.

"Well, you spelled vibes wrong. I hope you play better than you spell. It's a drummer we need."

I tried to dodge the issue. "I don't have drums at school." I had played drums maybe half a dozen times.

"That's no problem. Go down to Ace Music Store and pick out a set. Charge them to the theatre."

I figured what the hell. I had always wanted to play drums. The next day I picked out a set of silver-sparkle drums. I didn't know or care what make they were. They were cool. Kick and snare, hi-hat, ride, and crash, mounted tom, floor tom. I set them up on the side apron of the stage, next to the rehearsal piano.

Studio A was bizarre. Stages surrounded the audience on all sides. The audience sat in swivel chairs in a pit. There was a tall proscenium arch in front of two angled aprons and full-length side stages, which led to a rear stage and upper lobby modeled on the Shakespearian Globe Theatre, complete with balcony.

For the first rehearsal, the cast sat in the swivel chairs, sang the score, and read the script. Before every rehearsal and drama class we did warm-up exercises. Breathing, light calisthenics, and then verbal plosive exercises. It had a hypnotic effect and glued the class members and/or cast together. I did the exercises at the drum kit along with the cast.

The first number I played with the singing chorus was a march, the "New Ashmolian Marching Society and Student Conservatory Board." I rocked it out; the cast applauded. Later I discovered their last drummer had been a girl from the music school that everybody hated.

I was the designated bandleader. There was a female drama student playing rehearsal piano reading a five-line score. We added an upright bass and a second pianist, a jazz player improvising over the written arrangement. Later we added a clarinet, flute, and a three-piece percussion section for a Latin specialty dance number (missionary students who could jam). One bop-talked like a fifties hepcat. His name was Louie.

I spent as little time in the dorm as possible. I could not play my blues records without catching heat from some racist or student preacher condemning the Devil's Music. I hung out in the green room backstage at the theatre or across the street at James Café. One day at James Café I saw Merrell Williams, still wearing a white tennis sweater and shades. He had a problem. Jimmy Browning and Merrell were both sophomores, and had been roommates at the Catacombs the year before. Browning had gone to summer school and done stock at the theatre. He had a new roommate. Merrell asked me to share rent with him for an off-campus retreat. We were walking down 7th Street, just off campus, when Ivan Rider pulled beside us in his Thunderbird hardtop. "You boys look like two gentlemen looking for an apartment," he said. We both nodded. "I know the place," he added.

Ivan turned us on to a two-story a couple of blocks off campus. Merrell made eyes at the old woman who owned it. He thought all women were after him and most were. We moved in. He took the upstairs bedroom. I hooked up my record player downstairs and put up a Paul Klee print of "Sinbad the Sailor."

The theatre was great. I loved rehearsals and hanging out at James Café across the street. Despite being a drama major, I was the best underwater swimmer and third fastest in Physical Education. I signed up for European History with Bob Reed, a really good professor, and Old Testament Religion with Kyle Yates, a regal old gentleman with snow-white hair who had been one of the translators of the Revised Standard Version Bible and was a consulting advisor for the Hollywood film *The Ten Commandments*.

The rest of school was shit. The theatre kept me there. *Where's Charley?* was one of the best musical experiences of my so-called career. Our band was good. We set up stage left on the apron in full view of the audience. The cast was strong. Sharon Bunn, a sophomore, had the best voice in the show.

Every night Sharon stood in an amber spotlight in front of my drum kit and sang, "My darling, my darling, I've wanted to call you my darling for many and many a day." We started studying together in the old library and listening to records from files on headphones. She listened to contemporary, classical, highbrow music, like Charles Ives. I listened to Alan Lomax's field recordings, and first heard Blind Willie Johnson's "Dark Was the Night," probably the most moving and mysterious pieces of all music.

We rehearsed *Charley* for three weeks, built the set, and painted it. Students working the costume deck made turn-of-the-century getups that ran the gamut from student outfits to full dress for the Cotillion

Ball scene and South American Brazil dance costumes for the big fantasy dream sequence dance number, "Pernambuco." The dance sequence was in 5/4 time signature. I played the famous Joe Morello part from Dave Brubeck Trio's "Take Five." It was a showstopper. After dress rehearsal a Bible beater from the school administration censored the contraction moves from the dance.

Dress rehearsal. Ray Allen brought in the drummer from his off-campus jazz group to "give me some tips." I expected some bopped-out jazz-bo with killer chops and a North Texas State attitude. It turned out to be a hillbilly kid with missing teeth. He was nice about it. He could have easily eaten my lunch but instead showed me a snare and hi-hat "chase" to use on the title song. It became the signature driving beat of the number *Where's Charley?* "How's Charley? When's Charley coming home?" I played it faster and faster as the show ran. The last performance was so speeded up the chorus could barely get the words out and dance at the same time. I considered it a major accomplishment.

Rehearsal was fun, but performances were better. The shows ran Tuesday through Saturday, all sold out. The pit band was a hit. I wore my black, three-button gig suit and a skinny black tie. We played a second act overture, a medley of tunes from the first act, and always got a hand. Sometimes the audience applauded when we entered stage right and crossed to our instruments. It was a great feeling, like being somebody else: someone glamorous and mysterious who only existed during the show.

Night after night, Sharon Bunn stood in the amber spotlight; her auburn hair pulled up Gibson style, big breasted, and dressed in a wine-colored ball gown tightly cinched at the waist. Vera was still on my mind but Sharon tugged at my heart.

We would sing Jimmy Reed songs together. She had a great harmony voice. Louis, one of the South American musicians, played along with us. He thought the blues hysterical. I showed him the blues scale on guitar; he howled with laughter.

Nowhere else have I experienced the feeling of chance camaraderie and purpose as between members of a show cast. A temporary thing with a clear-cut beginning and end. People who may not like one another come together to entertain strangers they will likely never see again. You pull together, support one another, and give as much as you get. Your characters come alive with an emotion that shuts off the reality of life off stage. Theatre took over my life.

Where's Charley? was held over. We had a cast party at our apartment after the last show. It was happy, sad, and anticlimactic. Sharon had to choose between Carl, her stage lover, and me. She dumped Carl that night; the next day we hooked up at Browning's in the Catacombs. This was the last weekend before everybody went home for Thanksgiving. We sat on the steps to Jimmy's apartment and made out. I couldn't believe it. Sharon was open and giving, a free spirit. She smelled and tasted really good. I hadn't realized the extent to which I had accepted Vera's nonchalant lack of commitment.

I left Waco by bus for Dallas/Fort Worth, transferred to Memphis, and returned to the strangeness and familiarity of home.

Chapter 18

BACK AND FORTH, UP AND DOWN
(1960)

We crossed the river at dawn. City asleep. At the bus station I saw my parents' faces. At first they literally didn't recognize me. Then they did. I guess I looked pretty bad. Home was out of focus. My dog didn't remember me at first. Then he wagged his tail and rolled over on his back, like he was sorry. Where have you been, Jimmy? Huddie was there for the holiday. We ate breakfast. My mother let me smoke in the house, a first. I lay on my bed with the picture of Castro still on the wall. I thought about Waco, the theatre, Vera, high school, and slept until Thanksgiving dinner.

I came home with a bag full of laundry. All of my clothes were dirty. I cleaned up for dinner and put on some high school threads that felt funny. My father was disgusted, but we got through Thanksgiving dinner without a major incident. I figured I wouldn't push my luck, and got out of the house as soon as I could.

I cranked up the '53 Chevy and headed for the Toddle House. After a cheeseburger and a piece of banana icebox pie I felt more at home. A couple of guys from high school were there but it was mostly new people. Somebody was in my parking spot.

The next night I went to a drive-in movie with friends who were still in high school. We got drunk. At midnight, I went into the concession stand and called Vera on the pay phone. She answered, "I wondered if I'd hear from you."

"I don't know what to say." It was too late to call; the pathetic, humiliating act of someone losing it. It's easier not to remember what I said. I apologized. She said she'd see me at Christmas. I hung up. Vera haunted me through the years. I couldn't shake her phantom until I met my future wife.

The next afternoon I found myself in the chapel at my father's church. A memorial cross hung on the wall in memory of Bill Madison, my old friend who had been killed by lightning. I tried to clear my head. *Where's Charley?* was over. I was pretty much busted out of school. I loved the theatre but suspected it didn't love me back.

I had only seen Paul Baker on the first day of class. He was busy in Dallas at the new graduate school, the Kalita Humphreys Theater Center, designed by his friend Frank Lloyd Wright and built in the big-money Turtle Creek neighborhood. Virgil Beavers, the set designer with whom I had come to study, was full-time with the graduate program as well. My roommate, Merrell, was making noise about going to New York. Browning talked about how good it had been last year. Sharon had an old boyfriend in the music school at University of Texas who might rear his ugly head any time. Memphis had gone on without me. I came home to a different reality, but at least I was home. "Cross the river and through the woods." After the break, I returned to school.

Waco, Texas, is shrouded in mystery back to prehistoric time. Indians destined to be rubbed out by white devils. Frontier Texicans who fought bloody gun duels on Main Street in broad daylight.

> Always a natural home for
> Religious extremists
> Snake handling
> Unknown tongue speaking
> Shaking quaking
> And levitating
> Fire walkers
> With claims of faith
> Healing and raising of the dead.

It's like there is a spell cast over Waco, over its haunted landscape. No escape. Two rich and powerful families, who strove to minimize outside input and interlopers, controlled the town during the Depression. Factories and manufacturing facilities were discouraged. Bank loans were denied to new developers to keep the local blood pool untainted.

Baylor University operated as a world within a world. Like most colleges, the campus was surrounded with necessities of life. You could easily exist without contacting the outer world. The theatre was a microcosm within this dynamic. The polite Baptist student society isolated and shunned us. The "God Squad" put us on its prayer list and apologized, without being asked, for imaginary sins we were assumed to commit.

Tryouts were held for the second production, a play by a graduate student from Dallas and directed as a thesis project by another Dallas student. *Whistle in the Night* was a play within a play about an aspiring playwright and the inability to go home, very Thomas Wolfe.

I provided music for the show. I crawled up the catwalk holding the stage rigging and played harmonica on "Shall We Gather at the River" and "In the Sweet Bye and Bye." It was like *Tobacco Road* and worked well. It echoed through the space above the stage and hung in the air like the steam engine running through the graveyard.

The last open weekend before performances of *Whistle in the Night* started was something special. I discovered psychedelic drugs and pure grain alcohol on the same night. *Oso Negro*—Black Bear—was 190 proof. A little bear mascot key chain came with a half-gallon. Baylor! Drama students from Austin had come to party in Waco. Someone warned me about the pure grain alcohol, which I was mixing 50–50 like vodka, but I was too smart to listen. My head spun like a top and my entire lower body was numb. I sat on a windowsill, playing somebody's guitar. An actor from Austin spoke about a pill he held in his open hand. "This little pill will make you see the music, like colors floating in the air," he claimed.

I reached out, snatched the pill from his upturned hand, popped it into my mouth, and swallowed it, remembering Norwood Carter. The night opened up and swallowed me. When I returned to full consciousness, my head was in the upstairs toilet and I was puking purple. I was wearing different clothes than I remembered. My father's tan cashmere sweater had purple vomit down the front. Merrell was pleading, "Move your head. I gotta piss!"

"No," I said. "What day is this?"

"Sunday," he replied.

"What happened to Saturday?"

"We went to North Texas State."

"Who drove?" I asked.

"You did," he replied, relieving himself in the waste basket.

Hell, I didn't even know how to get to Denton, Texas. The pill turned out to be mescaline, an artificial magic mushroom. That was my first hallucinogenic experience.

Chapter 19

THE PLOT SICKENS
(1960)

Knowing how you are going to die is terrible. I had the same prophetic dream over and over. I am by myself and a knock comes at the door. A man I have never seen before is there. He says, "Are you Merrell Williams?"

I answer, "No."

He pulls a gun and shoots me.

Merrell would screw anything with a hole between its legs that wasn't its asshole. Young, old, short, tall, he took on all comers. One night he told me he was researching a new play. "I need to have an affair with a married woman," he giggled in a gleeful, almost sinister way.

Trouble started. His research subject was an upper-class drama major whose husband coached football. She was from a rich Texas family. A building on campus bore the family name. Her father was the chancellor's childhood friend. The scandalous affair quickly heated up and became hideously public. Before it was over she had moved out on her jock husband and taken their infant son with her. She moved into the Catacombs next door to Browning; the beginning of the end.

With a dramatic sense of when to exit, Merrell decided to move to pursue acting in New York. We had a farewell party at the apartment the night he was to leave. We drank, sang dirty songs, and whooped it up Texas/Mississippi style until we put him on the bus.

I couldn't afford to keep the apartment alone. I had learned to live on cheese and ketchup sandwiches, saving my money for liquor. There was no way to go back to the dorm, even though I still officially had a room, a shell I visited only under cover of night to change clothes or hide from prevailing evils.

I moved into the Catacombs, an antebellum mansion, replete with slave quarters, divided into two-room apartments. The Catacombs drew me in. Browning had an upstairs unit that stuck out over the driveway like a *porte cochere*. The overhanging room had windows on three sides so the dry Texas wind could blow through. I took up residence on the floor in front of the gas space heater, and spent many a night wrapped in an army blanket, curled up like an old hound dog in front of that heater. It was one of the happiest times of my life, but it didn't last.

Jimmy Browning was a real talent. Most of what I learned about Baker's Baylor Theatre technique I learned from Jimmy. He also gave me the foundation of my ongoing Texas education. He was from Breckinridge, a little West Texas town he loved. Baker's technique was rooted in childhood memories, a sense of place and region. One of Baker's big exercises involved "walking out your rhythm," a repeated hypnotic process that helped an actor access his character's inner core. We went to the Waco cemetery at night and would "walk out our rhythm." Jimmy organized groups of theatre students for trips to the graveyard. We drove through Cameron Park, a big weird city park on the Brazos River. There were long winding trails, landscaped gardens, and thick live oak groves along the river on a high rolling bluff. Browning was an instigator, a motivator. He wanted to become Scrooge McDuck, sit in his money bin, throw gold coins into the air, and let them rain on his head. Browning woke up every morning with a jerk, sitting bolt upright and saying, "God damn." I never asked him about it.

He was a rabid Goldwater Republican with no sympathy for my enthusiasm for Kennedy. He and Sharon were tight friends but argued about politics. She raked him over the coals: "Now, James Lee, you can't buy into all that fascist crap. You're too damn smart for that!" Jimmy believed the same "guns in the basement," anti-Catholic propaganda my parents did. Sharon told him, "All that garbage comes from a William Inge play!"

One Sunday we went to First Baptist Church in downtown Waco. Before the sermon, the deacons locked the doors. Then the preacher delivered a vitriolic diatribe against Jack Kennedy, the Pope, and all Catholics like nothing I had ever heard. Browning ate it up. It scared the crap out of me like the handbills with a big red cross that appeared on the windshield of your car if you parked downtown: "Be A Man/Join the Klan." Waco was the home base of the Knights of the White Camelia, an offshoot of the Ku Klux Klan. Ultra conservative DJ Paul Harvey broadcast eight times a day.

The presence of so much bigotry was tough on us misfits.

The institutional order of the University
The Baptist
Anti-Catholic prejudice
And anti-communist paranoia
The deeply
Ingrained
Political conservatism
Of my parents
And some of my good friends

Browning was an ROTC officer. He kept a borderline haircut that enabled him to slip by in ROTC and theatre. He had been an Eagle Scout like my father and an Order of the Arrow, the highly secret brotherhood exclusive to Eagle Scouts. Their secret rituals and running around naked in the woods were too much for me.

We were polar opposites but with one unifying desire. We both loved to party. Many a weekend night the apartment filled with theatre and art students and many bottles of wine. I brought my electric guitar back after Thanksgiving. When a party reached critical mass, I turned it up and played the Bo Diddley rhythm as long as I could stand it. A girl from Hawaii danced an incredible hip-undulating boogie that left little to the imagination. There is much to be said for so-called primitive cultures where the men play music and women dance in pre-sexual ritual.

Not wanting to repeat the grueling bus trip experience of Thanksgiving, I took the train home at Christmas. The girl who played the piano score for *Charley* was on the train, too. She was intimidating, a big beautiful girl with jet black hair. I didn't know her well, but we talked all night. Like me, she felt like an outsider at Baylor. Unlike me, she was making good grades. But the work was unrewarding, the Baptist sisterhood did not accept her, and she was disappointed with the theatre. She wasn't coming back after Christmas.

I told her I was frustrated, too. I felt directionless. I couldn't figure out if I wanted to concentrate on theatre, painting, or writing. She said I was lucky. Art was about conveying emotional information to an audience. If you managed to communicate your art to one other person, you were successful. It was what I needed to hear when I needed to hear it. She was an angel, like Dishrag, sent at a critical time to show me the way.

I never saw her again. We shared a cheese sandwich, doughnuts, and milk. I owed her a debt I couldn't repay.

When I got home I was on fire. My family was confused. My old friends were confused. I didn't care. I went back to White Station High. Mr. Cain let me lecture to speech class. I let them have it. Plosive exercises and all. I was in the best physical shape of my life from swimming and the exercises from *Where's Charley?* and *Whistle in the Wind* rehearsals. I was strong and wound up tighter than Dick's hatband. I had the Biblical strength of Samson. My hair was longer than it had ever been. I told my parents it was for a part in a play.

Vera was between Ivy League boyfriends so I was able to spend time with her. Her family Christmas tree had tiny red lights with one string that blinked off and on. I stared at it for a long time. It seemed to go in and out of focus. I thought about the campus and empty theatre. A few months ago my world had been small; all the people I knew were in Memphis, Little Rock, or Chicago. Now I knew people from all over. My world was growing, expanding, spreading out to touch the stars. I felt lost in Memphis. I drove around, looking for that safe hiding place behind the wisteria. It wasn't at the Toddle House. It wasn't at good old White Station High School. It wasn't at Vera's house.

I discovered a burgeoning bohemian scene at the Cottage Coffee House in Midtown. The Cottage served coffee, featured poetry readings, and flamenco guitar music. There was a chess game in the corner. It was a great place to hang. After hours, the friendly chess game often turned into cutthroat five-card stud.

I felt at home immediately. T.J. Oden, a frat brother from high school, sat on the stage. He had gone from being a clean-shaven, straightlaced frat boy to a hairy, bearded deviant, sitting in a coffeehouse reading a Lawrence Ferlinghetti poem. Another kid I recognized, Jimmy Crosthwait, was beating on bongos. I wasn't alone. Right after T.J. read his poem, I sat down at the out-of-tune piano and played something nondescript.

Back in Waco, I felt more comfortable at the Catacombs than at the dorm. The Texas winter inspired me to work on *Rain Summer*, the novel I started in high school. I brought my portable typewriter from the dorm, and started to rework and type the manuscript. I looked out the window of the old house. I could see the lights on the dome of the administration building. My book lay in stacks of paper all over the room. A sudden breeze blew through the rooms; the bamboo curtain flopped against the windowsill, and paper blew off the bed.

My participation in classes dwindled to a trickle. Grades were posted in the administration building. As anticipated, I had failed five classes. The surprise was an A in Drama 105. The twelve quality points from that A canceled out the Fs and Incompletes and kept me in college, a second chance I didn't want.

The most interesting member of Baylor Theatre was Dr. Juana de Laban, the movement teacher. "One does not walk or dance on the stage," Dr. de Laban said in a thick Hungarian accent. "One moofs!!!" She called her classes Movement. I signed up for her class second semester. First day of class she told me, "Dickinson, if you do not choose to wear zee dance belt, you have my permission to work in your blue jeans."

She focused on music I had done for the first two productions, and asked if I would help her with music for a piece she was to stage depicting the Creation of Life. Of course, I was delighted. We took classical music and ran it backwards on a tape recorder, adding percussion, bass, and drum hits slowed down to the wrong speed. She grinned with delight when I hit the top of my guitar amplifier and made the echospring reverb unit rumble in anger. "Very goot, Dickinson!" she exclaimed, "Very goot!!!"

University censors were confused and suspicious of Dr. de Laban's concept of creation; it was not strictly Biblical. She had dancers in material tubes, sometimes two in the same tube, like huge amoebas and protozoa, by far too Darwinian for Christian standards. Still, nothing was said. The administration had to respect Juana Baby. She was the coolest.

Chapter 20

SECOND SEMESTER
What the Monkey Saw
(1961)

The release form for an experimental workshop that would earn me an automatic pass in psychology lab mentioned inducing temporary schizophrenia. My hypnotherapist had already diagnosed me a paranoid schizophrenic. What could it hurt? LSD was just letters then. I had no idea.

Behind the post office was a small, cinder block building with a sign on the door: PRIMATE BEHAVIOR STUDY LABORATORY. Two clear plastic tents with a table and chair divided the front room. The next room contained barred animal cages. Student volunteers were tested against chimpanzees. We took standard psychological tests, putting pegs in holes and washers on the pegs, with one hand and then the other. The monkeys cheated, using both hands at once.

What looked like a thermostat hung on the clear plastic wall. From time to time a lab assistant dressed like the Gray Man adjusted the device. He wore a surgical mask, never spoke, and discharged aerosol spray into the air behind my head. Testing started with three males and three female chimps. Two males fought to the death and one female killed herself. I tested with a male, Clayton, who survived as far as I know.

Sharon had difficulty getting to Waco on weekends. She was a scholarship student living in a run-down off-campus rooming house. She didn't have bus fare and depended on other students for rides. I went by the dorm for clothes, and found a message. She wasn't coming. I felt tired. I hung around, fell into a deep, dreamless sleep, and woke in my clothes, disappointed Sharon wasn't coming. I heard the dormitory coming to life and escaped to the Catacombs and our private world. The air was cold and clear. My first cigarette tasted like straw, reminding me of burning leaves at home with Alec and my dog. I took another deep drag, held it, and reached into my pocket for my shades. Shake it off, big boy. You can fight but you can't win. You're trapped like a rat. All you can do is play it out.

Back at the apartment, Pat smiled and put in extra water for coffee. She looked good in the morning. She always looked good. She had checked out of the dorm for the weekend. Browning was asleep with the customary look of horror on his face. We sat at the small red kitchen table with our steaming cups.

"Sorry about Sharon," she said. "There was nothing she could do."

"I know."

"She'd be here if she could. She wants to see you."

I shrugged it off. We heard screaming—"God damn"—from the next room and knew Jimmy was awake. More coffee and new plans.

"Well, just 'cause Bunn's not here we don't have to roll over and die," Browning said. On other road trips we had visited Longhorn Cavern State Park, where we experienced total darkness. We had also visited Possum Kingdom Reservoir and experienced a lot of Oso Negro and Dos Equis Mexican beer. I didn't know what he had in mind. "Is Wortham, Texas, somewhere around here? Do you know where that is?"

"Of course I know where it is. It's in Texas," he huffed. "It's right down the road. What's your sudden interest in Wortham? It's just an old oil boom town that went bust."

I went to the orange crate that held community records and picked up an album. "Says here Blind Lemon Jefferson is buried in Wortham, Texas. I thought if it was somewhere close we might go see his grave. It's unmarked."

"In the first place I've never heard of Blind Lemon Jefferson and how are we supposed to find a grave if it's unmarked?"

"Well," I told him, suddenly taking interest, "There's this book I've got that describes how to get there with a picture of the graveyard."

I played the record. Blind Lemon is hard to take, unlike Jimmy Reed or B.B. King. It's hard counter-rhythm, strummed in an atypical series of patterns that doesn't resemble standard blues form. He recorded early and stood out from the more gospel-structured Delta style. There's a melodic counterpoint and ballad-like melody line that remains unique in the blues idiom.

I went back to the dorm and picked up my copy of Sam Charters's book *The Country Blues*. I showed Browning pictures of Blind Lemon, deserted downtown Wortham, and the lonesome windswept graveyard with the unmarked sunken space where Lemon and his brother were laid anonymously side by side between his mother's and sister's marked tombstones. "This is great. This is great!" Browning exclaimed gleefully. "Old man Baker would love this! Pure D Texas at its obscure best. This is it. We'll hit the road tomorrow. It's all set."

We spent the rest of the evening listening to "Black Snake Moan" and "See That My Grave Is Kept Clean." Browning had discovered another thing about Texas in which to take pride.

Sunday morning. Old timers could feel a "norther" coming in the water pipes. Campus was deserted. The rooming house on Speight Street was hung over. Pat made coffee. The stereo was turned down low. "Black Snake Moan" crawled in the room. We drank hot coffee and went downstairs to the car. The platinum blonde sat shotgun, silent behind her sunglasses. I shared the back seat with beer and a sack of ice. Jimmy pointed the green Ford sedan south. We crossed the Brazos River with the north wind on our tail and a Lord's Supper tablecloth commercial on the radio.

The scenery was a blur of rangeland, scrub oaks, and the Big Sky, as the locals liked to call it. Browning was from West Texas. His idea of "just down the road" and mine were different. Dilapidated oil rigs clustered in rusty bunches. Like good Baptists, they were not working on Sunday. Wortham was past the oil fields. We drove until we found an open gas station. The attendant was a kid. Jimmy did the talking. He said we were students from the college, writing a research paper. The kid pointed and mumbled something about "old men." The old men weren't hard to find. They sat on a bench around the corner from the Domino Parlor. One stood leaning on a crutch, his right leg cut off at the knee.

Browning asked if they knew anything about Blind Lemon Jefferson.

"Yah sah," the one-legged man said. I took over, telling him what I had read on the record cover: Lemon was born in Wortham, he had frozen to death on a street corner in 1930, and the record company had sent a man south with his body, but it only got to Dallas.

"No, sah," the one-legged man shook his head. "It was '29. I remember '30 was bad, but I never shall forget '29. Me and ol' Pete dug the grave." He pointed back to the bench. "It was us that buried him. The ground was solid froze. They had to lay out planks to walk on. We built a fire to thaw out the dirt enough to dig. New Year's Day." He gave us directions, "Past the 'white cemetery,' outside the city limits on the left."

We parked on the roadside. There was no gate. One strand of barbed wire was strung between the fence posts. A homemade sign twisting in the wind said CLOSE GAP. Blind Lemon's unmarked grave lay between his mother and her sister. The chain of events that stranded his coffin in Dallas also took the record company money for a headstone. He shared a grave with his brother, who was "Cut up in the sawmill. Buried in pieces in a cardboard box."

The afternoon sun was warm but a cold wind blew across the badlands. We huddled around the graves. Browning grinned with Texan pride. Pat stood shivering, arms crossed beneath her breasts, wondering what this was all about, what we were doing there. I remember the song Blind Lemon sang into the darkness, "There's one kind favor I ask of you. Just one kind of favor I ask of you. Only see that my grave is kept clean."

Back in Waco, at the old house, we drank, talked, and someone brought me the guitar.

Black and alone
Cars going by
Would not stop
Or know
And we killed them
By the hundreds
A night long ago
I sang my song
While the band played loud
And the world stood on its head
You give me someone
Half my size
And I'll whip
A room full of them
"Watch me
Stick a poker
In your mother."

Later that night, I took a blanket and retired to the back seat of Browning's Ford. I slept there breathing puffs of fog, protesting the cold and damp grayness that seeped in through vents and window cracks.

Chapter 21

SPRING POEMS
(1961)

I quit going to classes completely and tried to focus on *Rain Summer*. I became obsessed with the time element, and made elaborate charts and outlines. Without Merrell around to talk craft, I turned to John Logan, the hot undergraduate playwright who had worked with me in *Miss Carol* as the Cajun pipe rigger on the oil drilling platform in the Gulf of Mexico. He concentrated on play forms, had written little prose, and had taken up with Merrell's ex-femme fatale, now living next to Browning at the Catacombs.

Logan joined us on several of Browning's weekend road trips. In Dallas we saw an exhibit, "Art Through the Looking Glass," consisting of sculpture and collage, three-dimensional pieces with drawers, shelves, and hidden objects, seemingly of no connected relevance. I didn't think about it until much later when it haunted me.

One spring day Logan and I searched out collective memories of childhood experiences, and came across an old radio serial, *Sky King*. I brought up the secret signal ring promotional premium.

John said, "I still have mine."

"You what?" I exclaimed in disbelief.

"Yeah, I've still got it. I'll bring it back next time I go home," he grinned.

Green with envy, I tried to imagine the satisfaction and power I'd have if I had mine. I would be Ming, Emperor of the Universe, invincible and capable of anything.

My lack of direction grated on Browning. He was going to Pasadena Playhouse next year and trying for the Big Time in Hollywood. He would give it a year, and return to law school in Texas if he couldn't break into show business.

"You've got to get your shit together," he told me repeatedly. "You got to have a plan. You can't just go on wandering around from one idea to another. Theatre, music, painting. What the fuck is next? You've got to concentrate, to settle on a direction. You'll end up going crazy and accomplishing nothing." He decided I needed psychic help, researched the fortune tellers in Waco, and took me from one to another. The first was an old woman born with a caul over half her face (as Blind Lemon was said to have had). I sat on an old overstuffed bed beside her. She put her hand on my forehead and rolled her eyes back in her skull.

It was a load of crap. Nothing made any sense. She looked puzzled and told me, "Nothing is coming through."

I knew the feeling.

Ophelia Harwood was another story. She seemed to know me already. I thought about what she told me. My father was sick. He coughed up disgusting phlegm and had violent coughing fits, a "smoker's cough." But I sensed she was talking about something else. She told me my family would move, which seemed impossible, and that my grandmother would die. I didn't understand her talk about playing music. I had never seriously considered it since I could not read music and had no real training or knowledge beyond what I had absorbed from Dewey Phillips and Dishrag.

I dropped out of school and withdrew from classes to avoid further failure on my permanent record. I was sitting in the Green Room at the theatre when Dr. de Laban appeared.

"Deekensun!" she exclaimed. "Are you in or out?"

"I'm out, Dr. de Laban," I replied.

"Goot!" she said. Then she smiled a big Hungarian smile to let me know she meant it as approval and not condemnation. That was my official exit from Baylor theatre.

I planned to finish typing *Rain Summer* before I returned home. I worked all night and slept during the day. I looked worse than ever. I had shaved my head thinking it made me look like Jackson Pollock. I wore the same red-and-white-striped sweater and once-white toreador pants for way too long. I started drinking dark rum straight. I liked to drink alone in the dark. The words of Ophelia Harwood hung heavy in the Texas night.

I can't remember
That last week in Waco.
It's like a blank spot.
It might be the liquor
Or my sickness.
It might be

A residual effect
Of the acid test
With the monkey.
I'll never know.
It's all a blank.

I remember going to Breckinridge with Browning before returning home. Browning took me around his hometown and showed me off for shock value. He was strangely quiet, as if pissed off for my letting him down. I don't know what he expected but I had disappointed him.

Browning had an old friend, a younger girl he had mentored. Sandra Hudlow was smart, an actress, a trained piano player, and as life would reveal, a lightning rod for the troubled and the talented. Hudlow and I hit it off, which irritated Browning even more. The three of us went all over Breckinridge, seeing the sights. Browning was a local celebrity and loved the audience. Before a performance at the theatre he would go into the crossing tunnel under people's feet in the first row, lie against the concrete wall, and try to "feel" the crowd's vibrations. "They love me, they love me," he would say.

"They think they own you," I would tell him. "They bought a ticket and paid money. They think they own you."

"Oh, fuck you," he would reply, defensively. He loved the audience. It reminded me of the organ grinder with a monkey on the string.

Saturday night we ended up at the local hot spot, the Belvina Supper Club. The Bell, as locals called it, held Browning's hometown audience and he was putting on a show. There was no issue of I.D. or underage drinking. In West Texas things were a little wilder and more open than in Waco, the state's constipated center under the control of tight-assed Baptists. We drank openly and without repercussion. A black jump blues band, Big Daddy Pat and His Hot Brown Boys, played on stage. After a couple of sets I felt the music's pull, and remembered what the gypsy told me. I thought, "Okay, Browning, you want to see a show, I'll give you a show," and declared "I'm gonna see if the band will let me sing a song."

Hudlow looked surprised. Browning said, "Don't get up there and show your ass. I have to live here."

I told him not to worry and walked up to the bandstand. The guy I thought was the leader stood by the piano, shuffling through arrangements. He looked up. "Hey man, can I sing a song?" I asked.

"I don't know," he said. "Can you?"

I gave him my assurance. God knows what he thought. There I stood, head shaved, weird looking, white as sliced bread, and glowing in the dark.

He smiled, "What do you want to sing?"

"'Send Me Some Lovin'. You know that one? Little Richard."

"Sure we know it. What key?"

"B flat." I could see from his smile he thought it was a joke, expecting me to play the fool. The band hit the turnaround from the five chord, and I came in, "Send me some lovin', send it I pray."

The Belvina Super Club went silent.

"How can I love you when you're far away . . ." When we hit the bridge, I went up to a Little Richard note that made the whole joint vibrate. When the song was over I jumped off the front of the stage as the audience applauded wildly. I walked back to the table where Browning was grinning like the Cheshire Cat. Sandra sat, amazed.

The next morning I went to the First Baptist Church with Browning's family. Sandra played piano. I heard people muttering, "That's the boy who sang with the black band at the Bell last night." I sat in the amen corner, next to a little old lady. Sandra played straighter than my mother, without embellishment. Still, it was like an old friend, a little bit like home. I was going home, home to something familiar and unknown.

The strange, shriveled-up little old lady kept winking at me. Merrell would have been suspicious. When the collection plate was passed, I took it from the usher, and passed it on to the little old lady without contributing. The little old lady also passed it on, not putting in anything. She looked up at me and smiled. I bent over to hear what she had to say, knowing things were about to make sense.

She said, "You must be just like me. Saving up for the Lottie Moon Christmas offering."

Chapter 22

MORE BACK AND FORTH, UP AND DOWN
(1961)

Following my triumph at the Belvina Supper Club with Big Daddy Pat and His Hot Brown Boys, I snuck out of Texas like a dog with its tail between its legs and Lottie Moon still ringing in its ears. The train trip took forever. My mind went in and out of focus. At home my parents acted like nothing had happened. Nary a word was spoken about my obvious failure. My father saw my freshly shaved head and said, "Well, at least you got a haircut."

My parents put our house on the market (Ophelia Harwood prediction number one pays off). I traded my hated '53 Chevy for a broken-down Ford pickup truck. Alec, his huge friend Mule, and I started doing yard work. Mule had a pad of receipts liberated from a well-known Memphis landscaping company. We went around clipping and sweeping already trimmed lawns of the wealthy, and passing off bottom-land muck for top-dollar mulch. We drank cold gin and Thunderbird wine all day. Again Alec was doing his job, taking care of Mr. Dickinson's boy who had fucked up.

My drummer, Steady Eddie, was graduating high school, and wanted to make some music before he went to college. We cut Jimmy Reed–like demos at Berl Olswanger's music store, and took them to Rubin Cherry at Home of the Blues record store on Beale Street. I still sounded like Ricky Nelson, but Cherry liked it. He called me "Little Muddy," and signed me to Home of the Blues record Label with a one-page mimeographed contract with fill-in-the-blank lines for percentage and royalties still blank.

Rubin hooked me up with Gene "Bowlegs" Miller, a trumpet player with a goiter the size of a softball sticking out of his neck like a second chin. He became my producer. More importantly, Rubin got me a manager, a disc jockey from WLOK, the number two black radio station in town. His on-air name was Hunky Dory. My dilemma was calling WLOK and not knowing whether to ask for Hunky or Mr. Dory.

I didn't get far with Home of the Blues Records. I cut more demos at Fernwood, Scotty Moore's studio. Our hired-gun sideman guitarist couldn't hold his liquor and played the session flat on his back. My big song was, "I Was Just a Country Boy." I played harmonica on a neck rack while playing rhythm guitar. We had a good Jimmy Reed groove, racially limited as we were. Rubin would play the tape for a room full of people, all black, and then ask them which one of us was singing. They guessed everyone but me. It tickled the shit out of Rubin.

Rubin took me places where we were the only whites. Once, at an event honoring Rufus and Carla Thomas as Black Father and Daughter of the Year, Rubin didn't show up. I sat at a table with Bowlegs and Mrs. Bowlegs. The only other whites, Steve Cropper and the mayor of Memphis, were on the dais and kept looking at me, wondering who the hell I was. Bowlegs told me, "I'd let you dance with my wife, but I don't think the mayor would dig it."

I had a deep-seated kidney infection irritated by alcohol consumption and stress. It had relocated and settled in my prostate, and was difficult to treat. A doctor grew a culture and gave me experimental drug combinations. It was critical I stop drinking.

Friends started returning from college. Saul Belz, my old background singer and maracas player, came home from the University of Texas. He had joined a prominent Jewish fraternity and was living at the frat house. He always said that after high school he was going to cool his act and do what his family expected him to do: be a good Jewish boy. Fat chance, I thought. I was wrong. He was studying pre-law. After a couple of nights hanging out with him and his well-to-do contemporaries, I realized there was much of college life I was not experiencing. Saulie talked me into registering for summer school at Memphis State. It was too late to transfer, so I signed a release form agreeing not to attend Memphis State in the fall.

Sobriety and the relatively relaxed atmosphere of Memphis State (compared to Baylor) were a good mix, and I did okay in summer school. I used my bogus Oklahoma ID to get in the Plantation Inn. Even though I couldn't drink, there was the music. Ben Branch and the Largos—the house band—and the Del Rios vocal group and master showman Wild Charlie "Tennessee" Turner were performing. Wild Charlie, a "floorshow singer," rolled on the floor tied up in the microphone cable, and sang "Danny Boy" with mascara-stained tears running down his chocolate-milk-colored cheeks. He was openly gay, with a performing style that boarded on female impersonation.

One night I walked into the rest room, where Wild Charlie was sticking the cotton wick from a Benzadrex inhaler into his mouth, between his teeth and his cheek, like a squirrel with a plug of tobacco. "Speed Ball, little brother," he mumbled in explanation. "Works like a Bennie." Of course I had to try it.

Blind Oscar was the organist, Big Bell the drummer, with Floyd Newman on baritone sax, and Ben Branch on tenor. The two horns didn't make a full chord, but the guitar and organ filled out with so much space between the notes that the whole room seemed to breathe in and out in time. It wasn't what they played; it was the way they played. The tuning stretched out and pulled at the air with sonic tension. The beat was the same old strip tease bump-de-de-bump from the Harlem in Havana tent show.

> O Mother Africa
> The syncopated eights
> Over four
> With the sine wave push
> And pull
> That is more than swing
> But less than a full on shuffle
> Seeps into your soul
> If you live in Memphis

My parents sold the big house and moved to the city's eastern limits. They bought a new ranch-style stone and cypress house with no personality. I did pretty well at summer school, but since I had registered without transferring my transcript, I couldn't register for fall term. It was return to Waco or lose my 2S student draft classification.

My objection to military service was religious as well as political. I am an Orthodox Coward. I have had a long-standing aversion to uniforms since Boy Scouts. Marching in lines and regimented behavior seemed hellish to me. I had lived with the constant threat of military school since I first displeased my father. I had been trying to figure a way out of the draft long before Viet Nam. It was back to Baylor for little Jimmy.

I had to play it straight. I was on every conceivable kind of probation, and had to reside in the dormitory. I moved into the newly constructed Penland Hall. I kept my haircut and got out the old frat boy disguise of khaki slacks, powder blue button-down Oxford cloth shirts, and penny loafers.

My old adviser was surprised to see I had returned, and signed me up for a load of drama classes, thinking I could build up my grade point average. Old man Baker saw me in the Green Room and blew a gasket. He banned me from the theatre and all drama classes until I was off probation. I re-registered as a history major.

Browning was at the Pasadena Playhouse. Sharon was still at UT. Merrell was God knows where. Tommy Rodman, the bass player from *Where's Charley?*, and playwright John Logan had rooms in a small house off campus. ROOMS FOR BAYLOR BOYS, read the sign in front. The rest of the house was empty. When things got tense at the dorm I could hide out there. Rodman had two friends from high school, Tex Campbell and Jimmy Baird, who were both English majors taking folklore classes at UT Austin. They would come to Waco on the weekends and we became friends. They made tape recordings of me playing Tex's guitar and singing folk songs. Drinking was involved.

In the dorm I roomed with an older drama major, Reggie. He had been the butler in *Where's Charley?* and was one of the funniest people I had met. He could cheer me up, no matter what Baylor nonsense dragged me down. He tried to keep a low profile in the dorm, but it wasn't easy. He was trying not to be gay. Whenever the God Squad came to pray for us, Reggie chased them off by running down the hall naked (he slept raw and the Squad always arrived under the cover of night). Reggie worked hard to keep up his grades and was a good influence.

A spinet piano was by the exit in the dorm cafeteria. Two or three times a week one student would sit down unceremoniously and play Floyd Cramer songs, sometimes "Last Date," sometimes "Wonderland by Night." He could knock off the two-finger grace note technique perfectly. The cafeteria would erupt in spontaneous applause. It started to piss me off.

One day at lunchtime after the Floyd Cramer interlude, I walked to the piano and played "Great Balls of Fire" without sitting down. I walked out while they were still clapping and stomping their feet. It was necessary to make a hasty getaway; the devil's music was not to be played on campus. The Floyd Cramer boy followed me out, and quickly introduced himself as brother musicians do backstage on a gig.

"Hey man. That was really good. My name is Ramsey Horton. Who are you?"

"Jim Dickinson. I'm from Memphis."

"I got a gig Friday night," he said. "You want to make it?"

His band was all Baylor boys. The guitar player was pretty good with a Gretsch Country Gentleman. The drummer was dragging and didn't rock, and you couldn't hear the upright bass. It turned out Ramsey only wanted me to sing and front the band. He played piano himself, except for a few numbers he did on trumpet. Those songs were my only chance to play piano: "Cherry Pink and Apple Blossom White" and "Misty," instrumental ballads that weren't my thing.

Ramsey had the first piano pickup I ever saw that worked. It had three ceramic microphonic pickups that hooked to the metal frame of the sound board and sounded great! We played three or four gigs in and around Waco and hit the road. At our final gig, Wichita Falls, we were the opening act for the Bill Black Combo (Reggie Young, Bobby Emmons, Satch Arnold, Ace Cannon, and Tommy Cogbill). Cogbill hollered when he saw me, "Hey, Dickinson!! What are you doing' here?"

"I go to school in Waco," I answered. "I'm playing with the opening act."

We hung out and talked. Tommy was a great guy and a brilliant musician. He was really a jazz guitarist, but also probably the best electric bass player in Memphis. Reggie Young was so spectacular on rock 'n' roll guitar that Tommy was almost always stuck playing the Fender bass. Bill Black never played with the band, even though it was his combo. Tommy and I shared a couple of drinks, and he gave me a hit of speed. I was starting to feel at home.

The K-otics finished our set, and as we cleared the stage someone asked Ramsey if they could use his piano pickups for their set. Ramsey was so flattered that he agreed. We plugged the piano pickups into Reggie's Dual Showman. Bobby used an organ on most of the set, and asked me to play. My pill was kicking in. I did a Jerry Lee Lewis/Billy Lee Riley medley and blew up Reggie's amp. Cogbill said, "Well, Dickinson, you can take the boy out of Memphis . . . know what I mean?"

He shrugged it off, shaking his head.

We got stiffed on the gig and drove back to Waco in silence. The sun was coming up over the Brazos when we got back to campus. That was the end of my career with Ramsey Horton and the K-otics, but I had learned his Floyd Cramer licks, without which I would not have known what to play on the Rolling Stones' session in Muscle Shoals.

HOMECOMING QUEEN
It's Never Too Late
(1961)

After Barbara Teal moved to Cincinnati she wrote me simple, childlike letters, sometimes sad and always sweet. One letter was tear-stained with mascara blots on her perfumed stationery. It amazed me that this goddess would share her experiences with a worm like me. I wrote to her about art, books, and things I knew she didn't understand, but seemed to enjoy. When I returned to Baylor that fall, we continued to correspond. In one letter I invited her to Waco for homecoming weekend. She accepted. It was a gift from God. A friend from the dorm had a candy-apple-red '58 Chevy convertible. He drove me to Dallas to pick up Barbara at Love Field. She got off the plane with a soldier in uniform trailing her and trying to get lucky. Barbara saw me and ran squealing, arms open. Sorry, soldier. She was wearing a bright green wool suit and white gloves. Her hair was longer. She still tasted like strawberry soda. There was a zipper on the green suit dress from her neck to the crack of her ass.

I had arranged for an empty apartment at the Willowbrook, out by the lake, but with no heat. In the morning while I was dead to the world, Barbara got up and walked down the highway to get us coffee and donuts in a strange town with no idea where she was. Barbara had more guts than a tennis racket.

At game time, we walked to the stadium from the apartment house. She looked spectacular. I didn't look bad myself with my "H" Italian gig suit and a skinny black silk tie, like the one Ivan Rider wore on opening night. We made quite a couple. Cowboys from the dorm stood in awe. The crowd parted like the Red Sea when we took our bleacher seats. That was the only football game I attended in my years at Baylor.

Returning to the Willowbrook, the postgame party was on. I played guitar for a while. The drunks sang "Hot Nuts" and "Be-Bop-a-Loser."

Barbara and I split for the ice-cold apartment and proceeded to warm it up. We made up for lost time and didn't notice the lack of central heat.

Play every gig
Every song
Every note
Like it's the last one
One of them will be
Never throw it away
Or take it for granted
Put some bourbon in your coffee
Pour some gravy on the mashed potatoes
A little catsup on that T-Bone, please

Chapter 24

"BIG D" (LITTLE "a")
(1961-62)

It was not all a party. I put forth an honest effort in several classes. I had taken uppers or bennies on gigs to delay alcohol's effects before, but hadn't used speed as a study aid. Louie, the South American musician from the pit band of *Where's Charley?*, was my source. He made designer drugs, custom combos, and the acid for the psychology department LSD monkey experiment. I stuck to commercial varieties, like triethylamine sulfate #3 and dexamil. I elaborately outlined my history class notes, made charts of French and English monarchs and Old Testament scions. All night cramming sessions worked for me. I felt I was learning. I feared it was drug induced, but I developed a learning process of sorts.

I could always find one of the music department's practice rooms—cubicles with a spinet piano in each—to use for an hour or two. I could shut off Texas, and take the music back into my childhood. I pulled up songs from memory my mother taught me from sheet music. It was like gradually returning to familiar reality after waking from a bad dream. I played old songs only halfway right, and discovered a focus effect as the familiar melody's repetition let my mind think about the next note. It was therapy. Without those sessions, I would have been even more lost, especially since I was still banned from the theatre.

I vicariously continued what old man Baker called the "search for my integration of abilities," and soaked up as much as possible from Reggie and Rodman. Reggie was taking a costume design class from Virgil Beavers, the set designer I had come to study with, and having trouble with the class. He was a literalist by nature and had trouble with abstract thinking. I gave him ideas when I could, most of which Beavers rejected. Reggie squeaked by in the class, in large part due to my over-the-top suggestions.

Saul brought his black Dodge ragtop to school his second year. He stopped in Waco when coming up from Austin, and gave me a ride home for Christmas break. Family and friends wondered at the apparent change in little Jimmy; this new model seemed much improved, better dressed, and periodically sober. Nothing was said but I could hear the collective sigh of relief from everyone but Vera, who asked me who I was trying to be. I laughed it off. I was uncomfortable doing the old frat-boy act but it was getting me by for the time being.

Vera was a freshman at Emory. We had some good times that Christmas, probably our best. We spent more than a few hours at Yannie's, a new place owned by the bartender at the old Whirlaway. He had Edith Piaf and Yusef Lateef on the jukebox and killer hot peppers. College was showing Vera the world was more varied than her well-planned and methodically balanced universe. She gave me a little more room to breathe.

Once again, New Year's Eve was an eye-opener. The Royal Spades were now the Mar-Keys, and had a full-fledged national hit with their simple instrumental "Last Night." The Royal Spades' sound closely resembled the house band's from the Plantation Inn, and for good reason: most of the house band played on the recording. The band, under the de facto leadership of Packy Axton (his mother and uncle owned the record label now named Stax), had done several coast-to-coast solo tours and had backed Rufus Thomas's teenage daughter Carla, who had a hit, "Gee Whiz."

Steve Cropper wisely stayed home to work in the studio. Consequently, Charlie Freeman went on the road as a sideman for the band he had formed. The band fought constantly. They persecuted keyboardist Smoochy Smith, who had written "Last Night," a tune with two simple riffs and a sax solo added at Jerry Wexler's request when Atlantic picked it up and propelled it to national attention. Jazz player Bob "the Bear" Brooker replaced Smoochy. One night, in a scene out of Monday Night Wrestling, Packy hit Brooker over the head with a folding chair. Terry Johnson drove their VW bus into the ocean and the Mar-Keys were history, though the band continued to book jobs with pick-up sidemen fleshing out the band on a given night.

Packy opened a venue, the Junker Club, on Summer Avenue in Memphis. Packy had a black partner, "Bongo" Johnny Keyes, an unheard-of arrangement. On New Year's Eve I hit the Junker to see what the deal was. The band consisted of maybe half the old Mar-Keys and ringers. Ronnie Stoots was singing better than ever. They blew the roof off the small nightclub. They looked great: Italian suits, skinny ties, and high heel Spanish boots. They did the Plantation Inn show like Floyd Newman and Ben Branch, steps and all. Like a blackface minstrel show, these white boys were crossing the same old line in the sand Elvis and Al Jolson crossed. Every time it was crossed, a little more was rubbed out and harder to see.

I stood in my Ivy League disguise, seeing I had made a mistake. I was an audience member, a mark, a rube, one of the squares who come up to a musician after a set and to tell them how "cooool" they are. Packy didn't even recognize me. Stoots recognized me, grinned greasily, and shook his head. Could I get back over the line? In Memphis it wasn't as easy as sitting in with Big Daddy Pat and His Hot Brown Boys. I had blown it by going to Texas. New ideas formed in my brain. I couldn't see them clearly but they gnawed my ego.

Then a miracle happened. My grandmother talked my father into letting me take a car back to Baylor. My old truck's death had been long and painful. This was a family car, a '61 Chevy four-door fleet-model salesman special. I would have preferred a Crosby compact mini-model painted pink, but mobility would make existence in Waco much easier. Freedom! A man without wheels is but half a man.

Second semester. Things went smoothly in Waco. Reggie moved off campus to Rooms for Baylor Boys with Rodman and Logan. Merrell appeared as if returned from the land of the dead, and roomed with me in the shiny new Pentland Hall. Merrell seemed changed; not beat but beaten. He saw the wisdom of my slick-boy disguise and followed suit. He didn't return to the theatre and Baker's clutches but registered as journalism major and started to wear a little stingy brimmed golf hat and checkered sport coat. Like me, he costumed for his new role as Joe College.

One Sunday afternoon I made a startling discovery. To stimulate church service attendance, evening meals were no longer served in the dorm cafeteria on Sunday night. I found a little truck stop diner by Lake Waco that served a better than average chicken fried steak with fries and slaw. Say what you will about Texas, it is the home of the world's finest chicken fried steak. It was no Threadgill's, but it was more than adequate for a manly meal on a Sunday night. One night as I pulled out of the parking lot, I snapped on the radio and *Yours Truly, Johnny Dollar* drifted out. Yes sir. Waco was so backwards they still played radio dramas and shows long gone at home.

James Luther "Jim" Dickinson with father James Baker "Big Jim" Dickinson, petting zoo in northern California, 1942.

James Luther Dickinson wearing cowboy suit, North Shore, Chicago, Illinois, 1947.

James Luther Dickinson and his father, James Baker Dickinson, North Shore, Chicago, Illinois, 1947.

James Luther Dickinson and his mother, Martha Huddleston Dickinson, traveling overnight from Buffalo, New York, to Chicago, Illinois, 1948.

James Luther Dickinson, at home on Perkins Road, Memphis, Tennessee, Easter Sunday, 1955.

James Luther Dickinson with his grandmother, Margaret Huddleston "Huddie" Dickinson, Perkins Road, Memphis, Tennessee, Easter Sunday, 1955.

James Luther Dickinson and the Regents rehearsing at White Station High School, Eddie Tauber playing drums, Memphis, Tennessee, 1960.

James Luther Dickinson with Saul Belz playing maracas, talent show at White Station High School, Memphis, Tennessee, 1960.

Back view of talent show at White Station High School, James Luther Dickinson and Saul Belz playing maracas, Memphis, Tennessee, 1960.

Blind Lemon Jefferson's unmarked grave, Wortham, Texas, 1961.

Blind Lemon Jefferson's grave, marked with a broom, Wortham, Texas, 1962.

James Luther Dickinson, Waco, Texas, 1962.

New Beale Street Sheiks featuring (R to L) Sid Selvidge, James Luther Dickinson, Bill Newport, Jim Vinson, and Jimmy Crosthwait, Southern Avenue, Memphis, Tennessee, 1963.

The Katmandu Quartet featuring (L to R) James Luther Dickinson, Don Nix (above), Terry Johnson (below), and Charlie Freeman, 1965.

Another angle of the Katmandu Quartet, (clockwise: Terry Johnson, James Luther Dickinson, Don Nix, Charlie Freeman, 1965.

James Luther Dickinson engineering/ producing at "old" Ardent Studio, National Avenue, Memphis, Tennessee, 1966. Photograph courtesy of Ardent Recording Studios, Memphis, Tennessee.

The Tempters, #1 selling Japanese pop stars recording with James Luther Dickinson at Sounds of Memphis Studio, Memphis, Tennessee, 1969.

The Dixie Flyers: James Luther Dickinson's house band with Atlantic Records, (L to R) Tommy McClure, Mike Utley, Atlantic executive Tom Dowd, Atlantic vice-president Jerry Wexler, Sammy Creason, Charlie Freeman, and James Luther Dickinson, Criteria Studios, Miami, Florida, 1970.

James Luther Dickinson relaxing with his basset hound, Lightnin' Flash, at home at the Zebra Ranch, Independence, Mississippi, 2001. Photograph by Ebet Roberts.

It became a ritual. Sunday evening I drove out to Lake Waco and listened as old Johnny added up his expense account of danger and intrigue. An escape from Waco and Baylor; a return to familiar surroundings, long ago nights in Little Rock and Sunday afternoons in the Buick driving home from a family movie outing. Johnny always got his man within the allotted thirty minutes, added up his expense items, and signed off as the sun sank over the dirty shallow pond that passed for a lake in central Texas.

Chapter 25

BACK TO THE BURYING GROUND (1962)

Merrell's taste in women improved. His new squeeze, Sarah, had real class. She was the new schoolmarm in an old cowboy movie, a fair-skinned brunette with a moist glow around her. As karmic synchronicity would have it, she was from Wortham, Texas, where Blind Lemon was buried. She said her old family maid talked about Lemon all the time. She agreed to take me to meet the old woman.

This was it! I was going to get direct insight into the legendary figure about whom so little was known. Sarah Moody would be my portal to the past. One weekend in early spring we organized a safari. Sarah and Tommy Rodman rode with me to Austin, where we picked up Jimmy Baird. We were armed with a camera, tape recorder, 8mm camera, and Sam Charters's *The Country Blues*, the book in which I had learned of Blind Lemon and the Negro graveyard in Wortham.

The old woman was short and round. She sat in a rocker, looking out the window of her shotgun shack across the railroad tracks from what one could call "downtown Wortham." She was surprised to see "Miss Sarah." They oohed and aahed over each other with real affection. Sarah told her why we had come. "Blind Lemon?" the old woman said, "I was raised up with Blind Lemon. He was a child and I was a child. I was raised up with him. I can tell you all 'bout Blind Lemon." I showed her the picture in the Charters book. "That's Lemon. That's Blind Lemon! Like he was coming in the door. He was a child and I was a child. I was raised up with him. That's Blind Lemon."

We packed up the tape recorder and left the old woman muttering, "I can tell you all 'bout Blind Lemon." She did not do so. I started to realize that's all there was going to be. Baird was disgruntled, and grumbled as we got back in the car. Sarah was apologetic. Rodman was confused. I was disappointed but starting to get the picture. There was no doorway to the past. No Rosetta Stone to unlock the blues' secrets.

I drove to the old Negro cemetery where we had seen the neglected grave the year before. Things were different. Small tin markers with cardboard name plates were stuck in the hard Texas dirt over Lemon and his mother's graves. At the head of the weed-covered barren space that held all that was left of Blind Lemon was an old glass pitcher with two brooms sticking out of it. Inside the glass pitcher was a handwritten letter on what looked like a roll of adding machine tape. It told a rambling story of some pilgrim who was to meet with friends at the graveside. The letter was vague. The broom's symbolism was obvious, "See that my grave is kept clean," he had once sung into the darkness.

When I looked up from the strange letter I saw a group of elderly black folks walking toward us over dead grass and sunken graves. The leader wore a black suit and a ribbon banner across his chest announcing he was a minister. Sure enough, it was the pastor and the deacons from the church next to the graveyard. They wanted to know what we were doing. Sarah and Baird did the talking, being the most respectable looking. The preacher recognized Sarah's family name and warmed up right away. "We had some folks come looking for that same grave a few weeks back," he said. "One of 'em wasn't right in the head. They lef' that ol' stuff up by the grave. Police took that one boy off and locked him up. They got him in the hospital now. He's not right. I can see you folks is all right and not up to nothin'. You say you is from the university?"

"Yes sir. We're doing research on Blind Lemon Jefferson and regional music from the twenties and thirties."

"You folks needs to go see Trappy," the preacher said, receiving a nod of approval from the deacons standing behind him. "Old Trappy. He used to lead Blind Lemon around when he went to Dallas to make them records. Lemon taught him to play second guitar with him."

He gave Sarah directions to find the old man. She appeared to know what he was talking about. It seemed like we wandered all over central Texas before we found the little country store.

Trappy wore a white dress shirt and black suspenders. He sat in the shade behind a country store/gas station that had seen better days. Several old men sat nearby playing a silent game of checkers. They didn't look up.

"Can I help you folks?"

Baird explained (he was getting good at it). "We are students from the university doing research and were told that you had played with Blind Lemon."

Trappy was more forthcoming than the old woman. He had been Blind Lemon's lead boy and led the blind musician out of the Texas flatlands and up the old highway to Dallas. Lemon taught him to play second guitar. He had not gone on Lemon's fatal trip to Chicago. "I'da took better care of him, watched out, ya know? He'd get drunked up and pass out on the street. Wasn't so bad down home but up there in Chicago he just froze up and died."

I asked Trappy if he still played guitar.

"Lightnin' struck my cabin one night in a storm, knocked down my guitar from where it was hangin' on the wall. My wife took it as a sign from God and worried me 'til I gave it up."

I pulled my guitar out of the back of the car and strummed it awhile. "Why don't you see what you can remember?" I offered him the old Stella. He chuckled with a deep rattle in his chest, and took the instrument from me. "Lemme see can I chord that thing." His old fingers were clumsy on the steel strings reaching for an E chord. He plunked around for a while but seemed to get nowhere, "Nawsuh, I done forgot. It done been too long. You play somethin' for me."

The guitar felt funny in my hands, like a stranger rather than an old friend. I tried to play a line of "Black Snake Moan." He grinned toothlessly. "That's fine," he said.

As I drove us back to Austin and then Waco, I thought about the experience with the old woman and Trappy. I thought about the black minister and his deacons patrolling the graveyard, protecting it from "crazy white strangers" prying into their past. We were invading a private culture where we had no place. As badly as I wanted to learn the secrets of Blind Lemon, I did not want to trespass on this private history, this society that had produced music I loved.

The next day was Sunday. I went out to the lake and listened to *Yours Truly, Johnny Dollar* on the car radio as the sun sank in the west. When I got back to the dorm I tried in vain to crack a book. The old woman and Trappy were still in my mind. I could see Lemon being led by Trappy-the-child as they walked the streets of Wortham nearly half a century before. What was it in the eternal darkness of his world that had caused him to sing out? He was hell with the ladies, stumbling onto them to cop a quick feel. Poor blind boy, he wrestled, blind as a bat, in a traveling snake oil medicine show carnival. His songs were nasty, salacious, thinly veiled double entendre sexual humor, save for the one simple request, "See that my grave is kept clean."

Down the hall a brave soul played his record player. Devil music on the Sabbath. It was a far cry from Blind Lemon and yet part of the same American musical experiment in which the races reached for each other. The record's B side was a medley of songs my band had played two years ago in Memphis. I had seen an ad in the Dallas newspaper for the Mar-Keys playing at the Cellar. I had missed the boat. The gypsy's warning had come too late.

Chapter 26

ALL UP IN SONNY'S BED
(1962)

Checking out!
Making tracks
Waco, you're gonna be something
In my rear view mirror
Goin' home
Cross Ol' Man River one more time
And be where
I should have stayed

Imagine my surprise when my GPA and various probations converged and I could not transfer to Memphis State, sending me back Waco, into the beast's mouth, just barely getting my ass in summer school with one last chance. No room at the Inn dormitory, which was fine with me. I had my car and I found a two-room shack in a multiracial slum on the border area between school and city. A sign over the front door read SIN INN. I could only hope. I signed up for a medium load first semester: journalism and logic.

This was the first time I had lived alone. The little shack was surrounded by bushes and a driveway, making it feel isolated. The main room was all windows on three sides. I hung bedsheets over them. There was no AC but a "swamp fan" that blew hot air over tap water. It helped at night and made the air wet.

I picked up afternoon gigs with Dickerman (the jazz player from *Where's Charley?*), Louie, the drummer who showed me the pickup licks at dress rehearsal, and Ike, a Mexican trumpet player. Some gigs were on James Connally Air Force Base; others were at a roadhouse in Elm Mott. I saw the worst barroom fight I ever witnessed at that roadhouse. Two Mexican couples were dressed up like characters in the dance scene from

West Side Story; he-men in peg-legged zoot suits, women in crinoline pet-ticoats and teased lacquered hair in French rolls. They drank, danced, and had a high time until something went wrong. The two women scratched, bit, and pulled each other's hair. Then the straight razors came out. Blood everywhere. Somebody screamed the cops were coming. The two couples fled together. The dance floor was crimson with blood.

I was faking it on guitar with the three or four jazz chords I learned from Ricky. If I didn't know the song, I moved my hands with the volume down on my guitar. The gigs were fun but it wasn't my thing.

I embraced a solitary lifestyle of retrospective thinking, and started keeping a journal of random dark thoughts. Maybe it was the logic class's effect. I continued to correspond with Barbara, writing long lonesome letters that helped fill the hours after midnight. I invited her to visit me in my desert island domain.

Sunday night I had to study for a big logic test, essentially a midterm, which in the shortened summer school semester was a big part of the final grade. I listened to *Yours Truly, Johnny Dollar* at sundown and settled down to work. It was too hot. No rain for weeks. The heat had built up like a pressure cooker. The swamp fan blew the dry heat over the stagnant tap water in the trough below the spinning blades. Next day I blew the logic exam.

The rest of the summer was hot and uneventful except for one Satur-day afternoon. Tex Campbell wrote he had something important for me to hear. He wouldn't be more specific, only issuing an invitation. I drove to Austin Saturday morning, not knowing what to expect. Tex had turned me on to some very hip stuff, not just music but literature as well. He was an English literature major and smart as a fox. He had a wife and son from high school, and was strictly blue-collar.

With tears in my eyes I sat and listened to the voice coming out of Floyd "Tex" Campbell's record player. There it was. So obvious.

The answer:
Voice like a twisted
Rambling Jack
Language and words like
Nothing else
Leaking Ferlinghetti and Ezra Pound
Equal parts Charlie, Mingus, and Monk
I could hear Blind

Willie, Tex Ritter, Phil Harris, and Almeda Riddle.
A child's voice and the croaking of an ancient wise man
With glowing
Yellow eyes

It was all there.
The voice, guitar, and harmonica.
Flat in your face
Like seeing Elvis
At Ellis Auditorium
Or Will Shade
In Whiskey "Shoot."

There were old songs from the dawn of time
Talking blues
The ghost of Woody Guthrie
Alive in a new world
New songs he wrote himself sounded straight out of the Ozarks
Songs sung in box cars and barrooms
By nameless gypsy hoboes

In the midst of this music, what does he sing from its obscurity?
"I got one kind favor to ask of you
Won't you see that my grave is kept
Clean?"

I could feel the cold wind blowing
Across the Texas badlands
And see the nameless grave in the frozen ground.
Drawn there like the pilgrims
That put the ridiculous brooms
In the graveyard pitcher
What drew us there?
The crazy white boys
A story, a legend, an out of focus
Photograph in a text book
Yet there we were

The old gypsy was right
In not choosing,
I was drawn
To the path
I was once again
On the road
I had followed it here
I would follow it home
The music had been all around me
Though I had failed to consciously see it
I had soaked it up

The Sam Charters book
Where I had discovered
Blind Lemon
Was half about Memphis
What was I missing??

Who else was playing down
In the alley?
Or on the
West Memphis radio station?
Where was Will Shade?
Furry Lewis?
Thomas Pinkston, for God's sake?

It was all in the magic voice on the miraculous record
That Tex played for me that Austin afternoon.
On the back of the record jacket
Bob Dylan

Snarled into the microphone like Elvis or Hank
A look of resolute defiance, lip curled in contempt
This kid had the angel face of the corn belt heartland

The snap bill cap
The sheep herders' jacket
The turtleneck

The Martin D-28
The total package.

This was the missing piece of the puzzle—
Pointing the way to the future—
To the rest of my life.

Chapter 27

LOST IN THE WOODS
(1962-63)

I fell back into Memphis's easier rhythms and my old habits. Memphis State was like high school. I had to wiggle—rely on the "kindness of strangers"—to get myself enrolled. Baylor refused to send my transcript, a trick that could end with my ass in Vietnam. Somebody, somewhere in Baylor's bowels was pissed at little Jimmy. With the help of old theatre friends and Vera's mother, who was a placement counselor at Memphis State, I registered as a fifth-semester freshman, with no credits except those from summer school. I got the university's first-ever psychological deferment from ROTC.

I signed up for theatre history and anthropology, and found a place to hang out across the railroad tracks from school, aptly named the Campus Grill. Charlie Freeman was enrolled part-time and at the Campus Grill most afternoons. Bass player Tommy McClure showed up occasionally. Sometimes a whole rhythm section would be there.

I gigged with them a little. Roadhouse gigs on Highway 51 and in Arkansas. But mostly I had started doing folk music gigs. I traded my Rickenbacker solid-body for a Gibson J45 fire-engine-red sunburst, got out my old Jimmy Reed neck rack and harmonica, and fancied myself the poor man's Ramblin' Jack. It was easy. No band; no split the cheese. Talk, make sarcastic remarks, and tell lies to the audience. Hell, I was good at that!

I played the Bob Dylan record for everybody, like when I tried to turn my high school friends on to Jimmie Rodgers, the Singing Brakeman, or Blind Lemon Jefferson. Back then, some got it, but not many. They thought I was kidding with Jimmie Rodgers. It was the same deal with Dylan. Most folks didn't get it—yet.

I buddied up with Bill Newport, a kid I had known at White Station. His mother was my senior English teacher. He was a year behind me, in the same homeroom class with Vera and Steady Eddie. He was a good companion and co-conspirator. His garage-converted-pool-hall became my Room for Baylor Boys, a place of refuge and repose where we spent hours contemplating Eric Dolphy.

Memphis was beautiful that fall. The leaves changed slowly, gold to black gum red. I got a sheepherder's jacket at the saddle shop where I had seen Elvis cracking bullwhips with Nick Adams back in the fifties. I gave up the Ivy League Bruce Wayne disguise and settled back into jeans, Sears work shirts, and black Wellington lowtop boots.

Jack Kennedy had managed to get elected without my vote. I turned twenty-one later that fall. The year of Camelot. I "became legal," as we say down south. I could "vote and tote" (apply for a handgun permit), but more importantly, I could buy liquor and drink in a bar legally. I made full use of my new privilege. I drank my lunch at the Campus Grill, and caught a mild buzz before anthropology or philosophy class.

I searched for traces of the musicians in Sam Charters's book. The beginning of the civil rights movement made old black folks distrust the white boy asking questions even more. My old actor pal, Leon Rossum, found the first solid lead. He was a student at Southwestern, and had a teacher who claimed Gus Cannon was his family's yardman. They lived on Parkway, which had a tree-lined esplanade that had once bordered the city and now marked the beginning of Midtown. Gus lived on the place. He was tall and thin—old but not yet bent—baldheaded, with a Russian-looking fur hat and gold frame spectacles.

We found him bent over a gas lawn mower in the driveway. Two strange white boys walked out of the afternoon into the world of an old black man from another lifetime. We still didn't realize what would to happen to us. He led us out of the chilled October air and into his room over the tool shed/garage behind the big house. A gas stove overheated the small room. I noticed strangely painted lead pipes upright in a box in the corner. We sat.

"There was a fella here month or so ago to see me. White fella. You boys from New York?" Gus asked.

Leon shook his head. "Memphis." I wanted to say, "sir."

"I came to Mefus when I'ze 'bout yo age," he said. "Playin' in a medicine show. Fust seen a fellow blow a jug in Mefus—give me idea for them blowin' pipes." He gestured toward the pipes. They were painted multicolored and capped on one end with rubber can stoppers. They had old bottle caps and pieces of colored glass beads stuck to the long sides. "Pipe's got a mo' better sound," he added. "That New York fella had a machine with him and he recorded me. I used to make records ya know for de RCA Victor company. Yas suh. Folks don't believe me when I say that, but it's a fact."

"I believe you," Leon said reverently. Sitting in the afternoon sunlight, the old man rolled his head.

"You play music, suh?" he asked me. I nodded. "You have the look of a musician. Would you play fo' ol' Gus den? I don't hear near 'nuff music these days."

The old man reached under his bed and pulled out an ancient cardboard guitar case. He opened it slowly, removed the oldest Gibson guitar I had never seen, and strummed it once with his giant brown thumb. "I gots it tuned like a banjo, the fourth string down. You tune it to suit yourself."

I ran the string the way it was, making my E chord into a minor. I pulled up the G string to standard (like the Bo Diddley open D tuning, yet another secret code of their magical black music). I ham-fisted slow blues. Gus Cannon, onetime leader of the Jug Stompers, slowly swayed in the dusty light streaks from the setting sun, his eyes almost closed. After a few minutes he asked, "You like that music, white boy?"

I nodded.

"Don' mess with it if you don' like it. Dats ol' music and it sot in its ways."

It was getting dark. We said our grateful goodbyes, and he told us to come back anytime. He did not play for us that first time, but he would many times in the future. His banjo was in pawn. The man who recorded him sent him a copy of his record and no money. "I'd sho' like you gentlemens to hear my record, but I ain't got no playin' machine." As we left he asked if we were from the NAACP.

When my family moved from Chicago to Memphis in 1949, we lived outside the city limits, east of town, in Berclair, a little community that consisted of a drug store, a hardware store, a barbershop, and Mr. Baird's Big Star grocery store. Mr. Baird's son, George, was my age. George was a chronic epileptic currently under sedation, dulling some of his mental processes. Resulting drug addiction and extremely poor vision added to his handicap. By high school he had fallen several grades behind. He had a reputation for fist fighting, which he did his own way, like everything else. He wrote poetry he recited from memory in an awkward, childlike fashion. Like Alfred Jarry, Rimbaud, and Branwell Bronte, George invented his own infernal world. The walls of his condition locked him inside his own reality. He had a child's mind, forever a protégé.

He traps, hunts, and fishes.
He has an uncanny ability with animals,
Though he seems oddly cruel at times.
His world is not constant
And yet always the same.
Each moment is the same moment.
Every day begins at the same place.
Each morning though the same
Is always new.
Its God dumb.
To itself and its history.

George and I weren't friends growing up because I wouldn't let him trap squirrels in my yard. When our paths crossed ten years later, the first thing he said to me was, "Boy, Jimmy. I remember you. Never would let me trap your squirrels."

George had done little since high school. He couldn't drive. Bill Newport and I would take him to the pool hall. One night Jimmy Crosthwait, Newport, and I picked up George. We pulled into his long country driveway. He was in the backyard casting with his fly rod in the dark. I thought he was practicing his aim, casting almost straight up into the yard light.

"What are ya doing, George?"

"Fishing for bats."

"George," I said, amazed. "You can't catch bats like that." He smiled and held up a Mason fruit jar with six bats in it.

That fall we went on coon hunting safaris with George and his father's hound dogs, including

Old John
Who was supposed to be
The best hunting dog in Shelby County.
When you heard Old John tree
You'd be sure there was a coon.
Old John could follow a trail too cold for the other dogs.
Old John didn't hunt with the pack.

That was what first made me wonder about Old John.
He hunted way down in the bottoms
All by himself
And if he heard the other dogs tree something
Sometimes he came
And sometimes he didn't.
If he did come
He was liable not to stay,
Coon or no.
When George called them in
The other dogs came,
But when Old John heard the horn
He went further and further away.
He'd be way off across the river
And down in the bottoms
When the other dogs came in.
George called and called until
Finally we had to go get him
Put him on a leash and drag him to the car.
But he was still supposed to be
The best coon dog in Shelby County
Because when Old John treed
You knew there was a coon.

Maybe what Old John really liked was those last few minutes when the other dogs have come in, and he has it all to himself. He could hunt in the bottoms, bawl his old bawl that he must have known was worn out, and stay out until George finally got him. Those minutes when everyone else quit it were all his, until the night he never came back.

I was downtown one afternoon, walking by the Peabody Hotel, when somebody shouted, "Hey, Baylor Theatre." It was the writer from *Route 66* whom I had met in Dallas.

"What are you doing here?" he asked.

"Hometown," I answered. "What are you doing?"

"Shooting an episode. It's got a tall girl who rides a big motorcycle. I'll shoot a lot of pieces and put it together back in Hollywood. Don't suppose you could get me into Graceland?"

"Nobody gets in there," I told him.

They shot a fight scene at the Penthouse Night Club, a place run by my friend and future manager, Herbie O'Mell. He had the first integrated house band in Memphis, with Charlie Freeman and Duck Dunn playing with Little Willie John. Hot stuff. My future bride was in the show, jumping a horse in the fox hunt scene. We had yet to meet.

I dated around and still corresponded with Vera, now at Emory University, and Barbara Teal in Cincinnati. By Christmas I was pretty horny. On her first night home for the holidays, Vera made it clear she was only interested in being "friends." Fortunately Barbara came in town to visit her grandmother. We spent a couple of nights on the backseat of my white Chevy wrapped in a big king-sized blanket I borrowed from Harry Bowers, who was amazed by my good luck. Harry was hell with the ladies and still going with Anne Moss. But he could only dream of a woman like the fallen angel Barbara Teal.

After she returned to Cincinnati I felt the hole in my life more than ever. Vera drifted further away. I feared drifting back into the dire female psychodrama. I wrote long letters to Sandra Hudlow, who was matriculating at Baylor Theatre. I had seen her only twice, at Baylor for Nancy Barrett's farewell party and in Breckenridge at the Belvina Supper Club. Yet I poured out my intimate thoughts to this almost stranger. I neared desperation.

Amphetamines, my newfound study aid, helped boost my grades. I crammed and outlined all night. Newport was in anthropology with me. Our professor was called "Dr. Nash," even though he wasn't a Ph.D. He was a radical non-Boasian, which was rare, with a unique take on race and prehistory.

Crosthwait had become an artist. He painted and made sculptures of found object junk. He lived in a shack a local poet, Kenneth Bowdin, owned on the Arkansas side of the river under the old Harahan Bridge. He made his own clothes and grew his hair below his shoulders. We hung out a lot. He played trap drums in the Counts, but seeing no difference between the down beat (1) and the back beat (2 and 4), he was a little abstract for mainstream music. He had worked in the Ozark Mountains for a Buddhist monk, Brother Upaya, who was digging a bomb shelter in preparation for the Apocalypse.

My parents went to Little Rock on weekends to see University of Arkansas football games with old friends. During high school I went with them, but now I had the new house to myself on a semi-regular basis. More poker games with Newport, George, Bowers, and "Drive-In Danny"

Graflund, former King of the Toddle House, who was always up for six-packs. In high school, when my band played fraternity parties, Graflund would jump on stage and scream, "Suck fuck!" into the mic. One night he improvised a whole song as the band played "Johnny B Goode," one of the most creative things I ever witnessed. An ex–football hero and hardcore fraternity boy, Graflund had a creative fire that had yet to surface completely.

One weekend, Bubba Hardy, the toughest man I ever met, ran a poker game in the breakfast room. "Drive-In Danny" Graflund, Bill Newport, and I smoked paregoric-laced Pall Malls in my art room. We broke out the tape recorders. I played acoustic guitar, Newport beat a bass drum boosted from Baylor Theatre, and Graflund made up vulgar song after vulgar song, one of which contained the unbeatable lyric, "Rat shit, cat shit, suck your mama's tit, cocksucker, motherfucker, eat a bag of shit!"—a poetic verse that has served me well in many a hostile environment. The Paregoric Blues Band tape became legendary. A friend of Graflund's older brother expressed concern for Danny's soul and offered to pray with him.

That evening degenerated into a board-breaking competition. Newport used karate moves and laughed at Bubba Hardy, who used brute strength. They were breaking a nail keg. The competition proceeded without incident until George Baird broke a board across the top of his head. Later that night, during the poker game, George got too excited and had a full epileptic seizure, the only time I ever saw Bubba Hardy show fear. Newport bitterly took care of George; he was used to dealing with his friend's spells.

George's fit put a lid on the party. Andy Eudaly ("Tom" from *The Glass Menagerie* in high school) had been on the roof with a date. Andy was a lady's man. "Dickinson, your life is a circus," Andy said about the evening's events. "Let me get you a date with this girl I know. She's special."

His words had a familiar ring. My only blind date had been in Waco, helping out a friend with a beautiful girlfriend. He fixed me up with her best friend, a three-hundred-pound Mexican girl with a mustache. Especial! At the time Andy and I spoke, I was doing nothing but walking around all day in my old bathrobe, drinking sherry, reading Brendan Behan, and listening to *Sketches of Spain*. It wasn't working, so I told Andy to set me up.

Andy warned me, "This girl has class. Maybe you should dress up."

I dressed up, sporting a seersucker suit, blue Oxford cloth Gant dress shirt, and my black Wellington boots. I splashed on Royale Lime aftershave and picked up Andy. I followed his directions to my date's house in the heart of East Memphis, a couple of miles from White Station High School. My mother's friends lived across the street. I had driven by the house a thousand times. A big mimosa tree dominated the front yard and two Cadillacs were in the driveway.

My date was tall and thin, a mix of Audrey Hepburn and Mary Tyler Moore. She was a little young for me, a senior at Miss Hutchison's School for Girls. Mary Lindsay Andrews's eyes flashed with mischief. Not my type. Andy and I followed the two girls past a big white grand piano into a boy's bedroom with a stereo console in the middle of the floor, an overstuffed chair, a sofa bed, hand-drawn pictures of hot rods on the wall, and a set of Rogers drums in the corner. Mary Lindsay saw me look at the drums.

"Those belong to my brother."

"Who is your brother?" I asked.

"Al Stamps. He's my half-brother."

AL STAMPS!

"Andy says you play drums." Eyes.

"Yeah, I play a little bit." I looked at my boots.

"I dare you," she snickered.

I shook my head. She walked to the drums, sat, and played the drum part to Ray Charles' "What'd I Say" perfectly. Mary Lindsay was smart. Her conversation included talk of books, movies, and music. Like Al, her mother and half-sister played piano. Mary Lindsay was a jumping horse rider. Ribbons and trophies attested to her ability. She moved with a soft rhythmic grace and confidence that comes with mastery. I started to pay attention. As we talked she came over and sat at my feet. *Arpège.* Fresh and inviting. It stopped me in my tracks.

It was a school night for Mary Lindsay, so Andy and I made an elaborate exit before it got too late. We came back thirty minutes later, and parked where a mimosa tree blocked view of the car. We snuck up to her window, and popped out the burglar bars. She snuck out, and we talked all night. When I touched her, I felt a charge down to my toes, not a static electric shock, but like grabbing a hot wire and not being able to let go. I didn't want to let go.

I waited a couple of days to call Mary Lindsay. She was glad I called. We doubled with Harry Bowers to the Sky View Drive-In. I don't remember the movie. She tasted like peppermint candy. For our third date we went to the Oso coffee house, which Charlie Brown had opened after the Cottage folded. The Oso was smaller, darker, older, and sleazier. Blues legend Furry Lewis was playing. I couldn't wait. Charlie had found Furry living on Beale Street and working as a street sweeper for the city. Twice a day with a push broom and a garbage can on wheels, Furry Lewis swept Beale Street's gutters and cracked and crooked sidewalks. Armed with my Webcor tape recorder, I picked up Mary Lindsay and headed for the Oso in North Memphis. She smelled great and looked dangerous.

Furry Lewis, a small black man with white hair and blue eyes, dressed in a dark gray suit and Sunday shoes, limped to the stage on a cork leg, juggling his guitar as if he might drop it. I asked him if I could record his performance. He said, "No suh. I don't mind."

He sang everything: old blues, stuff older than blues, minstrel medicine show tunes. . . . He sang Jimmie Rodgers, "All around the water tank . . . waiting for a train," and after an abstract bottleneck solo, he yodeled. He sang church hymns and "St. Louis Blues" with no recognizable Handy lyric. He closed his last (of three!) set with "Let Me Call You Sweetheart," where in the melody both vocal and bottleneck went to a full four-chord change. Each time, Furry held the one and looked at his guitar as if it were missing the chord change all on its own. You couldn't tell what was in the act. He told stories between songs and recited poems, like George Beard. He opened the second set with

> Our father who art in Washington.
> Mr. Kennedy be his name.
> He taken me of off rat trap tobacco,
> Put me back on golden grain.
> 'Cause the sweetest flower in the world is the lily of the beech,
> And the worse whiskey I ever drunk
> Right here on Poplar Street.
> 'Cause the hoppa grass makes the hops.
> Honey bee makes the honey.
> Good Lord makes all the pretty girls.
> Sears and Roebuck makes the money.

"'Scuse me," Furry snickered.

He was an incredible entertainer. I watched a living montage, sixty years of American subculture I had been separated from by racial lines.

Now it was at my fingertips. Mary Lindsay could tell I was an overcharged battery. "That was something special," she said when we were back in the car. "I feel lucky to have seen that."

I drove aimlessly, not knowing where to go. I drove down the river. We talked. I told her about seeing the Jug Band when I was a kid. I told her about Gus Cannon. I told her about Butterfly and Dishrag and the "codes."

"You live an interesting life," she said. When I kissed her I no longer heard the music in my head.

Chapter 28

MARKET THEATRE
(1963)

I took Mary Lindsay everywhere. Movies. Plays. I took her to the Formula Junior Sports Car races in Stuttgart, Arkansas. Andy filmed the races. Mary Lindsay and I looked like we were in a French *cinéma vérité* existential modern romance. We dined at the Arcade, and watched the sunset over the river. She was always happy—no dire drama—and got along with my friends (no simple task). My quality of life picked up.

She was from an old Mississippi cotton family. Her grandfather was high up in the Crump machine; her role in the annual Cotton Carnival was part of her heritage. She was a member of the Queen's Court, and had a week full of parties. Her escort was an old fraternity brother from Tau. The last night I waited in the parking lot. She ran towards me in her flowing ball gown, laughing, happy to see me.

Mary Lindsay was scheduled to ride in the Germantown Charity Horse Show. She had been Junior Hunter Champion in the big fall show the year before. I fear I disturbed her and her horse's, Short Snort's, training. She looked great in her riding clothes; it was amazing to see this skinny little girl maneuver and manipulate her monster jumper around and over the fences in the ring. She was fearless and completely in control of this huge animal. She had been hurt several times, once rolled on and squashed like a tomato. She was unconscious in the hospital for eighteen days. An old scar ran down the middle of her face, twisting her smile to one side. It made her look mysterious.

I wasn't through with theatre. I felt unwelcome at Front Street Theatre and the local community theatre. Memphis State was a big letdown from Baylor, but Andy Eudaly encouraged me. He discovered a Catholic girls' school production of *The Glass Menagerie* in need of male actors. Andy took his old role of Tom. I designed the set and co-directed with the nun in charge, a rewarding use of my Baylor Theatre chops. We rehearsed for two weeks, and performed at Christian Brothers College for one night. Andy and I only had a night to construct the set. We took bennies and hammered it out. It was simple and abstract, without the scrim rear projections called for in Tennessee Williams's script. We had no time to fly the flats so we nailed them to the stage. Working into the morning, we got the set up.

We came up with the idea of doing summer theatre at the crack of dawn. We shared our idea with Phil Arnault, a well-established character actor in the Memphis theatre community. Gung ho, we borrowed money from my father and commenced. We found a great space: an old butcher shop in the Farmers' Market on Poplar at Crosstown. It was a long, low, crudely constructed series of sheds and shacks in which Mid-South farmers sold produce on weekends. Our space was at the north end of the line. With friends' help, we tore out walls, ripped out the old freezer and meat lockers, built a stage, and installed fifty wooden theatre seats we bought from a black Baptist church in South Memphis. Ricky built a light board with two switchable rheostat faders and twelve off-on switches. We made fake fresnels out of outdoor spotlights and tomato cans. I painted MARKET THEATRE in my best Baylor Theatre abstract lettering across the whole front wall. The place was really cool. We held open auditions, and wrung publicity out of the local newspapers.

Mary Lindsay had done a summer apprenticeship at Front Street Theatre and was a big help. She could handle the house and reservations, and was good with people. We were together day and night.

We opened the first week in June, which the Memphis mayor had declared Market Theatre Week. We had an invitation-only pre-opening for press and local dignitaries. Our first show was Eugene O'Neill's *Bound East for Cardiff*, with Phil and Andy in the lead. I directed. Folk music performers opened and each play was one act.

The evening started with the stage blacked out, and a spotlight shining on a solo guitarist. "Ladies and gentlemen . . . ," said a voice from offstage, "the Market Theatre proudly presents Jim Vinson."

Vinson vamped to "Make Me a Pallet on the Floor." His long blond hair flipped over and hung over his eyes, like Veronica Lake's in *This Gun for Hire*. Vinson played flamenco guitar and wore a bolero jacket. He had a sweet, semi-trained voice, and provided a stark contrast to my blue-collar, crazy white boy act. At the pre-opening I got my old friend, Barbara Anderson, then Miss Memphis, to stand in a white swimsuit, wearing her queen's crown and "Miss Memphis" sash. She looked like the girl from the *Creature from the Black Lagoon*. The effect was surreal.

We got plenty of good press. A respected professor from Memphis State directed our second show, *The Marriage Proposal*. We were heroes, cultural pioneers, new bloods breaking new ground.

One afternoon we were cleaning up for the evening show. A stranger walked in out of the summer sunshine, removed his shades, and shuffled his sandals. Meeting Sid Selvidge was a life-changing moment. He was an anthropology student at Southwestern from Greenville, Mississippi, a skinny blond ruffian with a guitar case and a Communist hammer and sickle belt buckle the size of a hubcap. Sid's voice—part Appalachian balladeer, part Delta field holler—was considered the best in town, equal parts Almeda Riddle and Jimmie Rodgers, with some Tex Ritter and Sam Cooke. Sid sang everything from "Captain Kidd" to "Ol' Black Betty." He did an a cappella "Boll Weevil" that can still stop a show. Sid's singing partner, Horace Hull, was truly amazing. Horace was from an old Memphis family, somehow kin to Boss Crump. He was the real deal, probably the most talented musician from my age group in town. Horace played long-neck mountain banjo and sang like an angel. The phrase "sing like an angel" gets bandied about, but Horace did truly sing like an angel. He even played pipe organ. He and Sid crossed harmonies like the Stanley Brothers, and went in and out of unison like the Everlys. It defied description. They were magic, without a doubt the best folk act I ever saw, bar none. But Horace's crippling speech problem made it difficult to perform in public comfortably.

One sunny bright afternoon, sitting in the back seat of Horace's Thunderbird, Sid passed me a joint. Marijuana, tea, reefer madness, the real Mezz!

"All right!" I said eagerly.

Horace stammered, amid laughter, "I knew you were a . . . h-h-h-head!"

Horace had recently returned from Morocco with his banjo case packed full of beautiful golden pot. Newport and I split a "lid," a Prince Albert tin can full. Street value in 1963 of $15. The good old days.

Crosthwait showed up at the Market Theatre as soon as we opened. He beat on oil drums, not tuned like steel drums from Trinidad, but just old dented rusty oil drums, turned over and jammed down over barstools. He chanted, chuckled, and played a dervish repetitious dance beat that seemed to recall a secret and sinister part of childhood. His act was menacing, unnerving, and the audience wasn't always kind. He screamed "God damn!" randomly. He made heavy, flame-charred wooden mallets, and wrapped them in rags to soften the impact and blur the attack of the note. His drums' sound was loud and amazing; it seemed nearby yet not right here, like an echo from a parallel universe, a bizarre dimension.

Two artists showed up at audition. Fresh out of Christian Brothers High School, Mike Murphy and Chris Wimmer were a brilliant comedy team, perfect examples of what I was trying to do with the theatre. They were my students. For the first time I was on the other side of the line. I was the director, the coach, the boss. It was my artistic statement, by all means collaborative, but I was the ship's captain; whether the *Titanic* or the *Flying Dutchman* was up to fate or fortune. I was Ahab. I was Professor. I was Baker.

I had the cast needed to do the show. The whole summer project was designed for John Logan's *Of Poems, Youth, and Spring*, the story of high school romance with an onstage Greek chorus and long sections of blank verse. It had been staged at Baylor the year before I arrived. I wanted to produce it myself. I found the female lead, Dorothy Ramspacker, at casting call. Barely five feet tall, she was a chestnut brunette with a sweet voice, a little like Mary Lindsay's. Mary Lindsay sang when she spoke. To a lesser extent, so did this girl. I did not want to direct Mary Lindsay, since the director-to-actor relationship is a dispassionate and dehumanizing procedure that might complicate our relationship. I got as close to Mary Lindsay as I could with Dorothy, changing her hairstyle and casting her as a late-fifties "girls' school" girl.

Mike Murphy was a younger Eudaly, a clean-cut all-American boy. I costumed him in a Sears work shirt and near-white wheat jeans. I made them create character background sketches and work from a nature object as we did in Drama X. I filmed it in 8mm for a pre-play silent film I edited together with black-and-white footage my father had shot from a hotel room in Wichita, Kansas, in the thirties. This was my "prologue." Jim Vinson sat off stage left, in full view of the audience, and played an accompanying score on gut-string guitar. One reviewer referred to it as "randomly ruminating," which pissed me off.

After that production I was through with the place. We ran *The Last of My Solid Gold Watches* and two plays by a local would-be author. The folk music aspect was taking over. One day something strange happened. A handful of us were shooting the shit in the lobby when suddenly the sunlight coming in the door was blocked out. Two big men in dark suits and sunglasses stood in the doorway. They looked like shaved apes, way out of place. Alien.

"Jim Dickinson around?" one spoke in a flat Yankee monotone. At least, I thought, he didn't ask for Merrell Williams.

Before I could respond, Chris Wimmer, a man always on top of the action, said, "No. He's not here. He won't be back until tonight, if then. How can I help you?" Chris was tall and thin with long blond hair. He smiled a toothy, obviously insincere smile, and took the two gorillas' reservations for the night's show (which they attended without further incident). Late that night I learned they were goons sent by somebody from Cincinnati called "Big Sid," whom Barbara Teal had apparently "run away" from. What the hell was she up to?

Amazingly, the fated classic inner theatre intrigue and drama transpired. Cliques formed between day people and night people. Jailbait theatre groupies came out of the woodwork. Drifters on their way through town showed up for a handout or a flop. The set for *Poems* initially had occupied the whole stage end of the theatre, redone into a black-and-white Franz Kline painting, but people gradually added text. It looked like a page out of a Baker 106 notebook, blown up to stage size. We started Sunday afternoon hootenannies (I have always hated that name, but the phenomenon was a super-popular moneymaker). We developed a Grand Ole Opry–like lineup of regulars: Sid, Vinson, Crosthwait, Collin and Cathleen (a man-and-wife act of pure traditional coffeehouse material), Bob Frank (a student from Southwestern who wrote his own historical Americana songs), Valerie Lord (a twelve-year-old girl with more chops than Joan Baez), Bob Knott (most interesting of all), and me.

Knott, from a prominent Memphis grocery family, looked as unobtrusive as a book salesman. In a button-down shirt and Buddy Holly glasses, he fingerpicked like a demon and wore a harmonica neck rack with a kazoo on the side. He also played a mean mandolin. He had a bone-dry wit; the audience never figured him out. But they didn't have to understand. He killed the house every show. He introduced me to Jesse "Lone Cat" Fuller and the wonder of the Fotdella, a mysterious bass instrument Fuller played with his feet.

Paul Craft's Memphis debut stood out. One Sunday afternoon he tore off the roof with a hot knockoff of "Foggy Mountain Breakdown." Craft became a songwriter in Nashville, writing "Drop Kick Me, Jesus Through the Goal Posts of Life," and the phone-sex anthem, "It's Me Again, Margaret." But he was most successful as publisher of the classic "The Gambler."

The Sunday afternoon hootenannies led to an all-music weekend with people hanging from the rafters. There were over two hundred admissions with only fifty seats.

At summer's end there was no way to keep going. It was hard enough to keep the room cool. It would have been impossible to heat. We had a closing party; then Newport and I went to Mountain View, Arkansas, to decompress. Mary Lindsay closed down the theatre.

On the way to Mountain View we saw a horrifying sight. As we rode by, the cornfield to our left began to move. A large section of cornfield opened and parted, revealing huge rockets aimed at the sky. We kept on trucking, feeling like we had seen something we were not supposed to see. Soon after, the Federal Government began constructing a huge nuclear power plant in Russellville, Arkansas, a few miles away from where we had seen the guided missiles. What in the Ozark Mountains needs that much power and protection? I don't think I want to know.

By the time we returned to Memphis, the Market Theatre was history.

We still owed the theatre's last month of bills, so I planned one last folk music show. I rented the municipal Overton Park Shell, where Elvis had played, and bought an ad in the *Commercial Appeal* newspaper. I went on the local Saturday afternoon *Dance Party* TV show; it was the first time couples from a local high school weren't featured dancing. Integration had changed the format; Memphis was not ready to see black teenagers dancing. To fill time, I was interviewed at length. I plugged my show big-time. I called it the First Annual Memphis Folk Festival, featuring the usual suspects: Jim Vinson, Colin and Kay, Sid and Horace, Bob Frank, and me. No one had heard of us.

I went to Little Rock for a couple of days before the show. My parents felt sorry for me; they thought no one would show up. We returned to Memphis just before show time, and there was already a traffic jam, with special cops directing traffic. My father was amazed. I charged a dollar a head to avoid entertainment tax. My father shook his head as a girl from the theatre went by, her skirt full of one-dollar bills, like an apron full of chicken feed. I paid the bills and split the money between all the artists. I never paid my father his original loan, one of many to come.

A review and a big write-up in the local press featured a picture of me playing my neck rack harmonica and guitar with a caption dubbing me the "Decibel King." I have never understood that caption. Just how damn loud can you play the harmonica and acoustic guitar? That write-up was one of the luckiest breaks of my career.

Chapter 29

OL' SAM HESS
(1963)

Back in the old days folks who played music in Mountain View, Arkansas, had gathered at the Stone County Courthouse on Friday nights for what was called The Sing. By the summer of 1963, local schoolteacher/celebrity Jimmy Driftwood had restarted the old tradition with hopes of attracting government grant dollars. Behind the national notoriety of his hit record, "The Battle of New Orleans," Driftwood appointed himself keeper and purveyor of the local ethnic musical scene. Musicians gathered in the courtroom, with the audience seated and the players in the jury box. One by one they took the witness chair and performed. Fiddlers and banjoists, little old ladies playing knitting needles . . . a man playing bagpipes paraded up and down the aisle as he wailed away. They performed familiar ballads from *Child's Book of Ballads* and unfamiliar songs learned within family traditions. My old partner from Market Theater, Phil Arnault, turned me on to it. I went whenever possible.

During my trips to Mountain View, I often visited cowboy folk singer Glenn Ohrlin at his small ranch. He had one of the best acts on the coffeehouse circuit. Born in Sweden, he came to the United States as a Merchant Marine and became a cowboy in Colorado. He played self-taught classical guitar (he had invented his own musical notation employing no bar lines), and sang cowboy songs in a cracked, emotionless voice. He had a show-stopping version of "Beautiful Morning Glory."

One night Bob Knott and I were at Glenn's ranch, and I did a little too much talking about Bookmiller Shannon, one of the regulars who performed with Jimmy Driftwood at The Sing. He was a pussle-gutted old reprobate who frailed his banjo (which had a picture of a canoe on a moonlit lake in the pines painted on its old head) delicately balanced on his flannel shirt–covered belly. It was getting to Glenn, who was typically serene. Glenn thought Driftwood was a phony and did not participate in The Sing.

He didn't trust schoolteachers. After I made one too many comments about Bookmiller Shannon's profundity, Glen grumbled and stood. He said, "You boys get up and come on with me. I wanna show you something." Glenn said he had to drive. We got in his car, a worn-out old Dodge with a push-button transmission stuck in second gear. Glenn lived halfway up a mountain overlooking Mountain View. We went up the blackest, darkest gravel road I had ever seen to what was surely a goat trail. The Dodge whined and strained. Headlights bobbed up and down, flashing into the nothing of the eternal Arkansas autumn sky. We drove up and up. Finally Glenn stopped and we looked around at nothing. We got out of the car, and stood in darkness as black as the bottom of the Longhorn Cavern. Out of the black stepped a tall, thin old man dressed in sun-bleached overalls and a shapeless straw hat. Glenn said, "Boys, this is Mr. Sam Hess."

We stood, amazed, still trying to adjust to the lack of illumination.

"Hidy," the old man cackled.

He reached down behind what I guessed was a fence post, and pulled up a crockery jug with a corncob stuck in the top. He withdrew this stopper and took a long drink. "Been breaking ground up the draw," he said.

I saw the mule he had been penning up when we arrived. He had been working until well after sundown, breaking new ground with a mule on a steep incline in the unforgiving rocky brown dirt. We followed the old man and Glenn up a rocky path to a little cabin glowing with coal oil lamp light. Walking through that door was like entering another time: wood stove, rocking chair, calico curtains. Everywhere I looked, on every flat surface and lined around the room, stood Bell topped mason jars full of fruit and unknown substances, three deep from the wall. Sam Hess declared, "Emmer's been puttin' up."

A tiny old woman standing behind the door chuckled and rubbed her hands together. She nodded her head in approval.

Glenn said, "Sam, these boys want to see yer banja." He nodded and led us to a closed door. We went inside what appeared to be a bedroom. He reached under the bed and pulled out an instrument case. I thought about Gus Cannon, but this was different. The air was full, like the anticipation in church as the organ plays nondescript chords before prayer.

Sam Hess removed the banjo from its case. It was a top-of-the-line Whyte Lady five-string standard scale banjo. His hands were disfigured by arthritis and lifelong labor. His knuckles looked like walnuts. His fingers were bent and broken. His hands moved like magic on the beautiful instrument. He frailed with the backs of his fingernails, playing the same style my French grandmother played. He sang in a pure falsetto, with a tone like cool creek water spilling over gravel. He sang "Barney McCoy," as if it was coming out of *Child's Book of Ballads*, "Oh where are you going, Barney darling."

I don't remember coming down the mountain. I couldn't even tell how we turned a car with only second gear around for the return trip. I only know the next morning Bob Knott and I stopped at Jimmy Driftwood's house for breakfast, and Jimmy's hair was dyed brown. As his wife served us breakfast, I saw the silver sparkles in her fingernail polish. Driftwood revealed that the ancient guitar he claimed his grandfather made out of a fence post and bed slats had actually come from a pawnshop in Nashville.

Glenn Ohrlin saw Jimmy Driftwood as an enemy. Glenn had explained most local musicians would not go to The Sing due to family feuds predating the "War of Northern Aggression." They did not trust outsiders like Driftwood, or talk of government money. Soon thereafter, the deal was done. A folklore center was built and a regimented annual Folk Festival was organized, bringing in musicians from hither and yon who had nothing to do with Ozark culture.

Dr. Nash, my anthropology instructor, called it the "Trobriander Effect." Scientists discover a primitive society living the paradise of pre-Western civilization. Through contact with the outside world, the balance and perfection of the community is polluted and eventually destroyed. Destroying the thing you love is an unforgivable sin.

Chapter 30

OSO AND DIXIELAND FOLK STYLE (1963)

My stage act was evolving. I found old gold-rimmed glasses my grandfather had worn and had my prescription put in them. I found dress shirts my father wore in prep school from Phil A. Halle, a men's store still active in downtown Memphis. I sold Selvidge my Gibson J45 and bought a Martin D28 (one of my dumber moves). I boiled and reshaped my father's old Chicago fedora and made a poncho out of an old hotel blanket.

I played semi-regularly at the Oso. It was low-key, to say the least. Charlie Brown let me do whatever I wanted. I started each show with a long drawn-out version of Froggie the Gremlin's "Every Time I Go to Town the Boys Kick My Dog Around," with an extended abstract kazoo solo in which I fancied myself referencing Sidney Bechet. I tried to establish as much distance between the audience and myself as possible. It was hostile. I spent my set break sitting on the sidewalk outside the front door, wrapped in my blanket/poncho (people crossed the street rather than walk by me). Mary Lindsay hated it. I could see it made her uncomfortable. Some nights she begged off and stayed away. She was having family trouble, some of it surely due to me.

Mary Lindsay was set to attend the University of Tennessee in Knoxville. I told her she wasn't going and bulldozed her into Southwestern at Memphis with the inside help from an old friend of my mother's. I think it spooked her. She was feeling manipulated, but I couldn't help it. We broke up. It was my fault. I hid under the bed and stupidly made my mother answer the telephone.

In the middle of my hibernation, my mother fielded a strange phone call from George Tidwell, the trumpet player from Al Stamps's old band. He was living in Nashville, working as an arranger for Bill Justis. Justis had seen the publicity about the Folk Festival at the Shell and wanted me to call him.

Justis worked for Mercury/Smash Records making "party records," instrumental cover versions of hit songs. He wanted to make an album of folk songs with a Dixieland band à la "Midnight in Moscow," a recent hit. He was looking for singers. "Get two more folkies and come up here next week," Bill said with his sarcastic, know-it-all hipster twang.

I called Colin Heath and his wife, legitimate folk singers with good voices. They could do the heavy lifting. We flew to Nashville. I hated to fly. Thankfully, it was a short flight. I had a bag of pot in my banjo case. We checked into the King of the Road Hillbilly Heaven next to the Pancake House down from Music Row, and met Justis at Ireland's Restaurant by Vanderbilt University. The first session was that night after a steak and biscuit dinner.

As Bill Justis and I walked into Columbia Studio "B" for the first *Dixieland Folk Style* session, Johnny Cash was leaving with his arms around two Carter Family sisters, who were holding him up like bookends. He took one look at me in my sheepherder's jacket and banjo case with a hidden bag of pot and snarled, "What's this? Amateur hour?"

Bill grimaced and grumbled as we passed. Bill saw the comment had hurt me. He smiled his hipster smile and said, "The Phantom of the Opry." Roger Miller was in the john wearing a tux coat and a black Bardahl T-shirt.

It was the real Nashville cats. Bill Purcell on piano, Bob Moore on upright bass, Elvis's drummer, Buddy Harman, on drums, wearing fingerless black gloves, Boots Randolph on sax, six different guitar players including Grady Martin and Fred Carter from the Hawks, acoustic, electric, baritone, six-string bass, and someone on five-string banjo with a flat pick. I couldn't play since I was non-union. All Justis wanted me to do was sing. It was like with Ramsey Horton and the K-otics. Hard for me to believe that's what he wanted. He had the fucking Jordanaires and three members of the Anita Kerr Singers working from five staff scores! My buddy, George, was in the bathroom frantically providing and copying parts. We ran the songs down a couple of times and took a cut. The musicians were fabulous; first-call session players, playing tight minimalist parts that fit like fingers into a glove. After the session I went to Printer's Alley to the Voodoo Club for a drink with Fred Carter, who got blasted and crashed a police barricade as we left.

I lay awake that night at Hillbilly Heaven, smoking dope and pondering the universe after the first session. This was IT. I had to find a place in the process.

The second day of the session was my twenty-second birthday. At home in the driveway was a new midnight blue Corvair Spider with four on the floor and a supercharger. I hadn't even driven it but I wasn't thinking about the car. I was absorbing as much recording magic as possible. We cut some corny folk stuff, "Michael Row the Boat Ashore," "Ten Thousand Miles from Home." I had a solo on "St. James Infirmary Blues," the song Vera's dad sang. Justis played trumpet, a rare occurrence, and the other players applauded.

Halfway through the day's second session, the big fire doors at the side of the tracking space burst open and a huge redneck dressed in black entered the room, talking fast and paying attention to no one. He walked rapidly toward the background singers, taking off Roy Orbison's dark glasses, still talking fast, "I'm sorry, baby. Couldn't make up my mind. Couldn't choose so I just bought both of them."

It didn't make sense to me. I figured someone would throw him out. The session ground to a halt. The stranger centered his attention on the flame-redheaded singer with the Anita Kerr Singers, still talking, "I'm sorry, Baby . . ."

Everybody followed the couple to the parking lot. He talked fast, pointing to a pair of Jaguar XKEs, a hardtop coupe and a ragtop roadster, both midnight-blue, like my yet un-driven Spider. He had bought them both, like cufflinks. He handed out little brown cigars with gold printing that ran from end to end, and read, "Shelby S. Singleton, Vice President of Mercury/Smash." "Who is this guy?" I asked my friend, George, standing by me.

"That's Shelby Singleton. He's the producer."

There it was. This guy hadn't been there for two-thirds of the session, and he showed up with two new sports cars. The producer. Finally, a job I could do. I watched him closely.

The session had been going pretty well but had gotten harder. More discussions; more nitpicking. Singleton took up a lot of space. He had shifted the air in the room. He was tall and overweight, with long greasy ducktails and mutton-chop sideburns. He never took off his shades. He was producing, I figured. We recorded "Blowing in the Wind." I asked him why we didn't cut "Don't Think Twice." He blew it off, shaking his head, "You'll never hear of that Dylan guy again. That one song was a freak accident like the Chipmunks."

I stayed an extra day after the tracking. The other singers had been dismissed. Justis wanted to do more vocal overdubs. Colin and Kay had been a bad call. He already had plenty of legitimate singers. He needed the edgy authenticity I brought to the party. Bill told me, "Give me some more of the 'Nig-a-Billy.'"

I returned to Memphis with much to think about. Making that album was like rehearsing for a play and then going into production through the last show. It wasn't like playing a live gig. I had contributed to something that would endure.

I missed Mary Lindsay. I wanted to talk to her about what just happened.

Barbara Teal came home at Thanksgiving to visit her grandmother. She was driving a new Corvette and had new store-bought tits. I asked her, "Barbara, where did you get the car?"

"My friends tell me what horses to bet on over at the race track."

Big Sid, no doubt. I didn't ask any more questions.

One night when Barbara had gone back to Cincinnati I was driving around East Memphis. Driving that little blue car was a pleasure. The Spider would wind out four gears smooth as silk. Maybe it was no XKE but it was a fine set of wheels for Handsome Jimmy. East Memphis was my backyard. I knew the streets by heart, knew how to dodge the stop signs and avoid the speed traps. Memphis opens west to east. All roads lead to God's Country. It had been cotton fields and truck farms when we arrived in '49. Now it was filled with subdivisions and shopping centers; suburban squalor swallowed the landscape.

One night I patrolled the streets behind White Station School. If I went left, I would pass Mary Lindsay's house. If I went right, it would be a different story. I went left. She was walking by the mimosa tree in front of her house, her hair and coat collar blowing in the wind. My car lights caught her full-on for only a moment. I knew.

It wasn't easy getting back together. Her friends were down on me. Her mother had discovered a letter from one so-called friend providing her with a little too much information about our relationship. I called Mary Lindsay. We had to sneak around. She talked to me in my car out behind the mimosa tree one night before she left on a date with someone else. We were on thin ice and meeting on the sly. She had dates for all the Christmas parties, but promised me New Year's Eve.

I went to Cambridge, Massachusetts, with Newport. He stayed with his freshman roommates and I bunked with Tex and his wife. Tex, the friend who turned me on to Dylan in Austin, was doing his Master's in English lit. He and his wife had an apartment off the Square behind the Harvard

Co-op. I attended classes with Tex, including a psychology lecture by B. F. Skinner of Skinner Box fame, and bought paperbacks of the *Quatermass Trilogy* at the Harvard Co-op.

Wet trees
Naked to the toes
Wave frosty fingers
And reach into space
This night,
As breath is held
And frog fires
Burn.
The white horse moon
Will slip like a pale stone
Slick in the backyard ditch
Down the mudbank of sky.
Crawling Christmas
Will newspaper itself
To every front porch and
Baste itself
To the stomach of the day
Tinsel and candle
Will Christmas tree
The passing possibility
Of the far gone eve
With the package of the morning
And the spirit of the night
Are tissue paper and gone,
Sailing in a ship-ly trinity.
The night is lost to ghosts of all the Christmas past
And we will hunt the coon,
We shall bay the moon
And woods,
Wander wild-eyed
With the spirit of old John,
Balling in the bottoms.
The glass star of childhood
And the red name-tagged stocking
Are sadly silent in the past.

Tonight the goal that I once reached backward to obtain will no longer
Suffice. It's behind her.
The answer.
Far to the rear of the blinking tree lights
That had no gift for me.

Walking back tonight
From the Harvard Square
In the falling snow
That may spend the strange holiday
For me in Cambridge,
I pass a building
In the basement
There are blue holiday lights
In two windows.
The rest of the building is dark.

Music was everywhere. Jim Kweskin's Jug Band at Mt. Auburn's
Club 47. Patrick Sky, the Indian activist, Mitch Greenhill, and farthest
out of all, the Holy Modal Rounders. Walking the street, I heard Travis
picking and harmonica wailing out of a dusty storefront. Young men who
looked like me, with long hair, scruffy, Navy pea jackets or fleece-lined
sheepherder's coats, blue jeans, and booted, plodded through the city
streets like rugged frontiersmen, carrying Martin D28s in black hard-shell
cases.

Before Christmas, I got a recording contract from Justis in the mail. I
called him. "Hey man, what is this?" I asked.

"Don't you want to make a record?" he asked.

"Sure," I said.

"Then sign the contract."

I showed my old man the contract. He shrugged. I signed it and mailed
it from Chicago the day after Christmas.

There had been a big snowstorm, but the blizzard didn't put a lid on
Mary Lindsay's partying. I later heard stories about her dancing on a table.
That's my girl.

Chapter 31

NEW BEALE STREET SHEIKS AND THE RETURN OF WILL SHADE (1963)

I proposed on New Year's Eve. We had been to Steady Eddie's house party. George Tidwell was there with his new bride, an airhead with an infectious, disarming Gracie Allen appeal. Mary Lindsay watched her and smiled. It looked like she was thinking about the future.

We had other married friends. Phil Arnault, from the Market Theatre, and his wife lived in Vets Village. She taught Mary Lindsay to make green pea casserole with mushroom soup and canned fried onion rings. It became the backbone of our early marriage.

Mary Lindsay didn't say yes right away. The second time I asked, we had doubled with Newport and Vera (not a really great idea). We were both pretty drunk. She said yes.

I was engaged. I was finally no longer a freshman in college, and had my second recording contract. I hoped to get a little further than I had with Rubin Cherry and Home of the Blues. Justis booked a recording session for me at Sam Phillips's studio. A week before the session, I got an envelope from Justis with a lyric sheet to a song written by *Playboy* cartoonist Shel Silverstein. Obviously, Bill meant for me to record it. There was no way. The song was "The Unicorn," which was later a big hit by the Irish Rovers. I couldn't hear myself singing the words "humpty back camels and chimpanzees." I acted like I never received it. I knew whatever I recorded had to be really good.

Whiskey Chute! Seeing Jim Kweskin's Jug Band at Club 47 had jarred my memory. I called Crosthwait and asked if he had considered playing the washboard. We went to a hardware store by Memphis State and got a Zinc King washboard and half a dozen sewing thimbles to use as picks. We drafted George Gillis, who had played bass on my Home of the Blues session, to play washtub. The New Beale Street Sheiks were born.

We rehearsed once, played a gig Friday night at the Pastimes Peanut Bar, and showed up at Sam Phillips's studio Saturday morning for the session. Nobody was there except Scotty Moore, Bill Black, and Rowsey, the repairman. Justis had failed to nail down the booking for the session, and Scotty wasn't buying it. We looked pretty bad. Crosthwait had hair trailing down his back. Gillis and I were hungover. I told Scotty to call Justis in Nashville. After he got off the phone, Scotty okayed the session and it fell to Rowsey to engineer. Later I found out it was his first and only session. We set up around a couple of RCA 77s and laid down four songs as fast as we could. While we were cutting, Bill Black called people on the phone to come over and laugh at us from the control room.

When we finished Bill shook his head. "Dickinson, this is the wildest thing you've ever done," he chuckled.

I tried to get the tape, but Scotty wouldn't let me have it. "I'll send it to Bill," I said.

"No, man. I'm going to Nashville tomorrow. I'll take it to Bill myself." Scotty still didn't trust me. More than a week went by, and I didn't hear from Justis. I called him. "What did you think of the tape?" I asked.

"Great, man! Great. The record comes out Thursday. Chet Atkins tried to buy it. It's a hit."

"Record?" I choked. "That was a demo."

"Oh, man, you could never do it that bad again," Bill said.

"Bill, you have no idea how bad I could do it," I said, with all my heart.

"What's that playing bass?" he asked.

"That's a washtub and a clothesline tied to a broomstick," I answered.

"A rope! A rope!" Justis shouted. "I went all over Nashville trying to EQ a rope!"

The record came out on Thursday. We got a *Cash Box* review and a pick-hit on the cover of *Billboard*. On Sunday, the Beatles were on *Ed Sullivan* for the first time. Our hour in the sun was brief. John R played it for two nights on WLAC. The first night he said, "Wait a minute, y'all. There's some kind of racket down in the parking lot. I'm gonna stick a microphone out the window and see what we can hear." Then he played the record. The next night he said, "I've been in the music business for thirty years and this is without a doubt the worst record I've ever heard."

Justis set me up with Ray Brown, the notorious booking agent who had aptly named Jerry Lee Lewis "The Killer." Brown, an ex–disc jockey, booked all of the Memphis artists: The aforementioned Killer, the Bill Black Combo, "Ace" Cannon, "Jumpin'" Gene Simmons, the Mar-Keys, and anybody else he could sell to a college fraternity, radio station, or nightclub honkytonk. His office downtown was an incredibly fun place to hang out. Ray had the same caustic sense of humor as Bill Justis. My act's strangeness appealed to him. He booked the New Beale Street Sheiks as a novelty. We played conventions and happy hours. Nobody had any idea who we were but it always went over. Jug bands have a universal appeal.

I quit doing my blanket act at the Oso: I didn't want to push my luck with Mary Lindsay. We were in the audience when Furry Lewis played and got to be friends with the wise old man. Charlie Brown had found Will Shade. After all those years, I would finally meet the genius from Whiskey Chute, the leader of the Memphis Jug Band!

It was another "parents in Little Rock" weekend. I was supposed to go to Nashville to meet Fred Foster, the owner of Monument Records, who distributed Southtown, Justis's label that had released "You'll Do It All the Time" by the New Beale Street Sheiks. The day before I was to go, Charlie Brown called wondering if I wanted to meet Will Shade. I met Charlie and Bailey Wilkerson (his partner in the Oso) at their joint, and we drove down to Beale Street. Furry lived in a basement unit in an apartment building on Beale. We climbed the stairs to the third floor and knocked on a door.

Will was dressed in a bathrobe, pleated suit pants, and suspenders over a wife beater. He wore old blown-out house slippers. His wife, Jennie Mae Clayton, stood mute at the stove with her mouth poked out. Will welcomed us in.

Furry had taught us that it was impolite to come empty-handed. Charlie Brown unsacked a fifth of Old Charter. The woman at the stove grunted. We drank and Will told stories. He went to his chifferobe, shuffled through socks, and pulled out a well-worn official-looking document. He shook it, and told us about suing Duke Ellington over "Newport News." He reached under his bed and pulled out what I swore was the same old Gibson I had seen at Gus Cannon's. He played big band block chords and sang in a whisper.

Furry appeared from out of nowhere. He bristled with anger, obviously pissed that "his" white boys were paying attention to Will. Bailey Wilkerson had a guitar with him. It was a nylon-string classical instrument totally unsuited to Furry's bottleneck style. I can still hear his aluminum conduit slide clacking as it bogged down on the neck of that Goya student model guitar. If anything truly deserved the term gutbucket, it was the awkward, chopped-off, no sustain of Furry trying to blow Will away. It was old-school head cutting. Furry played his repertoire and headed for uncharted territory. Will seemed oblivious to his competition. It wasn't pretty. Suddenly Will cried out, jumped up, and shuffled out the door down the hall. He didn't make it. When he came back he had pissed in his pants.

"Look at dat!" his woman hollered. "Yeah, now, look at that. You done done it." She was all over him. "Fuckin' around with white trash! Go on out of here! Get on out. Let me clean this ol' fool up."

Jennie Mae was once known as the most beautiful woman on Beale Street; duels to the death were fought over her. She had concealed her old friend Memphis Minnie in the county poor house, protecting her from the blues Nazis. She was a remarkable woman from another era, living out her days where she had been a queen.

Charlie Brown thought it was hysterical. I drove home in silence. Our house was empty and cold. I built a fire in the fireplace and watched the flame. I woke up in the morning in the den with my clothes still on and TV screen buzzing with snow. I did not go to Nashville. I never told Justis why. I called Mary Lindsay, who came over right away. We spent the weekend together. She never asked me what was wrong.

I couldn't put it together. Obviously there was a lesson here. These two old men, who in youth had lived and played peculiar music that spoke to me, made me think of old Sam Hess, though they could not be more different: Mountain country and city slicker, white and black, sons of Dionysus, who sang the music in their souls. I saw the common thread; the women, Emmer and Jennie Mae Clayton, living out their time with an almost forgotten musical treasure. We too were the common thread, crazy white boys, searchers, who invaded their world looking for hidden secrets. The two worlds only came together in what we sought.

Chapter 32

RAY BROWN
The Round Mound of Sound
(1964–69)

The best gig Ray Brown booked for the New Beale Street Sheiks was a hairdressers' convention at the Municipal Center auditorium, by the river in downtown Little Rock. I had not seen it on my many trips to Little Rock. They treated us like stars. A mixed variety show bill with a female comedian/ventriloquist opened, followed by the Bill Black Combo. The combo also backed Charlie Rich, who was brilliant, as usual. Tommy Cogbill shook his head when he saw me. We were the closing act, the headliners. I couldn't figure it. When we hit the first song, the audience went nuts. It was Crosthwait's hair. He let it hang down over his right hand as his fingers danced on his Zinc King washboard. He fanned it with the back of his hand and let it fly up in the spotlight. It was hypnotic. The hairdressers loved us. They got all the drug jokes and laughed in the right places. They wouldn't let us off stage. Charlie Rich was pissed. Ray Brown was a genius.

When Ray discovered I played keyboards, he booked me on legit gigs. He would book any six human beings who could hold instruments as the Mar-Keys. Usually there was one original Mar-Key, but not always. I played most of those gigs with Packy; sometimes with Wayne Jackson and Don Nix, but usually with Doug Kelly and the B Team. I wore my Italian suit, a skinny tie, and Spanish boots: my Mar-Key uniform. Those gigs were always great. Packy wouldn't play in the first set. He worked on his wine bottle. Second set, he played off the back of the stage, as if he was warming up. By the third set, after his pills kicked in and he was on his second bottle of wine, what he called "third set high" struck him. He soloed like King Curtis, cheeks inflated and eyes closed, with a Robert Mitchum forelock plastered to his sweat-drenched forehead. Fourth set he was over. He got a second wind after the gig, and always found a place for us to sit in. Some of the best barroom blues of my life was played in jam sessions in nightclubs with people I didn't know and never saw again.

One night backstage at the Theatrical Arts Club in North Memphis, "Bongo" Johnny Keyes poured grape Kool-Aid into Thunderbird wine bottles. Like a puzzled white man, I asked what he was doing.

"We're making port," Packy replied, as if it were obvious.

Here's how a typical Mar-Keys gig went. Packy and Kelly had turned me onto a new place to cop speed.

> The Oriole Drugstore glowed with a dirty yellow light,
> Almost warm.
> Its dust and grease-covered windows
> Faded smooth
> Into the nearly night.
> Downtown blacks on the corner
> Start the Saturday night boogie jive,
> But still too laid back
> For the untrained eye.
> The roaches crawled around the corner
> In their black and white.
> Be-bop bond daddies motorvate
> In deluxe limos with tinted windows.
> High school, heel-draggers and anchor-clankers
> From the navel base weasel
> By and fat, hot, hip
> Swinging hookers breeze up
> To and by,
> Cool as you please.
> I gave up the gold.

The old woman reached out of the dark counter corner and deposited a pill Bottle into my waiting hand.

> Jammed deep down the cuff of my coat-snappers
> Gonna carry me home.
> The dope up my sleeve.
> Down the street
> And away from the light,
> Drifting faceless stranger—

The invisible man.
Thus snatched from the cruel jaws of an awful death,
I snort my Benadrex inhaler
And step out into the night.
Black widow!
You red and black,
sweet-snappin' bitch.
Let me lick it.
Let me swallow you down
One little ball at a time.
No sleep for you, mother-fucker.
Stay up for the show.
Don't go down that long,
Dark hall.
The gang's all here.
The little pill that will never
let you down
And never is supposed to be a long,
Long time.
Standing to warm up now,
Charging up the big battery,
Winding up the old music box
Until that spring is as tight
As Dick's hatband—
SNAP!
Up through the top
And over the crest of the wave
Like the silver surf rider of the lonesome galaxy
Gone as the wild goose in winter
And sailing like the tail of a kite,
Guitar solo in Telstar.
Hallelujah, brother!
Saved at last.

I picked up Kelly and met Packy at Stax. Stax had long since moved
from the barn in Brunswick into an old movie theatre building on
McLemore at College, in an old neighborhood going black. Packy and
"Bongo" Johnny Keyes ran the Satellite Record Store in front of the studio
for Packy's mother, Estelle, or "Lady A," as they called her in the hood.

We met at the studio and jammed into two cars for the trip to Helena, Cape Girardeau, Lexington, Kentucky, or whatever hellhole Ray Brown booked. There was always some hassle or screwup. One night, the rhythm section and Don Nix made the gig in Lexington, but the horns missed the highway turnoff and ended up in Nashville. People at the high school prom were really pissed. I was wearing a silver lamé waist-length Beale Street cape from Lansky Brothers and looked like Captain Marvel. Nix put a pair of welfare-store blind-man glasses on me, led me onstage, and introduced me as "'Blind Luther,' the genius of the Hammond organ." We barely got away with it. I had to keep it up all night. Nix thought it was funny.

Driving home after the gig and mandatory "sit in," Packy delivered his usual speed rap: how Jim Stewart had used Packy's father's house as collateral to build the studio and how Jim Stewart was screwing Packy out of the share that by all rights was his and how someday . . . I knew the story by heart. It was true insofar as Packy was being frozen out in the studio.

It was the law of the jungle. Steve Cropper cooperated and worked closely with Jim Stewart. Packy was confrontational and not prone to compromise. Tom Dowd and cats from Atlantic were hanging around and working with session regulars. Sadly, Packy was shunned for his habits and personality. Packy had first brought black music to Stax. Jim Stewart was a country-fiddling bank teller. Black music was not what he would have recorded. He was still looking for the next Charles "Prove Your Love" Heinz. Packy brought the band from the Plantation Inn into the studio. Packy was the door to what would become Soulsville. Jim Stewart was smart enough to follow success through the door that opened in front of him.

Packy was already a far more talented arranger/producer than saxophonist. He learned to play too fast and took to the bandstand prematurely. He never developed a solid tone and played a little flat, like a French saloon singer, but in the studio he could pull an instrumental track out of the air and make a record out of nothing.

As Stax succeeded, it slipped further away from Packy. One night on a Mar-Keys gig in Missouri, a drunk frat boy stumbled to the steps and started arguing with Packy. "I been to Memphis and I seen the Mar-Keys and you ain't them," the drunk stammered. Packy was beet-red. "I don't care where you been or what you seen, I AM the Mar-Keys," he replied.

The Mar-Keys gigs with Packy were fun and edgy. Blues roots music was easy for me to play, but the new folk music and the protest growing around the civil rights movement spoke more directly to my psyche. Dylan's second album came out, followed by *The Times They Are A-Changin'*. Nothing had spoken to me so directly since Cowboy Tex Ritter's *Children's Songs and Stories*. *The Times They Are A-Changin'* was so intimate, like you were locked up with the singer in a railroad car or a jail cell, a confined space where Bob sang just for you. I bought the record at Poplar Tunes, where Dewey Phillips had broadcast and my old man played poker with Joe Cuoghi. I played the record once and called Mary Lindsay, wanting to share. I took it to her house (where I still wasn't exactly welcome) and played it without speaking.

Chapter 33

MARRIED, RETURN TO WACO, AND GOOD KID—THE ALL-TIME CHAMP (1964)

One spring afternoon, Newport and I were joy riding in East Memphis and smoking a joint. He was driving. I stared out the window at the upper-middle-class suburb we had been raised in. I saw a five- or six-year-old boy following a black yardman in front of a modern colonial-style house. The yardman walked and hummed; the little white boy ran to keep up. Newport said, "That's the story of your goddamned life, right there."

Mary Lindsay and I planned to marry at summer's end. She would transfer to Memphis State; that's as much as we had planned. Her mother was still after my ass. It was getting tight. One afternoon my mother started talking about the marriage. I assumed she was trying to convince me to put it off. I blew up.

"Calm down, Jimmy," she said. "This might not be the right time but it's the right girl. If you go on and get married this spring, your father and I will pay for summer school at Baylor." She still had faith in Baylor. I saw a way to get out of town for the first few critical months of our marriage. Mary Lindsay went for it. We had a formal wedding with groomsmen in morning suits. I had my patent-leather opera slippers' soles polished so I could kneel for the ceremony. Mary Lindsay wore an ancestral lace gown and looked like a storybook princess bride. We married in Mullins Methodist Church's chapel, where the shrine to Bill Madison, my friend killed by lightning, hung on the wall behind the altar. Charlie Freeman was there with Carol Jensen, the girl from art class, smiling like a fox. They married six months later.

We married the day after school finished, and two days later started summer school at Baylor. We ate our honeymoon dinner at the K.C. Steak House in Carlisle, and were supposed to stay overnight in Little Rock but didn't make it. We checked into the motel at Lonoke, Arkansas, and let

159

nature take her course. We watched *The Defiant Ones* on television and had cherry pie from the motel diner. Our honeymoon could not have been better.

Summer school: Jim Berry, my old dorm friend, fixed us up with a one-room apartment—with a kitchenette and a Murphy bed—out by the lake. We spent the summer in bed and ate lots of breakfasts. I associate that summer with seasoned pepper and Tabasco sauce on fried eggs, and Awake from a frozen orange juice mix.

I took the legendary Guy B. Harrison's famous Texas History class. He tried to talk me into coming back to Waco and doing my Master's on the local offshoot of the Ku Klux Klan chapter. No dice. Bad as campus had been, it was worse. Baylor Theatre was gone, torn to the foundations with salt sprinkled on the bare earth. A Sunday school teacher had brought a Sunbeam class to see Pulitzer Prize winner Eugene O'Neill's *Long Day's Journey into Night*, and made a written complaint of the profanity recited by the devilish Paul Baker's godless drama students. Baker walked out of the theatre spitting on the floor. He refused to be censored or controlled by the Baptist Pharisees, and took most of the theatre to Trinity University in San Antonio, Texas.

My bride and I took road trips. We went to Houston with Jim Berry, and he took us to the world-famous Cork Club. The owner, Gene Mc-Carthy (the James Dean character, Jett Rink, from *Giant*), was there in the flesh. Berry's old man was a big oil rig equipment supplier, well up in the oilman hierarchy. It was a cool weekend.

Courtesy of Tex Campbell, we visited blues guitarist Mance Lipscomb at his ranch in Navasota, Texas. We played music; first me, then him, in the proven white-boy tradition I was used to. We ate a late midday meal. When the women and children ate, he led me away to see his lean, wild-eyed racing dogs. Mance and I stood at his greyhound pen. A storm blew over the escarpment, headed east across the flatlands, and straight for us. We talked about Lightning' Hopkins. "It's the difference between me and Lightning. He don't act right wif folks, ya know. Folks come 'round and dey wants to know. It's an obligation we has to lead them in the light of days they never known."

His teenage granddaughter sat on the front porch next to a gut-bucket full of fresh, unslung chitlins. She looked nine months pregnant and stunningly beautiful, like the ancient black queen of the Nile. Mance drove us around and showed us off. He was a local celebrity with a new record on Warner/Reprise. "Frank Sinatra's label," Mance pointed out. He told the locals we were from California and had come to kidnap him. We got the evil eye.

At summer's end we got the hell out of Waco. I may be crazy but I'm not stupid. We both enrolled at Memphis State. The Dean of Men's wife loved my folk act and got us in Vets Village, twenty long clapboard World War II bunkhouses with three units in each barracks, located on the campus's north side. Terry Johnson, the Mar-Keys' drummer, and his family lived at the other end. Rent was $37.50 a month. We moved in with Lassie, the pet monkey Lucia Burch gave us.

Lucia, Mary Lindsay's childhood friend, was the youngest daughter of social activist attorney Lucius Burch, who had been brought in to break Boss Crump's political machine. I had followed his liberal exploits in local politics with interest for years. He had taken his daughter, Mary Lindsay, and Fred Smith (the man who would invent Fed Ex) to Ireland for a summer. I got to know Lucius through Mary Lindsay. He was one of the smartest men I have ever known. We ate many excellent quail dinners in his antebellum mansion in Collierville, Tennessee, where suits of Spanish armor stood in the entrance hall. He flew his private plane to Memphis daily. Oft' we sat in the front yard, smoking pot with Charlie Brown, while Lucius recited "The Stag at Eve."

Lucia was a truly unique individual. She and my wife were total opposites and dear friends. She was always up for a good time. She dated Newport, and later became Bill Eggleston's longtime mistress and companion.

We prospered at Vets Village. While we were in Waco, Charlie Brown had opened yet another coffeehouse. The Bitter Lemon, located just east of the Poplar Viaduct over Binghampton, was across the street from Melody Music, where I had seen Dishrag that second and final time. Charlie had partnered with artist/sculptor John McIntire from Memphis Art Academy. John owned a big rooming house in Midtown that everybody called Beatnik Manor.

The Bitter Lemon was Charlie's best effort. During the summer the finger-picking duo of John Fahey and Bill Barth showed up looking for old blues musicians. These two carpetbagging Yankees hornswoggled the local audience. The first time I saw them, I told hometown boy Gimmer Nicholson, "You play better than that." He looked at me like I was crazy. I took it as a challenge. I struck a deal with Charlie Brown and started playing regularly at the Lemon. I sold him my old light board from the Market Theatre. The audience was mostly kids. There was no liquor but plenty of pot in the parking lot. On weekends, Charlie booked Furry Lewis or Bukka White. Fahey drifted off but Bill Barth dug in his heels and stayed.

One of Lucia Burch's older sisters had married a New York television producer, who was coming to Memphis as the line producer for *Anatomy of Pop*, an ABC documentary about popular music. I would act as liaison to local industry members. I saw an opportunity to showcase old blues players at the Bitter Lemon but the television people wanted Elvis.

"Nobody gets to Elvis," I told the Yankee security over the telephone. "I'll take you out there but you won't get in."

The woman grumbled and complained in a nasal whine about the power of the press.

"Why don't you talk to Sam Phillips, the owner of Sun Records, the man who discovered Elvis?"

She lightened up. They could "fill in" with local color and maybe "some of the old blues guys." I tried to tell them about Stax and Hi Records, but they didn't get it. They had shot in New York and L.A., Detroit and Nashville. They were passing through Memphis, hoping to get an audience with The King. That was not about to happen. Their crew consisted of Lucia's sister's husband, a grizzly old cameraman, and a soundman, who was black and very uptight from the jump. They insisted on going to Graceland first, certain their ABC status would get them to Elvis. When we pulled up to Graceland, the gates were closed, signifying Elvis was home. Old Uncle Vester, Elvis's mother's brother, stepped out of his guardhouse in a blue and white guard uniform with a big EP on the front pocket and TCB (taking care of business) embroidered across the back shoulders. He shook his head. "What you folks want?" he crackled. His head kept shaking. "You got to understand," Old Uncle Vester explained earnestly. "Even I seldom enter his presence."

The New York crew returned to their motel in defeat. I told them an interview with Sam Phillips was set the next evening. In excitement, I fell off my Spanish boots high heels and badly sprained my ankle that night, which put me on crutches for the remainder of the shoot. It slowed me but wasn't about to stop me.

Charlie Brown rounded up the usual suspects: Furry Lewis, Gus Cannon, "Little Bit" Laura Dukes (a near dwarf novelty singer from the old Beale Street days), with Memphis Willie B, filling out a makeshift jug band. Charlie found Good Kid, the washboard player I had seen in Whiskey Chute as a boy. But Charlie Brown assured me the percussionist was way too fucked up to perform. "He was so drunk he didn't know his name," Charlie told me. Too bad.

Charlie was in charge of the phony jug band. I had my hands full explaining to these so-called journalist/experts who Sam Phillips, the man that invented rock 'n' roll, was. I had been around Sam a few times, but didn't know him well. I had no idea what to expect. They set up sound and camera upstairs in Sam's private office, which had a Wurlitzer jukebox, gold 78 records on the wall, and hadn't changed since 1958, when he moved from the original Sun Studio around the corner at 706 Union and Marshall. Sam was turned out, black business suit, white shirt, banker's tie, and a white silk square in his top coat pocket. He was "on" completely.

It was so heavy. I sat in the hall and listened through the open door. Sam laid it down, comparing Elvis to Sinatra; to "Big Chief," the bass singer from the Statesmen gospel group; and to the lead in the Mills Brothers, saying he originally had been attracted to Elvis as a ballad singer. He blew their minds. He talked about primitive rockabilly recordings as if they were high art, nuclear physics, or both. I felt triumphant at having helped him bring information about this music to the world. Hopefully these uninformed experts would recognize the truth when they shot the jug band.

I spent the next day in pain and on Percocets, hobbling like Tiny Tim or Long John Silver, trying to damage control the Bitter Lemon Jug Band shoot. Willie B's old lady refused to let him go off with crazy white boys and play the devil music, causing a last-minute freak-out. We were one brick shy of a load.

Charlie Brown forcefully recruited a local phony Rasta conga player, Chico Mazaratti, to play zinc tub bass. Charlie held a butcher knife to his throat in the Lemon's kitchen until he removed his shark tooth earring. We almost had a rhythm section. The decision was made to get Good Kid, no matter what shape he was in. At least he was a warm body. I couldn't wait.

The second time I saw Good Kid, he was rubber-legging through the Bitter Lemon's parking lot singing, "You are my sunshine. . . . I wrote that song, ya know . . . my ooooooooonnnly sunshine."

"Little Bit" Laura Dukes was kicking him in the ass. "Get in that door, motherfucker. Get yo' black ass in that door."

"I'm going, I'm going," he mumbled and stumbled, standing two inches from the open door. "Where de do'?" He looked around, helplessly lost. She kicked him and shoved him inside.

He was barely taller than Little Bit, who was four foot something. His clothes may have once been different colors; now they were all dirty gray. His pants' crotch hung to his knees. He staggered past the table where the black sound technician from the ABC documentary crew sat with his earphone clamped to his head. Furry Lewis and Gus Cannon were sitting at the same table, assuming that was where they were supposed to sit. Good Kid went straight to the stage and sat center stage, behind the microphone. We handed him Crosthwait's washboard and drumsticks. When he raised the stick to test the instrument, the TV crew hit the shooting lights. Good Kid recoiled, arms flung out like a Ray Bolger doing the scarecrow dance in *The Wizard of Oz*. "Let's turn de light down reeeeeeaaaaaalll looooowwww," he pleaded.

They took Good Kid off the stage. "If I take that back to ABC news, I'll lose my job," Lucia's brother-in-law said, giving me the first taste of the "fear" that cost me dearly in years to come.

As Furry, Gus, Little Bit, and Chico Mazaratti started "Next Week Sometime," Good Kid took a seat at the table with the black sound engineer, who was becoming more and more uncomfortable. The first time I heard the alien sound, I knew exactly what it was and pretended not to hear it. After a few seconds, the uptight Yankee director turned to me and said, "What's that funny noise? Do you hear that?" Good Kid was playing his nose. Old-timers call it "nose trumpet." I told him he had to stop. Good Kid turned to the black sound guy and mournfully said, "They done got me down here and now the white man won't even let me play my nose."

Later that night at the wrap party back at the motel, the soundman got drunk. He admitted he was from Atlanta, not New York, and tore open his Ivy League shirt to reveal an old razor scar. He said, "You gotta love the South. People let you know where you stand."

The documentary aired with no jug band, and sadly, no Sam Phillips. Tony Bennett was the show's entire second half. Sam was furious. Fortunately he didn't blame me.

That night at the Bitter Lemon was special and prophetic. All the right people, folks who deserved to see the clash of culture and commerce, were in the audience. Bill Barth laughed so hard I thought he would pass out. Lee Baker soaked it up. We talked about it often in years to come.

Chapter 34

GRANNY'S SEWING ROOM
(1965)

Ray Brown was booking a Mar-Keys tour of Europe. Charlie Freeman tried to talk me into it. I could go or stay married, but didn't see how I could do both. The choice was easy. Word spread I wouldn't go on the road. I was surprised when Larry Raspberry called me. Raspberry and his band, the Gentrys, had won the nationally televised *Ted Mack Amateur Hour* and made a record for Chips Moman at his new American Studio. The first thing he cut was the Gentrys' "Keep on Dancing," an old song by the Avantis, one of well-known Memphis lawyer and producer Seymour Rosenberg's black groups. It became a regional hit, Chips leased it to MGM for national distribution, and it was hot on the charts when Raspberry called. "Hey, Dickinson," he said. "I got a problem. Maybe you can help me."

It was nine o'clock at night. Wife and I were settled in our Vets Village cubbyhole, feeding nightly crickets to Lassie, our marmoset, who ate nothing but live insects. "What can I do for you, Larry?" I asked.

"Well, my record is #15 with a bullet and MGM wants an album, and half my band just quit to go to high school. Chips won't start cutting the album until I've got a band to go on the road. Will you go on the road with the Gentrys?"

"Hell, no, Larry," I said.

"Well . . . will you come down to the studio and tell Chips you will?"

That sounded like fun. Mary Lindsay and I drove downtown to American, launching one of our most meaningful adventures.

Lincoln Wayne Moman was called "Chips" due to his talent for gambling. His career began in Georgia with Bill Lowery. His first hit was as a songwriter. He wrote "This Time," a medium-sized national hit for Elvis clone Troy Shondell. Chips did time for tax evasion and moved to Memphis. He went to the West Coast with the Brenda Lee tour and replaced James Burton in Ricky Nelson's backup band, joining Johnny and Dorsey Burnette, who were also opening for Nelson. Old Memphis rockabillies stick together. Chips and Charlie Freeman lived together in Nashville while Chips did session work and Charlie toured with Eddie Cash's show band. Charlie played a Gibson Birdland and Chips liked to borrow it. When Chips came back to Memphis, he briefly hooked up with Jim Stewart in Satellite/Stax's early days. When that fell apart, he partnered with Arkansas soybean farmer Don Crews at American Studio, located at Chelsea and Thomas, in the heart of a North Memphis ghetto.

Chips was wiry and moved like a cat. He had a winning, good-natured grin, and flashing blue eyes. He could hypnotize a roomful of musicians in two minutes flat, and manipulate tumbling dice like no other white man.

My wife and I walked into the studio that night. Our lives were about to change. Larry Raspberry said, "Chips, you know Jim Dickinson." Chips looked at me and nodded. "He's going on the road with the Gentrys."

"Okay," he said and walked away. I talked to the other musicians, refocused, and realized Chips had locked the doors, ready to record at 10:45 p.m. He didn't unlock the doors until noon the next day. We recorded the Gentrys' whole first album and part of the second one. Chip's took me aside and said, "You're too good to go on the road with the Gentrys."

I agreed. We went next door to the Townhouse for breakfast, and made a deal. I had my first real job in the music business.

Chips, with a world-famous house band rhythm section, became the most successful record producer in Memphis music history. "Keep on Dancing" was the first of many hits. The American rhythm section began with the great Tommy Cogbill, Chips's bass-playing partner, and Clarence Nelson, a legendary black guitarist who swept and chased rats out of the echo chamber, and me. "Car-te-tur," a black would-be songwriter who slept on the couch in the front as a bodyguard, was there, too.

Mary Lindsay loved it and hung out whenever she could. Chips liked her, and sent her to get egg sandwiches in the middle of the night in the heart of the ghetto. I was proud she knew no fear. Chips's receptionist, Sandy Posey, was a high school senior with sad gray eyes. When no one recorded, Sandy went to the piano and sang songs she had written. She was not very subtle, but it ended up working.

We did sessions with the Gentrys, the Guilloteens, Ivory Joe Hunter, Pete and Repeat (a Sam and Dave clone), and produced song demos for various songwriters, including Joe South. Chips didn't want me to play full piano. Tommy Cogbill was a reluctant bass player and refused to buy an instrument. Chips's cheap Hagstrom bass sounded like crap. He had me double the bass part with my left hand on the piano. I was used to playing the bass part that way since my old band never had a bass player. Tommy had the only earphones, so he sat beside me at my left hand. He would add a convoluted bass part to every song to fuck with me; it became a signature. Those sessions tied my left hand in a knot. If the cut went well, and Chips's pill kicked in, he'd say in the talkback, "Jim, if you want to, you can chord on the bridge."

It made my wife mad he didn't let me play, but I learned what to leave out, the real beginning of my education. Play it over until it is right. I still hear Chips's voice on the talkback speakers: "Take it again."

Chips hated the telephone. I saw him rip the control room phone out of the wall and throw it out the door. He taught me an important rule: Never answer the phone in the studio. The client's record company might be telling you to stop. My calls are still screened when I'm recording.

One night Mary Lindsay and I were at the studio waiting for Chips to cut me a session check. We sat on the big black leather couch at the back of the control room. Football giant Roosevelt Greer sat beside us, waiting for Chips to do a horn overdub on his project. The backdoor flew open and in rushed Laurie, Chips's wife, wearing sunglasses, her hair up in curlers, spewing profanity, and leading a huge black German shepherd. Apparently she called to talk to Chips; whoever answered the phone put it down and left her hanging. She screamed, "Which one of you fucking idiots answered that phone?" Nobody replied. She shook her finger at Chips. The huge black dog sat on the couch beside me. I was flanked by the growling beast and Rosie Greer, who was deeply pissed. Laurie finished her hissy fit and left as quickly as she had arrived. Chips said, "Can't that woman understand that all I want to do is make rock 'n' roll records?"

I have always been glad my wife heard that statement and truly got it. We worked a session the night Cogbill's wife gave birth. Prioritizing is crucial in the recording process. It takes a special kind of woman to understand.

After the first Gentrys session, I got another fortuitous phone call. Bob Fisher, a high school friend, asked, "Can you write a song like the Kinks?"

"Sure," I said. Fisher worked as a salesman at Berl Olswanger's music store. I had dealt with him for years.

"Can you write one in the next forty-five minutes?"

I dug out my old Webcor reel-to-reel and went to work. When Fisher came to the apartment an hour later, I had a song demoed and ready.

"What's this for, Fisher?" I asked.

"I found this band. They are all fifteen and they play great. I'm going to take them into John Fry's studio and I need material."

Fry had recording equipment in his family's home. I had been there once. He and a few friends started a record label, Ardent, and put out a couple of local recordings. Fisher could have the song if I could go with him to Fry's studio. Fry had better equipment in his home than Chips had at American. Chips's setup was two mono machines with one pass overdub with a homemade console put together from Ampex mixers and guitar capacitor tone control EQs, all run through a Gates Level Devil limiter amplifier. Fry's studio was stereo with an Altec three-channel 250 SU board with Altec compression and graphic equalizers. The control room was in the family house, had an office/reception area with desks and phones, and a full wet bar. The tracking space was behind the house. We called it Granny's Sewing Room, alluding to its former function.

Fry remembered me and was cautious. I met the band, Bobby and the Originals, and got along with them right away. They were eager for help or advice. I played my song; they liked it. Before they knew what was happening, we recorded "Back for More." They were green as grass. Singer Bobby Lawson had a disarming Huckleberry Finn charm and good relaxed stage presence. He sang chronically flat. If a melody note went to a third Lawson was so flat that he took the chord to a full minor.

Fry's house was a great place to hang, less than a mile from Vets Village. I could hop the fence, walk down a drainage ditch, and come out in John's backyard. Fry had two partners in Ardent Records, Mary Lindsay's old friend Fred Smith, now attending Yale University, and John King, whose real interest was radio. King taught me a lot about the music business. He turned me on to Motown, told me about Huey Meaux in Texas and Cosimo Matassa and Johnny Vincent at Ace Records in New Orleans. I had never thought of regionalism and our role in Memphis in the tapestry of American music. King told me about Phil Spector.

This was it! Record production. The man behind the curtain. The phantom creative power of the recording session. Like Chips Moman, but far away in Los Angeles or Detroit, shrouded in mystery and arcane knowledge.

Fry considered himself retired from the record business. I was determined to drag him back. More semi-professional musicians started to

hang out at Fry's. Some were mutual acquaintances and shadier friends
of mine: Charlie Hull, Horace's little brother, Mike Alexander, a truly
talented bass player, and his partner guitarist, Lee Baker.

I wrote Bobby and the Originals another song, "If You Want Me, You
Can Find Me," which we cut with Charlie Hull on guitar, Mike Alexander
on bass, and Jimmy Crosthwait beating on a box with a pair of maracas,
a trick I learned from Justis. Granny's Sewing Room was an enclosed
garage behind the house. You could not see what was going on from the
control room. Once, as Crosthwait was overdubbing, Fry said, "Jim, is he
smoking marijuana out there?"

"Well yes, John, I believe he is," I said.

"I was just curious," Fry commented.

Things opened up in Memphis when Sam the Sham cut "Wooly Bully"
at Sam Phillips's studio. After the national hit with "Keep On Dancing,"
companies took Memphis seriously. The Bill Black Combo and Ace Cannon turned out instrumental hits. Stax had a red-hot deal with Atlantic
Records, and scored hit after hit on the R&B chart. Sam the Sham was
different, so off the wall local promoters started to take over-the-top acts
a little more seriously. Professional attitudes toward those of us far left
of center dramatically changed. I played on a couple of Don Nix sessions
during this period. Engineer Stan Kesler, who produced "Wooly Bully,"
took an interest in me.

I wrote a few songs I thought Sam the Sham could use and demoed
them at Fry's. We did the whole "Wooly Bully" riff thing: do-do, da-da
over and over on drums, portable organ replete with slap back, the same
Hully Gully hypnotic groove that made the Pharaohs famous. Kesler liked
the songs "Black Cat Bone" and "Mojo Man," both steeped in voodoo
references and magic hoo-doo, Sam the Sham's calling card. When we
played the songs for Sam, he freaked out and accused me of trying to rip
him off, beginning what would become a lifelong weirdness between us.

Chapter 35

FREE TEDDY PAIGE/MEMPHIS COUNTRY BLUES FESTIVAL (1966-67)

Teddy Paige, a.k.a. Edward LaPaglia, Edward the Troubadour, Medieval Knievel, now languishes in a mental hospital for the criminally insane in jolly old England, where he is incarcerated for attacking his next-door neighbor with a broadsword. My son Cody's young English friends befriended Teddy (whom they call Edward) and insist he is English.

I met Teddy in East Memphis in the early sixties through my neighbor, Mike Ladd. They were both really good aspiring blues guitarists. Teddy played old school while Mike provided a glimpse of the future with more of a rock style. Teddy was funny. He made rat faces at inappropriate times and loved to cause trouble. He was a thief. His Sicilian mother taught him to lie and to trust no one; she made him answer the telephone and lie when anyone came to their door. He developed a strange way of fitting into reality.

We played, in various aggregations, out at the naval base or the Moose Lodge. Teddy told crowds, "Here's another song you're not going to like." He claimed the Beatles ruined music and refused to play anything recorded after 1960. He liked my old boogie-woogie technique. I wasn't surprised when he called me for the session at Sun Studio.

It was supposed to be a demo session for the Jesters, a band Teddy had with Jerry Phillips, Sam's younger son. I had seen Jerry, who was four or five years my junior, around White Station High School. I noticed his long blond ducktails and the motorcycle jacket he wore in fourth grade. He was short, muscular, and strutted down the hall like he owned the joint. His older brother Knox was a little more conservative. Knox engineered the session. The Jesters' singer was Tommy Minga, a wild man with a pretty good stage act. They had not recorded anything Sam would put out on Sun Records. I had been to the studio once before, when we cut the New Beale Street Sheiks. Sam moved from the original 706 Union studio to Madison Avenue in the late fifties. Officially Sam Phillips Studio, everybody called it Sun.

The session took a long time to start because Minga, the vocalist, had not shown up. We talked and joked for what seemed too long. Knox was nervous, and ready to start. It became apparent Teddy had not called Minga for the session. Teddy asked if I would sing: "It's just a demo, man. Just a couple of songs. Help me out."

I agreed. Teddy pulled out lyric sheets. I sat at the piano, worked them out, and had a good time. The band was good. Teddy was great. The songs were old-school rock 'n' roll. One song, "Cadillac Man," was pure Chuck Berry. Jerry Phillips played maracas, like Jerome Green over Teddy Paige's Bo Diddley rhythm on Bill Black's Gibson Fretless Wonder. I took a hot piano solo. We cut three more songs, but "Cadillac Man" was the best by far.

Time went by before Knox called. Sam liked the session and wanted to put something out. He would have to file a union contract to release the record. We were to show up for a "smoker" session. I figured we would sit around and smoke. I thought filing a recording session was a union thing. When I got to the studio, Sam was busy notating microphones on a clipboard. He was in a suit and tie, and all business. We were going to record! Sam was fantastic. His eyes were wild. When he got worked up, the black of the iris nearly filled his whole eyeball. I couldn't help thinking that's how he looked at Elvis. Hell, that's how he looked at Howlin' Wolf! We cut another one of Teddy's songs and a version of Little Walter's "My Babe," which ended up on the B side of "Cadillac Man."

Sam asked if I had any material. I pulled out a song I had pitched Sam the Sham. He liked "Black Cat Bone"; it reminded him of the old days with the Wolf. I couldn't believe it. Later I figured out he was talking about the lyrics, not the performance, but his compliment affected my work on the session.

Sam wanted to release "Cadillac Man" on Sun. I believed I was contractually obligated to Bill Justis. Sam told me, "Son, you've got to cast your lot," and urged me to sign an artist contract and kick back my session pay, as customary.

"Sam," I told him. "I'm afraid my lot is already cast. I'm under contract to Justis."

"Oh, hell, man . . . Bill won't care."

Sure enough, Bill didn't care. The first time I heard myself on the radio, Dewey Phillips was down and out, working on a low-power AM daytime station in Millington, Tennessee. He said, "Here's another payola record. This piano sounds like Freddie Slack on Ella Mae Morse's records." I nearly wrecked my car when my intro to "Cadillac Man" blared out of the car radio. I was driving north on Front Street in Memphis, one of those moments you never forget.

I took the session check, which I did not kick back, and endorsed it to Charlie Brown. He used it as rent deposit for the Overton Park Shell, to put on the first Memphis Country Blues Festival in conjunction with Bill Barth and Robert Palmer. Palmer, a clarinet-playing blues scholar, and Randall Lyon, a fellow misfit-wannabe-artist, had showed up in Memphis from Little Rock. Barth and Charlie put on the first Blues Festival with my $65 check from Sam Phillips and a softball-size lump of Afghan hash.

The Memphis Country Blues Festival was a great idea, featuring blues musicians who had been rediscovered several years before. Like Charlie Brown, Bill Barth was good at rooting out old blues musicians. He and John Fahey had found Skip James plowing with a mule. Mississippi Fred pumped gas at a Stuckey's in Como, Mississippi. Bukka White had served a term in Parchman Farm, imprisoned for murder. Sleepy John Estes was in Brownsville, Tennessee (to which he had taken "that right hand road"), living next to a liquor store.

The first night of the festival the show was rained out, but musicians set up in the Shell's wings and played. Furry and Mississippi Fred McDowell were there, but the most interesting was blind Nathan Beauregard, who was "reputedly" 103 years old (he was actually born in the 1890s.) He played a cheap Beale Street pawnshop guitar through a cigar box–shaped amplifier. He was frail and mummy-like, with a face like an ancient statue's. The second night came off without an act of God. The performances were half old master Delta bluesmen and half crazy white boys. I performed with Teddy Paige on an upright bass, Mike Ladd on guitar, the drummer from the Jesters, and Jim Vinson on harmonica. Lee Baker played with a slightly edgier combo; the last act was an anticlimactic prediction of the future, the Insect Trust, with Bill Barth on slide guitar, Robert Palmer on recorder, Nancy Jeffries on vocal, and Randall Lyon dancing in a maroon robe.

The first time I saw a hippie I knew we were in trouble. Suddenly, my lifestyle was everywhere; what we had been getting away with was too visible. Two doors off Beale Street, Bill Barth and his crew had a place, the Sandal Shop, where they sold pot over the counter. One of Barth's buddies, a would-be trumpet player, "Electricity Man" (Warren Gardner), was arrested at the Gridiron, an all-night restaurant, for selling pot to an off-duty cop. That blew the top off.

Bill Justis called me again, and surprisingly, wanted a followup record—not that we had much to follow. After the experience at Sun with "Cadillac Man," I was itching to rock again. Even Dylan was plugged in and electric now.

One night on break at the Bitter Lemon, I looked in the window of Melody Music Store (where I had seen Dishrag). A beautiful fire-engine-red portable organ sat on the showroom floor! Next morning at 10 a.m., when Jack Boyden opened the door, I was there with my checkbook. Armed with my Farfisa Combo Compact, I was ready for my comeback. I wrote a few more songs. Justis booked Roland Janes's Sonic Studio to cut demos. I called Terry Johnson and Duck Dunn from the Mar-Keys rhythm section, booked Ricky Ireland on guitar, and Sid Selvidge and Jim Crosthwait to sing backup.

Roland Janes was the last of the best, the original Sun rhythm section guitarist who soloed on Jerry Lee Lewis and Billy Lee Riley recordings. He had toured with Justis, along with the legendary Sid Manker, behind "Raunchy," the first million-seller out of Memphis. He had fallen out with Sam Phillips, and had opened his own studio, Sonic, where he cut many local records and started hundreds of area hopefuls' careers. A true master, he could pull a performance out of a zombie.

We cut four songs that afternoon. The Farfisa sounded fantastic, like it was about to explode. Ricky dogged out on me, and barely played his guitar for whatever reason. I sent the tape to Justis and waited for his reply. Bill finally called. He wanted me to come to Nashville for a "meeting." Mary Lindsay arranged for us to stay with Lucia Burch's grandmother at the family's antebellum mansion in River Oaks. I walked around the fabulous ancestral home all day.

Justis finally called. I drove downtown to Music Row, and found Tuneville Music Publishing Company. Bill liked the material, the new direction, and really liked the bass player. Duck was uniquely powerful for the day. He was left-handed but played right-handed, putting his stronger left hand on the neck. He held the strings down so hard that he could pop them with his right hand's first two fingers, creating a snap on each note's impact. He started to come on at Stax, replacing Lewis Steinberg, the bass player on the original "Green Onions." Justis liked Duck so much he agreed to cut my master session in Memphis rather than Nashville, as planned. Arrangements were made and a date was booked with Janes at Sonic.

My brother-in-law, Al Stamps, was in town visiting the family. He kindly helped me work over the rough demos, making arrangements. He suggested the old false ending trick for "Monkey Man," where the cut seemed to end; then the voice came back screaming, like "Keep On Dancing" on speed.

When the day arrived, we got to the studio and I could tell something was wrong. I had heard rumors about bad blood between Roland and Justis. I didn't know what to expect.

"Can't do the session," Roland said, looking down at his super shiny military black, lace-up dress shoes.

"What's the matter, man?" Bill asked.

"It's broke, Bill," was the reply.

"Oh, hell, Roland. It's always broke," Justis countered.

"Yeah, but today it's too broke."

That put the lid on it. Roland booked us time at Sam Phillips. Sam greeted us at the door, "loaded for bear." Sam was dressed all in black, wearing dark sunglasses, talking a mile a minute. He and Justis fell on each other's neck. Due to Ricky's non-performance on the demo, I booked Charlie Freeman for the date and added Don Nix to the singers, which was lucky since Crosthwait got lost and never found the studio.

As we set up our instruments, Bill hit the talkback switch in the control room. His voice boomed out of the A7 Voice of the Theater speakers like the voice of Jehovah: "You boys want to cut this wet or dry?"

"WET!" we replied in unison.

Bill and Sam set up a barstool in the middle of the tracking floor and placed a fifth of Old Crow on it. When we emptied the bottle, a new one rose in its place. Things got pretty loose. By the end of the night, Duck Dunn had stripped to nothing but pants and socks. I propped myself up so as not to fall over the keyboards.

At one point, on break from tracking, Selvidge and I were in my car, smoking a joint in front of the studio. Freeman tapped on the window glass. "I thought that's what you were doing," he said, grinning. It was the first of many joints Charlie Freeman and I shared.

We cut "Monkey Man" and "Shake 'Em On Down" that night. Freeman played a classic Memphis guitar solo on "Shake 'Em On Down" that's discussed in guitar circles to this day. On "Monkey Man" I played the same solo as on "Cadillac Man" note for note, but the Farfisa's scream took it in a new direction. Sam Phillips, Bill Justis, and Fred Foster all loved it; the Katmandu Quartet was born.

I played two gigs with the recording musicians at a teenage nightclub in Midtown. By the end, the front of the stage was packed. Younger aspiring rock musicians stood with their mouths hanging open. Terry Johnson and Duck Dunn laid down a groove like no other white musicians on Earth. Freeman soloed like a jazz player in flight. Don Nix booked a gig at Clearpool opening for Jimmy Reed, a notorious no-show. Jimmy surprised everybody and showed up, dressed in a black plastic bowtie, shiny black cowboy boots, and an almost indescribable Kelly green suit made of what looked like canvas, with dress tails and a silver lamé military stripe down the leg with metal snaps in lieu of buttons. He was friendly backstage, dead drunk and mumbling. He was well-known for having his wife whisper the lyrics into his ear as he performed. She wasn't with him.

Nix asked him, "Hey, Jimmy, where's your wife?"

"She's back at the hotel," he replied. "She can make more money there than I can here."

I lived in two worlds, maybe more: college to stay out of the draft, Chips Moman's American Studio (whenever he called me), and John Fry's home studio. I watched Chips whenever possible. He had an uncanny way of projecting his ideas nonverbally. You knew what he expected you to do; everybody wanted to please him. He wanted instruments to fit together in the mix in a very specific way. He worked on intuition and gut feeling. His great taste in new material and way of inspiring performance got everybody to the right place at the right time. The pop/click of the talkback, and Chips saying "Do it again" continued until we reached that point.

Under my influence, Bobby and the Originals became Lawson and Four More, which I tried to turn into a rhythm section. Donati was rhythmically solid on drums and eager to learn. Joe Gaston was no Tommy Cogbill on bass, but was hip and ready for whatever. Guitarist Joe Lee was an innovator with more musical knowledge than you need to play rock 'n' roll. The wild card was keyboardist Terry Manning, a preacher's kid from Texas. Fry took charge of Terry and brought him along as an engineer. I was in charge of the other three. We cut song demos and experimented with local artists.

Behind the success of "Keep On Dancing," Chips put together a Gentrys session in Nashville at Columbia, where I had recorded with Justis.

Chips and Tommy drove up together. I rode with band manager Betty Hayes. Betty worked in Ray Brown's office, and was smart enough to sign a kid band that nobody took seriously. Betty drove, Raspberry sat shotgun, and I sat behind him. He slept, head back over the seat, and muttered, "Money, money, money," snoozing in a dreamland of rock stardom.

We met Chips and Tommy at Tree Publishing, owned by an extra slick operator, Buddy Killen, who talked a kind of Roger Miller-hillbilly-hipster-jive peculiar to 1960s Nashville. Tree was in an old house on Music Row, and had a demo studio run by John Hurley and Ronnie Wilkins, two people who became important in my formative music business education. They had written "Love of the Common People," a hit for Waylon Jennings and others. Ronnie was a South Carolina boy who grew up on gospel piano. John Hurley had the second best white voice I ever heard and a mysterious past. He had been a local TV child star in the Northeast and lied about his age. Later I saw a childhood picture that made him about ten years older than he claimed.

We cut their song, "Spread It On Thick," for the follow-up to "Keep On Dancing." During the session at Columbia, the Gentrys brought a TV set into the studio to watch their performance on *Hullabaloo*, the national rock 'n' roll prime-timer, enraging Chips. I don't think he ever forgave the band's arrogance.

The media was full of hype for the TV series based on the *Batman* comic book. Previews on the tube featured Neal Hefti's Batman theme. I thought I could do better. One night at Vets Village I wrote "A Call for Batman" as fast as I could move my pencil. We put together a girl group, with Mary Lindsay, Lucia Burch, and a local folk singer, and cut the band tracks with Lawson and Four More, with me playing twelve-string and guitar whiz Lee Baker playing a really hot lead. The band tracks were, without doubt, the best thing Fry had cut. After I put the girls' voices on, Baker wouldn't speak to me for a week.

Everybody cut a *Batman* record. By the time it was over there were fifty-two. Locally, Poplar Tunes/Hi Records owner Joe Cuoghi had one cut by Jumpin' Gene Simmons of "Haunted House" fame and written with WHBQ DJ George Klein, giving it the big Memphis push.

To get radio airplay we customized an old Buick into a Batmobile, and gave it away on WHBQ radio. A mechanic at a body shop that made hearses did the work. It had huge vertical fins, a metal bat outline on the front of the hood, spotlight sirens, and toy machine guns on the fenders that shot sparks. I drove the girls to local gigs, like the Mid-South

Fair and the annual Boat Show, in it. People got out of my way when I drove a Batmobile. I could park anywhere. The girls were stars. They wore black vinyl bat masks and black-and-white velveteen flared bell-bottom jumpsuits. We were rolling, but the TV production company enjoined everyone who had not obtained an exclusive use from DC Comics.

John Fry's family sold their house to Memphis State University. It became the president's residence. Fry's father found a rental property, a newly built storefront sharing the building with Brother Mac's Bible Book Store, in North Memphis in the old National Cemetery neighborhood. Like the Market Theatre, people volunteered to help set it up. I called Ricky. He jumped into the wiring and design. Fry purchased a prototype custom console from Welton Jetton, head engineer from Pepper-Tanner Jingles, who had just built a comparable board for Jim Stewart at Stax.

After succeeding with the Gentrys, Chips surrounded himself with a higher class of musicians. My days were numbered. Reggie Young, Gene Chrisman, Bobby Woods, and Bobby Emmons, who had been working for Stan Kesler at Phillips, came together with Tommy Cogbill and became the Tucker Street Band, the greatest of all southern rhythm sections. I missed the boat. My wife and I became Fry's first employees when Ardent on National was born.

We were still installing the new room when it was time to do a follow-up record on Lawson and Four More. The decision was made to go to Fred Foster's Nashville studio, originally built and owned by Sam Phillips. Again, I wrote the material and co-produced the songs with John Fry. I had just bought the first Fuzztone in Memphis. Sid Lapworth, Justis's old bass player on "Raunchy," called me from O. K. Houck's music store: "Dickinson, I got a piece of gear you're gonna love. It makes your guitar sound like it's blowing up," Lapworth told me.

Armed with my new Fuzztone distortion generator, my '51 Telecaster, and my Rickenbacker four tens bass amp, I was ready to rock. After listening to my guitar for seconds, the hillbilly engineer hit the talkback and said, "Boy, I believe that amp's broke."

I reassured him it sounded how I wanted it. He listened a few more minutes, came to the tracking floor, and turned my amp to the wall. We cut "Half Way Down the Stairs," a Stones-Yardbirds rip-off that still sounds good if you can get past Lawson's out-of-tune vocal.

I boycotted the second Country Blues Festival. The hippy fringe element was out of control. Lee Baker fronted an all-black band, complete with horns, called Funky Down Home and the Electric Blue Watermelon.

He burst on stage out of an exploding outhouse, riding a Harley Davidson motorcycle, wearing a polka-dot dress and playing "Stormy Monday" on an old Gibson non-cutaway archtop big band guitar. It was too much for me. Years later a recording of the event turned up. It was brilliant (as was typical of our many disagreements, Lee was right and I was wrong).

When I graduated from Memphis State we had to leave Vets Village. We moved into a rental property my father owned on the city limits, across from Memorial Park Cemetery. I engineered at Ardent and cut demos for friends I had backed up years before at the White Station talent show, Donna Weiss and Mary Unobsky, now fledgling songwriters working for Seymour Rosenberg, a buddy of Justis and Charlie Rich. Fry engineered all the legitimate sessions, including Pepper-Tanner jingle dates and jazz flutist Edwin Hubbard, who brought in the first big session.

I got the leftovers and the crazy people. Area bands discovered us. I cut the Sugar Cube Blues Band from Grenada, Mississippi. A Memphis manager, Parks Matthews, booked time for the Rapscallions with blues singer Bobby Ray Watson, whom I knew from the Memphis Country Blues Festival. Parks was overweight and cartoonish. He hung around American and Stax, and was always on top of local gossip and rumor in the studio community. Parks showed up late for the session. The band was setting up and rehearsing "Funky Broadway." He had a teenage titty dancer on each arm, a Styrofoam cooler, and an orange plastic bag in his hand. "Jimmy, Jimmy," he said. "I've been watching Chips and I got everything I need to make a record. I got the girls." They smiled gap-toothed grins. "I got the liquor," he said, holding up the cooler. He held up the plastic bag. "And I got the pills!"

That was my clientele. John Hurley and Ronnie Wilkins came in with Donna and Mary. John was the first client to request me as engineer. He wanted to stretch boundaries, and correctly figured I would go further out than Fry, whom he mistrusted. Hurley was hiding out, with felony warrants in two states for bigamy and fraud. Huey Meaux, the great Cajun record man, was on trial for transporting a teenage prostitute from Texas to the Disc Jockey Convention in Nashville. Hurley had driven the car. His testimony might have helped Huey, but would have done him no good. The legal jeopardy put an additional edge on the proceedings.

Hurley's session lasted fifty-two hours nonstop. Ronnie played the piano with a toothbrush and toothpaste on the music rack, which provides an idea of how long he expected to stay. A song by Donna Weiss concerned a returning Vietnam veteran visiting the mother of a fallen comrade. "Mrs. MacAbee" was pre-Nashville Phil Spector, complete with sleigh bells and orchestra chimes. Hurley wouldn't let the boy singer start until he was completely hoarse. Hurley literally beat the kid with a mic cable and sneered, "Sing, you miserable little shit!"

I learned much of what I know about the record business from John Hurley.

Don Nix had been to L.A. several times and was friends with Leon Russell, who was musical director of the rock 'n' roll TV show *Shindig*, and a first-call session player with Phil Spector's Wrecking Crew, along with Hal Blaine, Carol Kaye, and teenage Steve Douglas. We put together a reel of stuff we produced at Ardent, and went to Hollywood to play "show and tell." Fry sprung for plane tickets. Nix and I went with him. I hated to fly but couldn't resist.

We didn't accomplish much. Nix managed to sell a single I cut on Sam the Sham's old backing band to Capitol Records. Fry went home. I stayed a few more days. Oklahoma drummer Jimmy Karstein had a bedroom—really a closet—at Russell's studio home on Skyhill Drive. He was on the road so I crashed there.

Leon was cutting demos for the next Gary Lewis and the Playboys record. He had four-track equipment, much like Fry's. He taught me to bounce tracks together in a process called ping-ponging in order to get more room to record. At Leon's I met drummer Jim Keltner, who was just entering rock from the jazz realm. I met Delaney Bramlett, who befriended me as a fellow son of Dixie. Delaney took me to Nudie's and Frederick's of Hollywood.

Saturday night we left the Hollywood Hills for a pilgrimage to the Sunset Strip. Six or seven of us piled into Leon's Cadillac, and headed for the Whiskey a Go Go to see John Lee Hooker and Jimmy Reed. They were different in Hollywood, dressed like rodeo cowboy pimps. Hooker wore a gold lamé jumpsuit. Their performances were remarkably different from those I had seen at home, more distant and removed, almost formal by comparison. When I told my wife, she was disgusted. She couldn't understand how I could go to Los Angeles and see nothing but old commercial blues musicians.

One night I went with Leon, Nix, and their crew to the Palomino Club to see a Native American guitarist, Jesse Ed Davis. When we walked in, the crowd turned and stared. From the back of the room Bobby Ray Watson called out, "Hey, Dickinson!" I don't think Leon ever got over it.

Chapter 36

TOM DOWD AND KNOWBODY ELSE
(1967–68)

Packy Axton was barred from Stax after trying to strangle Jim Stewart. He started working at Ardent with his black partner, "Bongo" Johnny Keyes. John Fry cut the tracking sessions and turned them over to me for overdubs. Eventually I produced and engineered whole sessions. Packy put together a great young rhythm section, with Willie Mitchell's son, Hubby, on keyboards and Teenie Hodges from Hi Rhythm on guitar. The bass player was a kid, James Alexander, nicknamed "Knuck," as in knucklehead. The drummer, Carl Lee Cunningham, was the old shoeshine boy from Stax. (James and Carl Lee later formed the Bar-Kays.)

Packy cut instrumental tracks and "sold them by the inch," as he used to say. "Hip Pocket," his first local hit, followed "Hung Over." Folks at Stax heard Packy's work at Ardent and began working there, too.

One of my best cuts at Ardent was by two teenage boys from New York City, Steve Braverman and Albhy Galuten. Steve had a terrific white soul voice. Albhy, Irving Berlin's nephew, was an excellent keyboardist with a thirteen-note reach. We formed a production company and cut a session. I did strings, horns, and rang orchestra chimes, like John Hurley. We pitched it to Atlantic Records. Years later Jerry Wexler described it to me as "typical, overproduced Southern crap, baby."

Dale "Susie Q" Hawkins came to Ardent, looking for somebody who played electric saw; they called me. When I arrived, he had forgotten what he wanted, but assumed I was part of the program producing the Gentrys. I contracted the session, hiring local musicians. He also worked on a personal artist album, *LA, Memphis and Tyler, Texas.* He had cut tracks in Tyler, Texas, and Hollywood. The L.A. material featured a good teenage slide guitar player, Ry Cooder. Dale Hawkins gave the world James Burton and had a way with guitar players.

Knowbody Else, a band from Manila, Arkansas, was my high-water mark at Ardent. They had longer hair and more outrageous clothes than any of our local boys. The lead singer looked like a pirate in high-heel women's boots and a Perez Prado bolero shirt with puff sleeves, open to the waist. They had the first Super Beatle Vox amp I worked with. Homer Ray Harris had thrown them out of Lyn-Lou's studio for playing too loud. Chips wouldn't let them in American. I couldn't wait. Within twenty minutes of them starting to play, everyone at Ardent fled in self-defense. Even my wife left.

Soon to become the hit band Black Oak Arkansas, Knowbody Else was the most original group I ever recorded, like nothing I've heard. They had seen photos of the Jefferson Airplane but never heard their music, so they played how they imagined it sounded. Lead guitar, twelve-string guitar, bass, organ, and the most unique drummer. He had learned to make the sound of backwards hi-hat from the Beatles records.

I told them not to worry about money. I recorded them anytime they showed up. They lived communally in Jonesboro, Arkansas, and were 4F, from felony convictions for stealing the high school gym's public address system. They wrote a song about it.

When I finished Knowbody Else's album, *Soldiers of Pure Peace*, I figured I had it made and quit Ardent. I arranged to play my masterpiece for the great Tom Dowd, who worked in town at Chips's place. I took Charlie Freeman with me. We had heard stories about Tom Dowd. He engineered many classic early rock 'n' roll records and immortal jazz recordings. He was an ex–nuclear physicist who had helped build the first atomic bomb. He came to Stax and worked magic on the old home-rolled gear. Now he worked with Chips Moman's rhythm section, recording Solomon Burke, the King of Rocking Soul.

He was more than cordial. He led Charlie and me into the control room and put my tape on the playback two-track. The crackling rumble of my recording exploded from the speakers. Dowd cocked his head, closed his eyes, seemingly absorbed in the music. In the middle of the second song, he punched stop. The tape jerked to a halt. "Does anybody else in this group sing?" he asked, smiling.

"No." Knowbody Else's whole sound was built around Jim Mangrum's cartoonish, neo-operatic yowl.

"Well, I hate this guy's voice. But I want to listen to all of it because I recognize this as a tremendous engineering accomplishment."

His opinion of Mangrum's voice devastated me, but his assurance of my engineering swelled my head with pride. Dowd listened to this whole thing with the enormous Solomon Burke waiting in the studio. When finished, Tom said, "This is mountain music." I had told him nothing about the band. "What they need to do is mix their ethnic roots."

That stopped me in my tracks. It was the smartest thing I had heard about recording music. I took it to heart and spent the next few years mixing my ethnic roots. Little did I know that I was preparing to work with Ry Cooder.

Things got tough. Without the pittance I received from Fry, we were up against it. One afternoon I sat staring at my feet. My wife bluntly stated somebody had to make some fucking money.

"I'm getting a job," Mary Lindsay said simply. "What you are doing is important. That night you recorded Furry Lewis was important. I watched my brother give up on his music and I don't want that to happen to you." She had graduated from college and tried to work at a bank and at a photo shop. Then we got lucky. She found a job as a horse trainer working for True Jacobsen at a stable in Collierville.

True, a lanky, dishwater-blond Texan ten years my elder, was the only other person I ever ran across from Baylor Theatre. By observing True work in her stable/boarding barn/riding academy, I determined one could apply Mr. Baker's Integration of Abilities widely. True's operation was pure Baylor Theatre. Mary Lindsay trained an ancient Shetland pony to walk in a circle with a child on its back. True showed the spectacle to proud parents with too much money and told them their precious child was a "natural talent." She was good. My wife gave her the tools she needed. Mary Lindsay loved training and showing the high-end thoroughbred hunter/jumpers True's clientele owned. We drove to horse shows in New Orleans and Jackson, hauling a horse trailer, which is worse than pulling a U-Haul with a Hammond B3 in it. Mary Lindsay showed a client's jumper and won first place. She looked beautiful astride the handsome beast, wearing riding britches and shiny tall black boots (throw in a riding crop and I'm helpless). I loved welcoming my wife home after a day training horses at the barn.

I got a job as head engineer at Onyx Studio in South Memphis, but didn't take it seriously. If I didn't want to cut a session, I said it was "too broke." Nobody knew the difference. Onyx had a hot salt-and-pepper rhythm section. Ronnie Moore played a three-string bass upside down and tuned wrong. Bobby Manuel was the guitarist I had held by the ankles while he stood on his head and played with his teeth. They were white boys. "Crazy" Ronnie Williams on B3 and "Baby" Joe Gray, who played left-handed on a right-handed drum kit, making it really easy to mic, were the Brothers.

The best session I cut at Onyx was on a novelty keyboardist, Ironing Board Sam. Sam played a homemade organ on an ironing board. He brought the thing in, and hooked it up with a lamp cord and alligator clips. When he turned it on, it shot sparks. All the notes played at once, like the music of spheres. He said, "Don't worry, brother. We jes' gotta wait forty-five minutes." I was dubious. Forty-five minutes later the multi-scale cosmic hum shut off clean. Sam, or "Board," had a teenage drummer, Jerome Miller, a three-hundred-pound black guy with a spiked dog collar around his neck. We cut a song, "Non Support," that charted.

For the third Memphis Country Blues Festival the "crazy white boys" house band duty fell to Sid Selvidge and me. Lee Baker, the original Funky Down Home, couldn't play. He had been busted for selling marijuana and resided on the Shelby County Penal Farm. The Electric Blue Watermelon was the backup band and supported the ever-increasing Insect Trust. The band included Charlie Freeman; bass man Tommy McClure; drummer "Baby" Joe Gray from the Onyx house band; horn players Robert Palmer, Trevor Koehler, and Warren Gardner from the Insect Trust; and harmonica player extraordinaire Ed Kollis. Kollis, hired as American Studio engineer by Chips Moman, later engineered *Elvis in Memphis* and toured the world with Leonard Cohen. Selvidge and I sang two songs. When I walked off stage, Bukka White rushed up to me. "You got some twist in you," he said, grinning like a possum.

He walked me to Mississippi Fred McDowell, sitting on the stage apron. "You hear that? Fred, did you hear this white boy singing?" He could hardly have missed it. Fred looked up and grumped in disgust. I wasn't about to put it over on him.

Seymour Stein, a New Yorker, recorded the third Memphis Country Blues Festival, the first release on Sire Records, when it was part of London Group.

Chapter 37

IN MY YOUTH I SOUGHT THE TRUTH
LIKE STANLEY BOOTH
(1967–69)

I had seen Stanley Booth at Memphis State University, and knew him from an article in the *Tiger Rag*, the campus newspaper. I knew he held a black belt in karate, a degree in art history, and tended to show up at local art community events. He and I crossed paths one afternoon at Stepherson's Big Star grocery store in East Memphis. We were both cashing checks. He wore a burgundy leather jacket and tortoise-shell dark glasses with a red bandana nattily knotted around his skinny neck. He looked like he was out of an ad from *Gentlemen's Quarterly* magazine and was obviously stoned. We exchanged pleasantries and phone numbers. He was living with my friend, Jan Bradford, the deadpan comedian from *Strange Flowers*. Soon Mary Lindsay and I were hanging out regularly at Stanley and Jan's. He had a great stereo jazz collection. He was friends with Charlie Brown, Hunter George, and many local underground art types. We smoked pot and listened to music.

Stanley, a fledgling journalist, had published his first piece in *Playboy* magazine about Furry Lewis and a piece on Elvis was about to run in *Esquire*. His information on both pieces came from Charlie Brown. He was trying to sell the *Saturday Evening Post* an article about a Korean War army deserter just repatriated to Memphis. Instead, the *Post* assigned him the topic of Memphis music. "Who could possibly be interested in that?" Stanley asked with contempt.

That pissed me off. I listed Memphis music personalities—Chips Moman, Steve Cropper, Dan Penn, Willie Mitchell, Sam Phillips—for him to interview, and told him, "Go talk to these people, and then tell me they aren't interesting." Stanley got interested pretty fast. He witnessed the "Dock of the Bay" session, days before the tragic plane crash that killed Otis Redding and all but two of the Bar-Kays. The sad event became the story's focus, and ran in the last edition of the *Saturday Evening Post* magazine. The article established Stanley as an up-and-coming rock critic, something he didn't relish. He was assigned to cover Brian Jones's (of the Rolling Stones) drug trial in London. Stanley formed a relationship with the Rolling Stones that changed our lives.

Charlie Freeman started working for Stan Kesler at Sounds of Memphis studio, built in an old tobacco warehouse by Sam the Sham's former manager. Charlie, Tommy McClure, and Arkansas drummer "Slamming" Sammy Creason from the Bill Black Combo touring band reformed Kesler's rhythm section. Charlie wanted me to record his "big song" if Stan fronted the studio time.

It was an ordeal. The damn song was so long. The recording tape ran off the reel but we worked on it for so long Stan Kesler got used to me. We went for coffee together, a privilege reserved for the inner circle. One afternoon in Dobbs House Coffee Shop, I asked Kesler for an engineering job.

He said, "Man, I just hired B.B. Cunningham as my assistant. I wish I could hire you but I don't have room."

"What about as a session musician?" I asked, hopefully.

"I've got a blues session coming up on Albert Collins and I've already booked Hooker Brown on organ, but if you want to hang out and try to slip in on the date, go for it."

I showed up with Charlie Freeman. As we walked to the studio, we saw a Kelly green Cadillac convertible with California plates and two fishing poles sticking out the back window on the driver's side. Charlie said, "If that's not a blues player's car, I'll kiss your ass."

The session started in chaos. Sammy Creason was wadded up on the studio floor in the throes of a kidney stone attack until an ambulance carried him off. Kesler called Tarp Tarrant, Jerry Lee Lewis's longtime drummer. Freeman had worked with him when he toured with Jerry Lee's band, the Memphis Beats.

Bill Hall from Houston produced the session with Leland Rogers and did the heavy lifting. Leland, dubbed "the Silver Fox" due to his white hair, was Kenny Rogers's older brother and ate up with cool. He wore a safari hat and a white jumpsuit. He produced with an easy style, friendly and smooth. I sat at the Wurlitzer electric piano and played along with the first tune. Leland walked by and told B.B. Cunningham, "Put a mic on that."

I had weaseled my way onto the session.

We cut for three days; then Stan brought Wayne Jackson and Andrew Love in to do the horns. After the Albert Collins session, Sammy Creason returned and we came together as a rhythm section. Hooker Brown and McClure couldn't get along, so Creason replaced Hooker with B3 player Mike Utley. We became the Dixie Flyers.

Albert Collins's album, *Trash Talkin'*, was nominated for a Grammy as R&B Instrumental of the Year.

Charlie Freeman married Carol Jensen, the girl from my art class. They lived in the midtown ghetto across from the Mid-South Fairgrounds. Money was tight. We held ritual fried chicken and mashed potato dinners—to which we added our pea casserole—at our cottage by the cemetery or their "little house on Inez." We were brothers in arms.

Charlie knew my musical limitations. On a session, I could count on him to give me the note outside the triad. He did it without the other musicians noticing. He pulled me out of the hole time after time. Charlie said there was "no such thing as a wrong note." The right note was only a half-step away in either direction.

The Sounds of Memphis studio was temporarily in a warehouse that naturally sounded great. After Albert Collins, we did sessions on Billy Lee Riley for the Sun record label, which Shelby Singleton had purchased. On the Riley session I played the Wurlitzer again. We cut "Kay," a country song about a Nashville taxi driver (Billy changed it to Memphis). We got a good cut that Sam Phillips himself called the best record Riley ever made.

I was in heaven. Billy Lee Riley was my original inspiration as a kid. I thought "Red Hot" was the best rockabilly record ever made. During our session Riley's Indian wife got pissed because he was loaded. She departed in a huff, leaving Billy Lee without a ride. I took him home. We rode around northeast Memphis until dawn before he remembered where "home" was.

We recorded Bettye LaVette, a seventeen-year-old black girl from up north, for Leland Rogers. We cut our best track yet, "He Made a Woman Out of Me," on her. Bettye had a crush on Wayne Jackson from the Memphis Horns. She gave Charlie and me our first hits of cocaine. Charlie said, "Well, there goes a few brain cells."

The most interesting session we did with Kesler was an R&B pop artist from Japan. Kenichi Hagiwara—known as Shoken—was the lead singer and guitar sideman of the Tempters, a group of pop stars from the Land of the Rising Sun. They had Beatle haircuts and wore hooded zipper-front mink jackets. Very cool. Two older Japanese businessmen, producers from the publishing company, were with them. The producers spoke English; the musicians did not. We cut them like a typical R&B date. The vocalist sang phonetic English and wept bitter tears on the ballads. Kesler overdubbed the Memphis Horns and the Holiday sisters, who sang on *Elvis in Memphis*. After each take the producers came into the tracking space and bowed to each of us. They had a briefcase full of hundred dollar bills and paid in cash after each session. Freeman asked what musicians' scale was in Japan. They seemed not to understand. Charlie asked again, "What do you pay musicians in Japan?" "In Japan, not pay musicians," one replied curtly. Some things are the same wherever you go.

I met Duane Allman the first time I went to Muscle Shoals Sound Studio in Alabama. Jan Wenner, the publisher of *Rolling Stone* magazine, was producing Boz Scaggs, the "blue eyed soul man." I had heard stories of Florida guitarist Duane Allman from Mike Ladd, Mike Alexander, and John Hurley. Ladd and Alexander knew him from military school, and Hurley used his band to cut demos in Nashville. Duane looked different from the rest of the good ole boys from Shoals. He had long hippy hair and played bottleneck slide like a demon from Hell. They called him Skydog, reflecting his conscious state.

We talked about Mike Alexander. Mike was a con man who told people he owed money from dope deals to meet him at a certain time and remote location. At the appointed time, he would be boarding a plane elsewhere. He was famous for selling "treasure maps" leading to the motherlode dope stash. Duane laughed, and pulled a Mike Alexander dope map out of his trucker's wallet. Duane was a kindred spirit and soulmate. I knew we would meet down the road.

The second time I went to Muscle Shoals I met Jerry Wexler. Wexler was recording the Arkansas-transplanted-to-Canada rockabilly legend Ronnie "The Hawk" Hawkins, a man among men. Hawkins got off the plane in Muscle Shoals with a cardboard box full of liquor bottles and a woman who looked like a cross between a Playboy bunny and a serial killer. The expression on her face could curdle milk. She looked like she was smuggling the front bumpers of a '49 Cadillac in her sweater. She had the old familiar Ann Moss rocketship tits up. She was a former Miss Toronto, a hardcore lesbian, ex–roller derby star who Hawkins would sic on eager groupies and road whores. A large man in a beat-up cowboy hat, Hawkins told Wexler, "I got the pills, pot, and pussy. I'm ready to rock 'n' roll."

"Cool it, baby. This is a dry county," Wexler warned.

I drove to Shoals with a songwriter, Bob McDill, from Bill Hall's operation with Dickey Lee and Allen Reynolds. McDill and I had written a song, "Sanctified." Kesler set it up for us to pitch Hawkins the song. I didn't think he would cut it but I wanted to meet Wexler. Chips and Kesler put the idea in my head that all you needed for success was the Atlantic Records production account, like Stax had. I would discover the fallacy of this concept.

We met Wexler at guitarist Eddie Hinton's house by the lake. I said, "It's an honor to meet you, Mr. Wexler."

He said, "Call me Jerry, baby." I often wondered what would have happened if I had said, "Okay, Jerry baby."

Wexler liked the song, which was full of Ronnie Wilkins's gospel licks. Ronnie Milsap finally cut it. Wexler and I got along right away. He loved southern musicians, but I don't think he had met one with whom he could discuss William Faulkner and Flannery O'Connor. We stayed up all night, telling lies and drinking Jack Daniels, each trying to impress the other. When Bob McDill and I drove back to Memphis, the world was different. I had met Jerry Wexler.

Our next session was a doubleheader. Leland Rogers brought Bettye LaVette. Hank Ballard came too. Hank sang a shuffle no matter what groove we played. BB Cunningham was full-time tracking engineer. I knew BB from childhood Sunday school class at Bellevue Baptist Church. He had made guitar instrumental records as a teenager, had been the organ player in the Hombres, and the vocalist on the big hit, "Let It All Hang Out." We did okay with Bettye LaVette, but never beat "He Made a Woman Out of Me" from the first session. We re-cut "Thrill on the Hill." Leland never worked us hard and always let us off early.

The Memphis Country Blues Festival had grown to be a three-day event. Bill Barth pulled together more real bluesmen than had ever been assembled: all the regulars, Furry Lewis, Bukka White, Mississippi Fred McDowell, the fabulous Reverend Robert Wilkins and family, plus Joe Callicott. Lee Baker was out of prison, having done time in Lexington, like Tim Leary. Baker formed Moloch with Eugene Wilkins, the little brother of the screamer from my Blue Ridge vocal group. They were loaded for bear. Barth scheduled our Sounds of Memphis rhythm section to back up Albert Collins. Collins did not show up, so we took the set. Ringers like Johnny Winter, the albino white boy from Beaumont, Texas, who had nothing to do with area music, showed up.

The festival was being filmed by national television for Steve Allen's series, *Sounds of Summer*. Gene Rosenthal of Adelphi Records and public TV reps with clipboards and clearance contracts negotiated with the bluesmen backstage at rehearsal. Rosenthal spoke heatedly to Marvin, lead man and protector of blues mummy Nathan Beauregard. Suddenly, Marvin produced a .45 automatic from his suit pants and stuck it in Rosenthal's face. Negotiations halted. Later I complimented the ex-gravedigger, now keeper of a blues legend, on the smartness of his move with his piece. He said, "Thank ya, suh. Weren't nothin." I shook his huge brown paw of a hand and started to introduce myself. "Oh, I knows you," he stated in no uncertain terms. "You is Mista Dick'son's boy. You live out there by the graaaave ya'd."

When a TV stooge tried to get Reverend Robert Wilkins to sign a release form, Baby Son, the Reverend's youngest boy and tambourine player extraordinaire, said, "Daddy, these folks ain't sanctified."

Our band was booked as Soldiers of the Cross and we were scheduled to perform gospel material. Barth also booked me to play with Sleepy John Estes and Yank Rachell because I played like the guy who recorded with them back in the day. It was great. Sleepy John told me, "Man, you plays jes' like Knocky Parker." I took it as a great compliment, until I discovered Parker was a northern white stride player.

When Stanley Booth met Jerry Wexler, I felt them start to click. I figured between the two of us we could get a clean shot at Atlantic. One weekend we did blue mescaline over at Stanley's house. I had only done psychedelic drugs once since Baylor and the monkey tests. This was a mellow trip. We listened to the first *History of Rock 'n' Roll* broadcast on FM 100. With the drug's aid, I realized the continuity of what I had witnessed firsthand in Memphis of the fifties. I told Mary Lindsay it was time to quit her job. We were on our way to the real thing. I felt it.

Stanley was going on the 1969 world tour with the Rolling Stones as the authorized biographer. Brian Jones was dead. Stanley had what amounted to his suicide note and the beginnings of a detective story involving sex, drugs, and rock 'n' roll. We were to meet Stanley at a Holiday Inn in southeast Alabama, drive to Auburn University, and attend the Stones concert as guests.

The next part of this story is my wife's to tell, but this is a thumbnail sketch. Neither Stanley nor the Stones were at the motel. Mary Lindsay talked the motel manager into putting us next to Chuck Berry, who was one of the Stones' opening acts. We checked in. I took a shower and let my baby work. Mary Lindsay knocked on Chuck Berry's door.

Chuck wasn't alone. A tall blond white girl wearing a sundress was sitting on the bed. Chuck said, "Come on in here, sweetness," and dove into the girl's crotch. My child bride kept her cool. She claimed she was Stanley Booth's sister, and desperate to hook up with him before the concert. Chuck Berry chuckled, "Yes, darlin'. I've been on this tour for a month now and I done met a couple of Stanley's sisters." He agreed to drive us to the gig. Having done hard time for transporting a minor for sex, he welcomed a white couple accompanying him across the state.

At the venue, Berry opened the trunk of his rent-a-car and walked away, leaving me to carry his guitar case. It worked. We sailed by security and found Stanley standing next to Keith Richards.

The show was great: Chuck Berry, Ike and Tina Turner, T. Rex, and finally the Stones. They rocked the house, playing hit after hit. Middle of the set they broke down, and Mick and Keith did Fred McDowell's "You Got to Move" as a duet. The band returned with "Midnight Rambler" as a theatre piece. Mick, down on his knees in prayer, beat the stage with his silver-studded black leather belt. WHAP! "Talking about the Midnight Rambler." WHAP! "The one you never seen before." It was dynamite. Ivan Ryder could not have done better. Part Rudolph Nureyev, part Howlin' Wolf, part Muddy Waters, and part Stravinsky, staged by Bertolt Brecht. Marat, de Sade in Boystown, *Ciudad Acuna*. Richards's guitar churned the rhythm, like a belly dancer's drummer boy.

Back in Memphis, we could tell the first session we cut at Kesler's new studio wasn't right. The tobacco warehouse's good, natural sound had spoiled us. A new Electrodyne with multicolored fader modules and lighted switches had replaced the old Universal Audio console. It looked cool but sounded flat. Nobody said so, but everyone was disappointed.

We were recording the great James Carr, the best soul voice I ever heard firsthand. James was so out of it that a uniformed nurse was with him at all times. I don't know what he was on but he was high as a monkey. On one song he would get to the song's bridge and get lost every time. At one point, we realized James was missing. Panic ensued. Somebody found him on the two-story studio building's roof, staring down at the parking lot. They talked him away from the edge slowly, and the session, such as it was, continued. It was discouraging. We had waited so long for the new facility. This was a letdown.

One telephone call changed everything.

Chapter 38

STONES IN MY PASSWAY
(1969)

Here's the setup: November 27, 1969, Thanksgiving Day. Wife and I were sitting down to turkey dinner midafternoon, when the phone rang. It was Stanley Booth. He said, "Somebody here wants to talk to you."

The next voice I heard said, "This is Jerry Wexler. Hello, baby."

Wexler's next words blew my mind, "How would you like to move to Miami and be a rhythm section?"

If you have read Stanley's book, *Dance with the Devil: The Rolling Stones and Their Times,* you know some of this. To paraphrase Mark Twain, "Mr. Booth told the truth, mostly."

While having Thanksgiving dinner in New York, Wexler and Stanley listened to the Albert Collins album we recorded at Sounds of Memphis. Wexler said, "I wish I could have a band like that to use down in Miami."

Stanley, God bless him, said, "Well, that's Dickinson and Charlie Freeman."

Charlie had been banned from the studio for firing his shotgun in the control room. We were looking for another job. Working for Chips and Kesler, I had become convinced all you needed to be successful in studio work in the South was the Atlantic account. From Stax to Muscle Shoals, wherever Atlantic went, success followed. This seemed like a dream come true. I called Charlie. Tarp Tarrant had played drums on the Collins album due to Sammy Creason's kidney stone attack, but Charlie convinced me we had to offer Sammy the job. We thought his wife would not want to move, but Sammy jumped at the opportunity. Tommy McClure and Mike Utley were eager, too. The deal was made. The contract was signed. We kept it secret in Memphis. We were stabbing Stan Kesler in the back and knew it. Like Br'er Fox high up on Chinquapin Hill, we lay low, preparing to move to Miami Beach and Criteria Studios in January. Stanley was on the road with the Rolling Stones. He called in the middle of the night.

"The Stones have three days off at the end of the tour," he said. "They're looking for a place to record. Can they record in Memphis?"

In those days a foreign band could get a touring permit or a recording permit, but not both. The Stones had been denied permission to record in Los Angeles and needed a place without a strict union policy. The Beatles had been unable to record at Stax due to an insurance policy. I could think of no place in town where a secret session could be pulled off. I told Stanley, "No."

"Where could they record?"

"Muscle Shoals Sounds," I said without hesitation. "Nobody will even know who they are." I could tell it made Stanley mad. He snapped back, "I don't know any of those people. Who could put that together?"

"Call Wexler," was my answer. I didn't hear back from Stanley for a couple of weeks. My phone rang in the middle of the night again. Stanley said, "Be at Muscle Shoals Sounds on Thursday. The Stones are recording."

I didn't drive my too-well-known, lime-gold, fastback Mustang to Muscle Shoals. I took my wife's nondescript tan Plymouth station wagon, incognito. Secret mission. The parking lot was empty. What the hell. I went to the back door and knocked. Jimmy Johnson cracked the door and peeped out, "Dickinson, what do you want?"

"Here for the Stones session," I said.

"Oh, hell, does everybody in Memphis know?" he asked, his voice high-pitched with excitement. I assured him nobody in Memphis knew. I was there to meet Stanley.

"Come on in, man. They just made it to Muscle Shoals airport. The largest plane that ever landed there and three people got off." We waited together.

Keith. He walked into the room like a scarecrow, mumbling to himself and chuckling over his private joke. His skin was greenish blue or bluish green. His best tooth hung from his left ear and formerly belonged to a cougar. Tied scarfs and bracelets hung from his skeletal arms like ragged, bloody bandages on a wounded soldier. The front of his projectile spiked hair was peroxide orange, like a high school harlot from 1957, the kind of girl who wore mouton. Keith Richards was a pretty picture.

Charlie Watts and Bill Wyman were tiny. That's the first thing you think when you meet the Stones. They seemed so inappropriately small. They were friendly. Stanley was with them, thank God, but Jagger and others were not. They accepted my presence as Stanley's friend. We shot the shit, easily and comfortably. Before long Keith and I were sitting at the studio piano playing Hank Williams songs. They had just met Gram Parsons, who turned them on to country music. I think somehow Keith associated me with Gram, which warmed him up to me naturally, bullshitting and talking to me good-naturedly, musician to musician. Wyman and Watts were beautiful. Bill was quiet, lurking with his gorgeous brunette wife all covered in white bunny fur like the ice princess. Charlie prowled the studio, checking everything out, mics, speakers, etc. He seemed like an old school jazz cat.

Ahmet Ertegun, the big he-bull himself, appeared grinning through expensive teeth. You knew, instantly, every hair in his beard was precisely the same length. Ahmet was starting a R. B. Greaves day session while the Stones would record at night. He seemed to be waiting for Mick to split.

By the time the rest of them arrived, I had passed the test and was part of the session crew. Jimmy Johnson was the engineer. No one else was inside. Business was about to pick up.

Late arrivals: Mick Jagger, Little Mick (Taylor), road manager/piano man Ian Stewart, and Tony-the-bag-man. Not Spanish Tony Sanchez, but a Black Panther from Detroit who shows up in the Altamont video with his arm in a cast. He broke both fists at the ill-fated gig. Once Jagger settled in, things began to pop. They started to run down Fred McDowell's "You Gotta Move." They were doing it in their live set as a Mick/Keith duet with acoustic guitar and vocal. When they started to play it as a band, it wasn't working. Stanley and I retreated to the control room with engineer Jimmy Johnson.

Wyman played the Wurlitzer electric piano and no one played bass. It wasn't coming together. I thought, what a drag, after all this I'm going to watch the Stones blow it. Stanley had become romantically involved with the little sister of an old Macon friend, and was anxious to go to the motel and telephone her, which would give me a chance to smoke a joint. The Muscle Shoals boys were paranoid about dope since the state police had recently busted another local studio. Things started pretty tight, but they soon loosened up.

Stanley and I headed to the Holiday Inn, each with our own agenda. When we returned to the studio not forty-five minutes later, the Stones were gathered in the control room for the first playback. Charlie Watts was smiling. What issued forth from the speakers at the old coffin factory was a far cry from Fred McDowell at Hunter Chapel. Jagger's voice put an ominous tone on the old gospel song. Keith hammered the hook-riff in a way that sounded more like Bo Diddley than Old Fred. "When the Lord gets ready," Jagger snarled, "You got to moooove."

His accent seemed oddly appropriate. He mutated his young man's English voice into the world-weary moan of an old black fieldhand from darkest Mississippi Delta. Delighted, Keith overdubbed the guitar hook that announced every vocal line with any guitar he could find—a Telecaster, a twelve-string Stella, and whatever else Eddie Hinton left behind. The guitar riff started to take on the whip-crack chain gang sound of the "Midnight Rambler" I had heard when Mick beat the stage with his silver-studded belt. The drums sounded a sort of death march; the electric piano rumbled with a distorted vibrato like a drunken gig at the V.F.W.

"You see that woman, who walks the street. You see that po-lice man out on his beat? But, when the Lord gets ready, you got to mooooo-ve," Jagger mooed like a lonesome cow from hell. It was pure Rolling Stones. In the brief time Stanley and I had been gone, they had turned the ragged beginning of a disaster into a Rolling Stone classic. They forever owned the performance, as surely as Fred and the Hunter Chapel Singers owned their version.

The next night was different. They started with a heavy guitar. Keith was in G tuning, but he didn't sound like Furry Lewis.

The inversion of the intervals
In what is actually a 5 string banjo
Tuning creates a meat-heavy twang
That somehow propels
The beat of the music
Like a melodic drumbeat,
Somehow mean
And hard
With a sexual strut
Like a belly dance rhythm.
D tuning is not the same
(D is bluer,
More lonesome
Somehow,
Not as familiar
Or primal and jungle).
The middle of the chord whangs,
Almost losing tuning.

The bottom of the chord rumbles
Deeper than standard
And the top treble creeps out
Like a scalded alley cat
In the middle of the night.

It is the perfect tuning for Richards and the Stones, swinging with an arrogant snake drive that instantly takes you to a midnight party in the Moroccan whorehouse. The riff Keith introduced that night in Muscle Shoals in the old coffin factory was perfect, hitting the augmented five chord of the blues progression, creating the turnaround pattern to hook the lyrics and push the verse back to the top of the form.

Keith sang what weren't words but grunts and groans, painful and sexual. Jagger wrote on a green steno pad as if taking dictation. He was translating. When he had the idea, he walked away, humming to himself. He circled the room like a buzzard over a carcass. After what seemed like not enough time, he turned over three pages of finished lyrics to "Brown Sugar." Some say it's about Claudia Lennear, the Ikette from Ike and Tina Turner's Revue, who toured as an opener for the Stones in '69 (later she showed up as a member of the Space Chorus on Leon Russell's Mad Dogs and Englishmen tour). Be that as it may, Jagger had responded to his environment. He soaked up the Old South's ghosts and the deep Alabama accents that surrounded him. In the first verse he refers to "Sky-Dog Slave-Trader." Sky-Dog was the nickname the Muscle Shoals gang had for slide guitarist Duane Allman. (I have seen a lot of songwriters in my day, but I have never seen anyone compare to Mick Jagger.) When he finished the lyrics, he stood in the center of the room with a handheld mic and ran it down with the band until they had an arrangement. Then he went into the control room with Jimmy Johnson to work on the sounds as the band played the song instrumentally.

Satisfied, he retreated to the vocal booth and recorded it maybe three times. They listened to a couple of playbacks. The eighth-note tom-tom ride in the "A" verse rubbed harmonically with one note in the bass pattern. Somebody said, "Charlie, you need to tune the tom-tom, so it doesn't rub the bass."

Charlie said, "I never tune me drums."

Ian Stewart, the road manager and sideman piano player who had been with them since the beginning said, "Wait a minute. You can't say something like, 'I never tune my drums' and just go on."

"Why should I tune something I'm going to go out there and beat on? I'll hit for a while and it will change," Charlie said, and walked off into the studio. He did and it did. Two more takes and they had it. That was the second night.

They stashed a vial of cocaine in the tack piano in the back corner of the studio. Not Spanish Tony slept on a nearby couch, guarding the goods. Keith offered Stanley and me a line. Charlie Freeman and I had done coke with Bettye LaVette on her session at Sounds of Memphis but I didn't get it. It made me feel supernormal, taking away brain clouds I carefully constructed, but I was polite, taking my share.

That night somebody brought barbeque sauce and containers of pulled pork. As we made sandwiches, Jagger and I ended up together. "Don't you think you could stand to lose a bit of weight?" he asked. Before I could reply, Charlie Watts answered, "He ought to kick your ass."

Mick picked up a container of meat and walked away, eating it by hand. The same thing happened when you passed him a joint: he walked away with it. The privilege of celebrity.

The Stones wanted to play a free gig, which seemed simple enough. Their touring permit had run out; they wanted to promote it themselves. They wanted to schedule a gig in California. Jann Wenner helped them over the telephone from San Francisco. It wasn't going well. Keith had visions of state police troopers blocking his entry to the festival ground. He was looking forward to the confrontation like some bizarre civil rights demonstration.

Albert and David Maysles, documentary filmmakers, showed up for the third night of sessions. They maneuvered around without speaking. They had filmed the Stones' first concert of the tour in New York, and were following the band to San Francisco for the free concert.

My mother read in the Chicago newspaper an article with the headline, "WHERE ARE THE ROLLING STONES?" Nobody knew. Another thing nearly nobody knew was that their recording contract with EMI/London Group was expiring. They had signed early in the "British Invasion" and did not receive high royalty front money. Ahmet Ertegun and Jerry Wexler knew it. Wexler flew in for the last day of the session to talk turkey. Ahmet was the supercool jetsetter; Wexler was the snake charmer, old-school record man who could sweet-talk the most extreme hard bop blues musician hip to record industry hype and typical bullshit jive. Before you knew it, you had signed the napkin and given him your first-born.

When Jerry arrived the stage was set and the cast was complete for the Stones' final act at Muscle Shoals Sounds. Everybody else was at the Holiday Inn. I was day-sleeping at the Kings Inn, a truckers' motel on the Birmingham highway. It was impossible to sleep. I had signed to Atlantic Records as a session musician and was moving to Miami Beach with no idea what would happen next. I had watched the Rolling Stones write and record what would surely be one of their biggest hits.

I dressed carefully for the last night session. Black and white striped bell bottoms, black Spanish boots, a purple button-front undershirt, and a shiny black jacket-shirt with a multicolored paisley print scarf tied around my neck. I looked like the Summer of Love.

As different as the second night had been from the first, the third night was different still, lower key. The studio was more relaxed, settled in, yet with the feeling this was the last act.

The curtain.
Like a production in theatre,
Studio sessions take on a "play life."
A chance camaraderie
That has forever
A life
Of its own.

The recording
Is a document
Which tells the story
In the future.
Only the players share the truth.

There is a predictable
Sadness
To the end of
The session
The play,
The end
Of the game
Yet it is the goal, the object of the whole process.
As we started
It was already over.

The song was different, too. Keith had fathered a son, Marlon; this was a lullaby. "Wild horses couldn't drag me away" was about Keith not wanting to tour. He had a fully developed melody and chord progression, a complete chorus, and sketchy non-word verse melodies. Jagger took his green steno pad and walked to the lounge where the old beanie-weenie machine and coffee pot were located. This song took him a little longer.

Celebrity gossip columns had carried a story about Marianne Faithfull, Mick's old girlfriend, and her rumored marriage to Lord somebody, unconfirmed. Jagger was like a high school boy about it. He turned the simple lullaby into a metaphoric tale of unrequited love and betrayal.

As they started to run down the song, Ian Stewart rose from the piano and started packing gear that wasn't being used, as if leaving. "Well," said Jagger. "I assume we need a keyboardist."

He stood with Wexler and me. Wexler said, "Baby, we could call Bewey Beckett," in his Jewish Elmer Fudd voice.

I said, "I don't think that's what he means." I didn't find out for ten years why Stew didn't play on "Wild Horses."

They were too out of tune for the studio's concert grand and the Wurlitzer. I couldn't see giving Keith the old E-note tune-up routine. I didn't think that would work. I sought the old upright tack piano in the back of the studio where they had their cocaine stashed. When I started to play, Not-Spanish Tony woke from a deep sleep and moved the stash, making for a nice little dramatic scenario. I found a section of the old piano just out of tune enough to work with the Stones, and started trying to interpret the chord chart I had gotten from Keith. It was instantly apparent something was wrong. Keith had just learned to write a "Nashville-system" chord chart, where the chords are represented by numbers and look like a phone number.

Bill Wyman saw me having trouble, and said, "Where'd ya get them chords, mate?"

"I got them from Keith."

"Pay no attention to him," he said. "He has no idea what he's doing. He only knows where he put his fingers yesterday." This is the best description of rock 'n' roll guitar playing I have heard.

Once I figured the song out, it all made sense. The song was in the key of G but the progression started on B minor, which Keith had called #1 on his chart, throwing the following chords up a minor third. Bill and I rewrote the chart. Little Mick came over, snatched my copy of the chart, and walked away. Fuck it, I thought, and started to play.

The song had a sort of cowboy ballad feel. All I had that would fit was my old Texas Ramsey Horton/Floyd Cramer licks. I had two. Starting with a one-note bass and an open fifth after the downbeat minor sixth, I applied my Floyd second-interval grace-note phrases wherever they fit. Charlie was dropping out for whole "A" verse patterns and coming back in like a drunken sailor falling down the stairs. Several times in the song I was literally leading the changes in the form. We struggled along for say forty-five minutes, playing the changes instrumentally with Jagger in the control room with Jimmy. I heard the click of the talkback and Jagger spoke the words that I had been dreading. "Hey, Keith," he snarled. "What do you think about the piano?" Silence. And then Keith replied, "It's the only thing I like." I breathed a sigh of relief and put in my second Floyd Cramer lick with silent thanks to God and Ramsey Horton.

We got the cut quickly. Jagger was pleased with the track. Jimmy Johnson set up to overdub vocals. They took the songs in the order they were recorded. Mick and Keith were in the vocal booth on the same mic, passing a fifth of Jack Daniel's Black Label bourbon whiskey back and forth, singing background and lead on the same pass. They were redoing "Brown Sugar" during a break in overdubbing. Stanley and I were in the control room. I thought we were alone. I said, "He's leaving a line out that he was singing last night on tracking. And it's a good one."

"Tell 'em." Charlie Watts's voice came from the couch in front of the console. "Tell 'em," he said, again, more emphatically.

"I'm not going to tell him," I stuttered. Charlie rose from the couch and pressed the talkback button. "Tell him," he ordered.

"Mick, Mick," I said. "You're leaving out a line that you were singing last night."

"What is it, then?" Jagger replied.

"'Hear him whip the women.' Last night you were singing 'hear him whip the women' as a pickup to the chorus of the first verse."

"Who said that?" Mick asked. "Was that Booth?"

"Dickinson," Charlie replied through the talkback.

"Same thing," Jagger replied. I've never figured out what he meant, though I'm sure it was a put-down.

With the vocals finished, Jimmy Johnson and Mick set about doing rough mixes. Jimmy Johnson had been playing guitar on the daytime R. B. Greaves sessions and cutting the Stones overnight. He had been awake for at least three days. His eyes were bugging out like a tree frog's.

As they mixed, I couldn't help notice the Maysles brothers setting up two light trees pointing at the control room window from the tracking side of the glass. They had been shooting with available light only, which was lacking. My vast theatrical training at Baylor Theatre led me to realize that whatever they shot with lights had more chance of making it to film. I studied the situation.

Nobody was on the big couch where Charlie had been hiding. The lights and the camera aimed directly at it. I had the last joint. Keith knew it. As they started working on "Wild Horses," I put the joint behind my ear and sat down on the couch. Keith joined me. The light came on. Tape and camera began to roll, and I was in the movies.

Two shots from the Muscle Shoals session survive in *Gimme Shelter*: a shot of Mick and Jimmy Johnson behind the mixing console and the shot of Keith and me on the couch, eyes closed during the "Wild Horses" playback. Thank you, Baylor Theatre.

We all met at the Holiday Inn restaurant for a farewell breakfast. Jagger disappeared for twenty minutes. When he reemerged, he had changed clothes for the first time in three days, now wearing a white suit, a long red and white striped scarf, oversized golfer tam, a cartoonish bebop-cat hat, and dark glasses. He had also managed to get high as a kite. His voice had dropped at least an octave. He sat between Wexler and Ertegun and started talking about eighteen million dollars.

During our time on the couch, Keith asked me, "What do you think about Atlantic?" I gave him the old party line. We had just signed on to the Dixie Flyer deal and I was a true believer: tradition, catalogue, musical and genre knowledge, Tom Dowd, the atomic scientist engineer. I gave him the hard sell. Now with Jagger talking turkey with Wexler and Ahmet, it started making sense. They were negotiating the Stones' new record deal.

I was sitting in a booth with Bill Wyman and his white-bunny-fur-clad ice princess, who spoke not a word. A waitress asked, "You boys in a group?"

"Yes," announced Wyman. "We're Martha and the Vandellas." The girl shrugged and took our order.

The Stones (and Stanley) went to Altamont. I went back to Memphis with a 7-1/2 ips reel-to-reel tape copy of "Wild Horses."

"Don't let your disc jockey friends copy that," Mick warned.

"He ought to kick your ass," Charlie Watts grunted.

Chapter 39

"YOU GOT TO MOVE"
(1970)

It was hard to keep cool. Jagger loved the recording of "Wild Horses." He played it over and over on a Wollensak portable. The Stones flew to San Francisco and Altamont. The Summer of Love was gone.

As I drove home, I wondered what would happen next. No one knew about our Atlantic deal, and absolutely no one knew about the Stones. We were screwing Kesler and felt like rats, but the band was jazzed. The Atlantic job was the opportunity of a lifetime. Jerry Wexler and Tom Dowd came to town to ink the deal. The cat was out of the bag. Big spread in the local news; lots of speculation. Kesler took it like a man. He had one last session booked at the new studio for Leland Rogers. There was no artist. It was a going away party for us, the deserters. Leland had a fruit jar full of Ambar amphetamines that looked like M&Ms and a case of Cold Duck burgundy. We partied down. As the night went on, Leland called us into the control room. "I don't mean to put a jinx on you," he said. "But I'm afraid you boys have already done your best work."

He predicted the future but we couldn't hear. My wife gave me a gold sleeve to put over my left canine tooth for a Christmas present, a mark of my getting the Atlantic deal. Before we left town my old teacher, Alec, came to say goodbye. I am lucky to have had good teachers.

Christmas came and went to our little cottage across from the cemetery. I traded in our cars and bought a new canary-yellow Ford Torino with racing stripes, a full race cam, and three on the tree.

I had no idea what to expect in Miami. I envisioned driving a dune buggy over palm-treed beaches. Hawaiian cotton shirts. Cool rum drinks with umbrellas and fruit. New Year's Day my child bride and I struck out on our biggest adventure so far, a giant step into the total unknown, Atlantic Records. As we drove the new yellow muscle car further south than I had ever been, the Rolling Stones in the old coffin warehouse seemed like a dream. Yet it was not to be undone. The lights were on; the camera was rolling. I had the 7-1/2 ips copy. "Wild horses couldn't drag me away." It wouldn't be real to the world until it was released, but it was real to me.

Charlie Brown had moved to Miami a year before, and would help us get settled. He lived in Coconut Grove, a beatnik retirement community full of folk singers and old commies from the fifties. Criteria Studio was on South Beach. Charlie and Carol quickly found a house nearby. Mary Lindsay and I crashed with them and began looking. Rent was so high. We wanted something with at least a swimming pool to represent my new-found status. Mary Lindsay has a talent for real estate and found a great place. The house was blocks from the studio and had a round-bottomed pool that moved with the lunar tides. The former tenant was a high-dollar hooker; cops had battered the door off the hinges. AC vents had been pried off the walls. There was a double king-size bed with zebra-striped sheets, where undoubtedly the dirty deed had been done many times. The place had a strong vibe. We moved in and lived like we were in a movie.

There was a "welcome" party for the band at the studio. Everything was decorated in pastel. The teenage engineer wore a pink dress shirt and flip flop rubber shower shoes. The studio owner wore safari clothes and seemed nervous. We drank. They wanted to hear us play. We did an up-tempo shuffle in A that should have been a piece of cake. It felt funny. The "pocket" was wrong. It wasn't just Sammy and the drums. It was all of us. It felt forced, phony, by the numbers, more like Stax than we normally sounded. Utley was all over the B3, rumbling mashed pickups from the five. Freeman crackled and honked with bridging feedback and distortion. I hammered at double octaves like Leon Russell on Dexamyl, but something was not right. Only Tommy McClure sounded like he had in the alley at the old tobacco warehouse on the Albert Collins or Billy Lee Riley sessions. I considered geographic significance. We titled our first performance composition "Let Me Put My Condominium in Your Pastel Concrete Box."

Before we moved to Miami, Albhy Galuten expressed plans to visit Charlie in Memphis again and was surprised to learn of our new jobs, especially my playing piano for Atlantic's house band. He considered himself a much better player. Albhy was waiting on us when we arrived in Miami. He sat at my feet, rolled joints and made chord charts until he figured out why I got the job and he didn't. Wexler wondered who the hell he was. He avoided Dowd. Albhy didn't care. He knew an opportunity when he saw it. He ended up getting more out of Miami South than anybody.

Wexler wanted to name the rhythm section. They had fired the "Cold Grits." We kicked names around. New Year's Eve before we left Memphis, Mary Lindsay and I had seen *The Reivers*, a movie based William Faulkner's last novel. I bought the book on the day of Faulkner's death, my last summer in Waco at the Sin Inn. Eudora Welty claimed that with Faulkner, "You got to clear the tracks for the Dixie Flyer." I didn't think they would like the name but Wexler loved it. Sammy thought it sounded like a hockey team.

The Dixie Flyers got off to a slow start. Wexler wanted to sign Tony Joe White. Tommy McClure and Mike Utley had played on his hit, "Polk Salad Annie," his first album, and toured with him. Wexler was heavily courting Tony Joe for an artist contract and arranged for Mr. Poke Salad to produce some kid band he was interested in. Eric Quincy Tate sang with a guitar player who looked like fish out of water. They were over their heads. The songs were amateurish. Tony Joe produced at the level of "B" team Nashville assembly line. No Wexler, no Dowd. We worked with Criteria house engineers who thought we were hillbillies. If this was the big time, it sucked.

Our second victim, Jerry Jeff Walker, was a big improvement. Jerry Jeff was methodical but laid back, smart enough to work the band with loose reins. Donnie Brooks, a noted harmonica player with a real grip on Jeff's material, was with him. Jerry Jeff had experienced unexpected mainstream success with "Mr. Bojangles," cut at Sam Phillips's studio. He felt a kinship with us Memphis boys.

Jerry Jeff lived in Coconut Grove, one of several old folkies under the enormous artistic shadow of Fred Neil, the de facto Great Kahuna of the Grove. Neil had an engineer they called Bob "The Fox." The two seldom cut music, and if they did, Freddy erased it before his New York manager could get it. The Fox was paid not to record, the perfect gig. An elaborate underground of smugglers and pleasure boat captains hung out at the Gaslight, a famous old-school folk music venue. Vince Martin and a kid named Jimmy Buffett also hung around. Charlie Brown was respected by musicians and smugglers alike, as he had been in Memphis. He hooked us up. We could buy a grocery bag full of un-pressed Colombian gold for $300, which was great.

Jerry Jeff's recording went well and the music was good, but there was no sign of Wexler or Dowd in the studio. Mary Lindsay and I would see Wexler socially. We went to Jerry's for sit-down dinners. He liked my wife and hired her as his executive assistant. We were in what he called his "brain trust," and memoed on all the goings-on. But Wexler had been conspicuously absent from the studio.

Wexler had a yacht, a deep-sea fishing vessel with a two-man crew, aptly named *The Big A*. He took me out when he wanted me to agree on a deal that otherwise would have resulted in conflict. I'm subject to motion sickness. Add to that, Wexler was taking us into the Bermuda Triangle. Great. Although I did the typical fishing of a Southern boy, I had long since struck a deal with all God's creatures, be they fish or fowl. They leave me alone. I leave them alone. Deep-sea fishing was a compromise, to say the least.

Claudia Creason, Sammy's redheaded wife, hated the personal relationship developing between my wife, Wexler, and me. Claudia had a bogus publishing company and her own agenda. She had moved two pet songwriters to Miami. Wexler didn't like them. Her favorite songwriter sang in falsetto, which Wexler particularly hated and associated with Motown, a word one couldn't speak in his presence. Seeds of unrest were planted.

Our next scheduled session was weird. It was with Warner Brothers artist Taj Mahal with his guitarist Jesse "Ed the Indian" Davis, whom Charlie and I both knew from Hollywood. Taj Mahal's first record had the real shit. There was that magic guitarist again, an unforgettable name, Ry Cooder, the guy from crazy Dale Hawkins's record who had showed up in Captain Beefheart's Magic Band on the classic California art rock recording *Safe as Milk* (containing "Autumn's Child," a rare ballad and my favorite piece by the good Captain).

We jumped in bed with Taj Mahal. He played the crap out of an old green-gray National Steel-Bodied Standard guitar. He shucked and jived in his African robes, "dancing out the beat" when Sammy had trouble coming in on the "up," not the "down" beat, a weakness that reared its ugly head in the future. Jesse and Charlie bonded in the brotherhood of guitar. Charlie was inordinately proud of his Indian blood. If he was high enough, he turned red. We cut half a dozen good tracks. The record never came out. Soon afterward, Taj disappeared for a while somewhere on the Continent.

We waited for the other shoe to fall. Rumors of working with Bob Dylan circulated but we had yet to really work with Wexler or Dowd. We floundered in the new stereo earphones, feeling like we were floating in space. Then things got real serious in a hurry.

We were booked to record with Aretha Franklin, the Queen of Soul, arguably Wexler's most significant artist. Her recordings at Muscle Shoals resulted in big hits, but the situation had been volatile, replete with racism and sexual harassment. The story wasn't told and certain names were spoken in only whispers. She had supposedly sworn never to record in the South with redneck soul musicians again. We worried Aretha wouldn't show if she found out we were white boys.

We were out on the damned boat. I hooked a hammerhead shark when the radiophone brought word Aretha had landed. Everyone panicked. After much hurry and many phone calls, we convened at Criteria, ready as we would ever be for Lady Soul. Aretha traveled with a thirty-person entourage in a caravan of limousines. It looked like a funeral. They parked on the grass in front of the studio, kept the motors running, the doors open, and the lights on.

At that time in the R&B community, it was hip to associate with Sam Cooke's relatives. Aretha had two, including a twelve-year-old boy who sat beside her on the custom piano bench, swinging his feet which failed to reach the floor. It was quite a show. She played the huge studio piano with a tray of little prepackaged tin can gin drinks, Orange Tommies, in front of her on the music rack.

It took a while to get started, but once she heard us play, she was all smiles. Wexler was pleased and relieved. Wexler and Dowd added Arif Mardin, an over-trained Turkish jazz producer who spoke like Bela Lugosi doing Dracula, to the production gumbo. They buzzed around, trying to accommodate the Aretha situation. All we musicians really had to do was follow her lead.

Aretha Franklin is a force of nature. Her pure gospel voice, trained from childhood by her famous pastor father, and her unbelievable mastery of the piano keyboard are devastating to experience firsthand. Her chubby fingers are capable of making fourteen-note chord patterns, two notes with each thumb and little finger. I was as useless as tits on a mule. But Aretha reacted to my gold tooth and Moroccan floor length robe. I played Wurlitzer and Fender Rhodes. Utley hid behind his B3 and silently prayed for help.

On the first song, as our luck would have it, we hit the old upbeat intro problem we had with Taj Mahal. Over and over, Sammy missed the pickup. Finally Aretha said something about "trouble with the drummer." Sammy turned red as a fire engine. He sucked it up and nailed the tune. *Spirit in the Dark* became our biggest chart hit.

Charlie and I had developed a code. If we ran up on jazz chords beyond my normal triad, Charlie gave me the outside note on the sly. If Charlie put on his sunglasses, I knew to look out; if he said he wanted to play "acoustic" in the vocal booth, it meant I should play electric guitar so Charlie could nap. When I saw him put on his shades during the Aretha session, I couldn't believe it. Sure enough, he said, "I'm going into the vocal booth and play acoustic." O.K., I thought. Aretha had a black guitarist with her, but I figured I had better follow Charlie's lead, so I strapped on my new Gibson 335. I pulled it off, moving seventh chords up and down the neck of the hollow-bodied jazz guitar like I knew what I was doing. The result was "Don't Play That Song," which won Aretha the Grammy for Best Female R&B Vocal Performance.

To get the track and live vocal for "The Thrill is Gone," we cut down to piano, bass, and drums. Wexler kept talking about the solo, anticipating Freeman's contribution. Duane Allman had recently done an over-the-top outro for Wilson Pickett's "Hey Jude." Wexler went on and on about it. Whatever Charlie was going to do, I knew it would be far from Duane. By the time they got the track and were ready to overdub, Charlie already had his shades on. Charlie had a childhood injury of cut tendons in his left arm that put a twist in his grip resulting in a funny tension on his guitar strings. He had to tune his instrument into the pressure put on his strings by his slightly turned left hand. When he drank a little too much, the muscles in his forearm relaxed and his guitar went out of tune. Charlie said his guitar was "getting drunk." This was already the case.

As Wexler churned with anticipation, the tape started. During the first verse, he didn't even touch his instrument; it buzzed, un-grounded in his lap. Top of the second verse, he answered the vocal with slightly out-of-tune Wes Montgomery octaves. I thought Wexler was going to have a heart attack. When it played back, Wexler said, "Baby, believe me, I have worked with the finest guitarists of two generations. Charlie Freeman is the only one who can take a true solo." Everybody in the room thought, "What about Reggie Young?" As if reading our minds, Wexler said, "And that includes Reggie."

Charlie soloed like a saxophone player. I think that was what Wexler thought. Charlie was the man.

The Dixie Flyers did a five-day week with each artist, with a possible sixth day if needed. Aretha didn't want to stop, but we were booked with jazz artist Carmen McRae the next week. Aretha moved into the larger "A" studio, and brought in Cornell Dupree and a hodgepodge rhythm section to keep her going. We had held our own and survived the Aretha-meets-the-white-boys test.

Carmen McRae was great: dressed to the teeth, multi-shaded, theatrical lipstick, full makeup replete with false eyelashes, and lacquered wig with huge golden gypsy earrings. She worked from sheet music, a five-staff orchestral score. We made chord charts from demo tapes, as always. She was puzzled. "Hey, Arif?" she asked. "What are they doing?" referring to our primitive practice.

"They are making chord charts," he replied in perfect Turkish vampire.

Still puzzled, Carmen said, "Won't it sound funny if all they play are chords?"

"Wait and see," replied the Lord of Darkness.

We got the first cut right away and went to the second song. Carmen McRae said to Arif, by then safely in the control room, "Hey Arif? Is this how Aretha does it?"

"Yes," he answered over the talkback.

"Shiii-iiit," she said. "This is easy."

That first night, out of respect, Charlie and I smoked a joint in the parking lot, rather than firing it up in our "recovery room." We noticed we were not alone. Someone was at the other end of the parking lot, also smoking. Carmen McRae! She had a brother in Jamaica who sent her the good ganja. She relaxed right away.

Second day she showed up with her head in a rag and wearing house shoes. She told us stories about being backstage with Billie Holliday and tying her arm off so she could shoot up.

It was my favorite session, though they had us cut two or three Tony Joe White songs (incredibly inappropriate for the artist), and despite Arif Mardin's mindless, condescending attitude and obvious contempt for us. It pissed Mardin off that our process was primitive and ignorant, but efficient.

There are two cuts on the album *Just a Little Lovin'* that remain my favorite work for Atlantic. On "Live the Life I Love" and the Beatles' "Something," my piano intro to the solo turns into King Curtis with the New York Symphony strings.

Our next record was our first full-on production of an official Atlantic artist, Lulu, a former child star from England who recently had been #1 on the U.S. pop charts with the movie theme "To Sir with Love." We got along great with Lulu, who was a redneck at heart. She killed the country songs. We made an interesting album titled *Melody Fair*. "Hum a Song

(From Your Heart)" by Lulu and the Dixie Flyers topped out at thirty on
Billboard's Hot 100 pop chart. We were on our way.

Let me add that when Dowd moved to Miami full-time, and Wexler
started splitting his time between Treasure Isle and the Hamptons, Atlantic South seemed like a good idea to them. But not to Wexler's partner
Ahmet Ertegun, to whom it was already a failure. It was tough. Wexler
told us one thing and Dowd told us another. Most of the time, it didn't
make sense. We used different terminology. Wexler repeatedly talked
about the "channel" and the "middle 8" when we worked in twelve-bar
patterns. I never did find out what a "channel" was.

Wexler and I had begun to get tight at the Stones session. He was
another giant among men, like Sam Phillips. However, our friendship put
me in the position of speaking for the band. The band was freaked out.
Every time the weekly paychecks were late, the band called me. I had to
call the company. If the earphones were shit, which they were, the band
bitched and moaned to me. I had to complain to Tom Dowd, whose job
it was to solve problems. It put an early strain on my relationship with
Dowd, whom I admired tremendously.

Wexler encouraged us to develop our own group artist project. He
envisioned a mix between Booker T and the MGs and The Band. Charlie
and I had worked on songs since Soldiers of the Cross. Sammy wanted
to be the Bill Black Combo, and his old lady wanted us to cut publishing
demos.

Wexler was a big believer in publicity. He brought in New York rock
writers to interview the strange new Southern swamp music rhythm
section. Lisa Robinson interviewed Charlie and me for *Hit Parader*. We
formed a friendship that carried into the future.

Enter Jake the Snake, who worked for the video production company
at Criteria Studio. He was the first person I saw with a gold coke spoon
hung around his neck. Previously, I found cocaine boring. It gave me a
supernormal feeling I avoided. Charlie loved it. He could stay awake and
drink. Boring though it was, I was willing to take my share. I still dream
about it. I can taste it in my sleep, but I haven't done any since a Keith
Richards session in Memphis nearly twenty years ago. Charlie said it was
the Devil.

Miami had yet to become coke capital of America, as it did with the
birth of disco and the arrival of Crosby, Stills, Nash, and Young, but Jake
the Snake had plenty. It gave the band an edge. Sammy liked it because it

was like speed. There are rare examples of the Flyers-on-coke where we are on the same page and the groove is intense.

After fumbling around, looking for a direction acceptable to one and all, our next company session was with Brook Benton. The Cold Grits's only hit was Brook Benton's "Rainy Night in Georgia." Atlantic wanted to follow it up, but Brook was so happy to be current and pertinent again he couldn't have given less of a shit. He stood in the middle of the tracking floor, singing into a handheld mic, and drinking Scotch out of a hip flask. The more lubricated he became, the more he turned into Kingfish from *Amos and Andy*. "Hello dere, brother Andy," he said into the microphone. "How is you doin'?"

Arif was the producer. I questioned his familiarity with the old black radio/TV show, which my old teacher, Alec, referred to as "that ol' funny show." Between Benton's Kingfish and Arif's Dracula, the interchange between the control room and artist was hysterical. We bit our tongues. The happier Brook Benton got, the more he would slip into "Saturday Night Fish Fry," in his Kingfish voice. It was by far the best thing we hit on in the session but too racially offensive for the Turkish producer to tape.

Next came Sam and Dave. We had heard horror stories, tough tales of the Soul Men who ate white boy musicians for lunch. But with the backwards good luck of the Dixie Flyers, we came closest to doing our thing (breaking the prevailing curse of Leland Rogers) on the Sam and Dave date. Unfortunately, the record did not come out for twenty years and then in Japan, which is another story.

Sam and Dave were slumlords in Miami Central, the for-real hood. They feuded notoriously and only tolerated each other's presence when doing the act. I see nothing wrong with this situation; the Dixie Flyers were not friends. We seldom interacted socially. When we did, it was forced and unpleasant. But when somebody counted to four, we were there. We anticipated every curve and corner. We subdivided the space in a twelve-bar structure without saying a word. Even Sammy, who disliked or mistrusted everything that I represented, told me, "Man, I never had anybody play the turnarounds with me before." It was true and as close to a compliment as he could get.

We blew Sam and Dave's socks off. They canceled other work and cut for a second week. On one song, "Knock It out of the Park," we hit our old Sounds of Memphis syncopated retro groove with the wah-wah Clavinet and machine-gun guitar. Another soul ballad, "When a Woman Needs a Man, She Needs a Soul Man," had hit written all over it.

Sam and Dave, like Brook Benton, never went into the vocal booth. They worked handheld microphones back to the rhythm section, facing the control room glass like a live nightclub performance. I have never seen another performer do it, yet it seemed so natural. They performed for Wexler and an unseen audience of future listeners. "When a Woman Needs a Man, She Needs a Soul Man" was such a performance that they threw their mics down, and walked out to an imaginary audience's applause and screams. They walked down the hallway, out the front door, got into their cars, and drove away. Elvis has left the building.

Dave's car was an XKE roadster with an embossed leather top that read "Soul Man" in print only visible from an overhead helicopter. Dave took more dope than any other human I ever witnessed. Charlie and I followed him into the bathroom and watched him unfold two $100 bills on top of the urinal, one full of coke and the other with glowing blue heroin. Without removing his shades, he bent over and hit each side of his huge nose with controlled substances. He turned, went out of the john, and sang as if he had just brushed his teeth.

Sadly, Dave is no longer with us. He was the fast-dancing, funky, low-harmony singing Soul Man, the second best R&B voice I ever experienced, the first being James Carr.

The Sam and Dave session turned out so well, Sam and Dave broke up. They could not face touring. As with Taj Mahal, some of our best work remained unheard. Fate? Destiny? Or just hoodoo?

Bonnie and Delaney Bramlett came and recorded with their own band. Bobby Whitlock from Memphis, the B3 player, sang high harmony. He had been an angel-voiced, teenage Memphis star with several bands when Delaney found him before their first Stax recording. The high voice listeners assumed is Bonnie is, in fact, Bobby. They also carried Jerry Scheff on bass and Ronnie Tutt on drums, who eventually became Elvis's backup band in Vegas. We knew Tutt as an Ivy League jazz drummer from Memphis who worked on the Pepper-Tanner jingle session assembly line, supercilious and square as a box. I had previously engineered an Eddie Hubbard session, where Tutt played drums in Bermuda shorts watching a football game on a portable TV on his floor tom. This could not be the same guy. But it was. He was Creason's idol. Sammy's post-jazzoid idea of how to play rock 'n' roll drums was to imitate Tutt. He couldn't believe the new Ron Tutt that showed up. The new model had hair to the middle of his back and a new, teenaged hippie wife. It was too much for Creason to handle. Creason also had a problem with the fact Delaney requested Tommy and me for the session since he knew us from Leon's house in Hollywood. Delaney was a good old Mississippi boy with incredible drive and ambition. Bonnie was equally dynamic. They could sing their asses off. Add the almost superhuman choirboy top end Whitlock supplied, and you have unequaled southern soul vocal power. Delaney was also a bandleader in the biblical sense of the word.

Wexler produced a studio visit from Little Richard, the Architect of Rock 'n' Roll. Richard didn't want to play but Wexler coerced him to the piano. Suddenly, everybody was a guitar player. Engineers, assistants, and random people, all would-be guitar players, wandering the hall appeared to say they had played with Little Richard. We cut "Miss Ann" before Little Richard escaped. Richard did not like Tutt. As good as Ronnie was, he was white as Wonder Bread. He does a multiple-impact, continuous sixteenth-note roll that seems poised on top of the beat, conspicuously un-funky.

Delaney was not happy with Scheff and Tutt, and fired them after the Little Richard incident. He overdubbed Tommy McClure, top to bottom, on every track, while the crew packed the band's gear. Sammy hated the whole thing, being excluded and seeing his idol with feet of clay. There was an additional piece of bad luck. Delaney's roadies took Charlie Freeman's beloved and irreplaceable Gibson 355. Mac Emerson, the studio owner, crawled up his own asshole apologizing and swore to make good. I went with Charlie downtown to Ace Music Store to look for a replacement. Charlie asked if they had a Gibson stereo, like B.B. King played. They showed him a room full of Gibson stereos. He didn't like any of them. He found a '58 Les Paul Custom he liked, but it was not for sale. He made Atlantic rent it. It was heavy for Charlie's light frame, but he liked the way it played. Atlantic shipped guitars in from New York and elsewhere, but Charlie would have none of them. It went from bad to worse.

The Bob Dylan session almost happened. We heard he had looked for us in Memphis but we were already gone. Wexler saw Dylan as the ultimate American artist. He was to record at Criteria. This was our shot. Charlie and I showed up early. Dylan was a Columbia artist and CBS was a tight union house. All Columbia artists were required to use a Columbia house engineer. Two Columbia engineers were in the reception room when we walked in. There were also two bodyguards with what looked like gun cases. Everybody was there but Bob Dylan. His manager, Albert Grossman, the Benjamin Franklin-lookalike godfather/manager of hippieville, had pulled the plug. Grossman and Wexler had negotiated artist rights for the *Woodstock* album, on which none of Grossman's artists appeared. As revenge he strung Jerry along and then canceled. That was it for the Dixie Flyers. The handwriting on the wall glowed in the dark.

Chapter 40

"ONE MORE SILVER DOLLAR"
(1970)

Florida wasn't all work. We hung out in the Grove whenever we could. Charlie Brown worked for Haas, the famous snake doctor at Serpentarium, his snake ranch in the Everglades, where Haas experimented with poisonous snake venom as a cure for various diseases. The main building's entrance was through a huge King Cobra. Charlie also had an old smuggler friend, now a celebrity bartender at the Light House, a luxury motel in Key West. We would hide out there with our wives, spending the day drinking Singapore Slings and listening to tall tales of drug running in the Caribbean.

We started to have visitors from home. Lee Baker, fresh out of prison, showed up with Eugene Wilkins, little brother to the screamer from Blue Ridge who had lifted my arrangement for "Money Honey." They were looking for a record deal. Baker was ready to conquer the world after completing a stint in the Lexington drug rehabilitation facility, in order to avoid hard time in the Federal pen. They hung out for a few days, soaked up the Miami sun and weed supply, and met Wexler. Their band, Moloch, was a little too hard for Jerry. They ended up on Stax.

Charlie and I played off-the-books Fred Neil sessions, recorded in an old church in the Grove with a Scully four-track and a Shure mixer. After each session Fred erased the tape. There was more and more cocaine.

Our next official session was with an old Gulf Coast rocker, Dick Holler, who had been the bandleader for Jimmy Clanton, Ace Records' star white boy. Holler wrote the novelty hit "Snoopy and the Red Baron," the garage band classic "Double Shot of My Baby's Love," and the last hit for Dion, "Abraham, Martin, and John," which Wexler had just cut on Wilson Pickett, altering lyrics to emphasize the civil rights movement. In order to change the lyrics, Atlantic signed Holler, the song's original author. Phil Gernhard, who had worked with the Bellamy Brothers and whose business card read "South Florida's Most Successful Producer," was producing. He wanted to make records for grocery-store sack boys instead of twelve-year-old girls. On Wednesday Dion, of Dion and the Belmonts, showed up unheralded, and slam, bam, thank you ma'am, we recorded "Your Own Back Yard," an anti-drug anthem, for Warner Brothers. When it came out with our name on it, Charlie didn't remember it and claimed it wasn't us. Ironically, it was our last chart record.

My listening room was subterranean, literally below sea level. One day, I listened to my treasures after a record-buying orgy in Coral Gables. I discovered Ry Cooder's debut album. The cover displayed a tall black caped figure leaning against a shining silver Airstream trailer, looking like a young Gary Cooper. Cooder had played on the Dale Hawkins album, Captain Beefheart's *Safe as Milk*, and with Taj Mahal in the band Rising Sons. The music was from Mars: backwards reverse suspension, convoluted mountain melody spun together into a soup of folk-oriented space blues sung with a dry, croaking, cartoonish sarcasm. We had finished Aretha Franklin and Sam and Dave. Not bad, but I couldn't help wishing I was working on this high-end Hollywood art rock.

Wexler pushed for a Dixie Flyers record. We recorded ourselves for a week. To Sammy's chagrin, I was the band's de facto vocalist. I pushed Utley to sing but he gave up after one attempt. In Memphis Charlie and I had written blues rock songs for Soldiers of the Cross. One had morphed into a Led Zeppelin–like screamer, "Old Time Used to Be," a title we got from Duane Allman. It contained a midsection breakdown to guitar and vocal, a classic sing, sing, play, play, Plant and Page extended call and response, where the band fell out for a whole verse leaving just me and Charlie, leading up to a big crescendo explosion where the band kicked in for a final climactic verse. The band broke down with no problem. When we punched in the overdubbed guitar and vocal section, one track was left out of sync. I sang through a Vox guitar amp with heavy vibrato in which one vocal track was heavily affected and one was clean. Charlie's guitar bled into the amped vocal. When the engineer hit the record button, the out of sync situation created a psychedelic delay factor; the vocal dragged behind the guitar, like a stuck-in-the-mud motif. We heard it and responded intuitively. When it was over, the band failed to kick in, sitting there with their mouths open. It was spectacular. When we played it in the control room, the band listened in silence. Finally Sammy said, "If we put that out on a record, all my friends back in Jonesboro will think I came down here and started taking drugs."

Without thinking, I replied, "Well, Sammy, you did." McClure didn't talk to Charlie or me for three days before deciding it was cool. Not Sammy. Never. It drove the band apart.

To make it worse, Dowd loved it. Tension eased between Tom and me. He had a stepson from his first marriage with a drug problem. They were having trouble getting him into a rehab program. My old friend from Baylor, Tommy Rodman, was in New York working at Phoenix House, a Synanon-based addiction treatment center specializing in an experimental program treating drug addiction as a disease. I called and got the kid accepted. Dowd was grateful and warmed up to me, despite the space between his cold, hard, logical physics background and my voodoo-centric, Baylor Theatre–style creativity. We still argued about the relative importance of moon phases and elevation above sea level as applied to recording, but it was friendlier.

The Allman Brothers were in Studio A, working on their second Atlantic/Capricorn album. It was really good. They recorded live instrumental tracks and overdubbed lead guitars and vocals. I remembered one of their two drummers, Butch Trucks, from his first session at Ardent on National. I don't think he remembered me. Duane was super friendly, as usual. It was the first time I met his little brother Gregg, whose voice still held traces of the great John Hurley, who had trained them in Nashville. I wondered if John had used the mic cord technique I witnessed on Gregg. Duane ran a tight operation, keeping his band on a short leash.

One morning I walked into the studio, and Dowd was behind the receptionist's desk. "Dickinson," he called out. "Just the man I need." What was he up to? "We're doing vocals and we need a falsetto on high harmony. You've got a falsetto. Come in here and help us out."

I played along. I knew he didn't really want me to sing but didn't know what he actually wanted. I followed him into Studio A. Gregg and their guest harmonica player, Ace, gathered around the microphone behind a windowed baffle. They looked nervous. Dowd started the tape. I got my first taste of "Midnight Rider." It got to the release before the hook; the melody went up a full octave. Gregg wasn't quite getting up to the note on "One more silver dollar." I hemmed and hawed but clearly could not get close to the note. Then I realized what Dowd wanted. I pulled out a joint, lit it up, and handed it to Gregg. He grinned and looked relieved. Soon he sang the now-familiar high note, like a lonesome coyote in the Georgia piney woods on a dark night. When he sings the note today, he stays in the lower register of the lower octave. Dowd, the master of compromise, had triumphed again.

Since Dylan's no-show, Wexler had pulled back from the Dixie Flyers. We started working with the salt-and-pepper "B" team, Dave Crawford and Brad Shapiro. Brad was funny and later enjoyed success with Millie Jackson, but Crawford, a bitter black man who got drunk during sessions, wanted to play piano. We didn't like each other. We recorded with Dee Dee Warwick (Dionne's sister) and "Little" Esther Phillips, who both had good moments, but neither record was particularly good. One Saturday morning we did an industrial film for Dowd, his first venture into film. It was not an Atlantic project. It was for the Playboy Club, showing Bunnies shooting pool with lots of phallic pool cue imagery and balls rolling in slow motion on green felt. We also did demos for Toni Wine, who performed the black girl's voice in the Archies. Her song "Groovy Kind of Love" (recorded by Wayne Fontana and the Mindbenders) had reached #1 on the charts. She played Wexler like a cheap guitar. It was cool to watch this super sharp lady manipulate the old master. She was cold as ice and worked the rhythm section like a consummate pro. We were doing "busy" work, obviously marking time, moving ever lower on Wexler's priority list.

One day out on the *Big A*, Wexler asked me the question that would drive the final nail in the coffin of my time with the Dixie Flyers: "Baby, do you think Sam the Sham has another hit in him?"

Sam the fucking Sham! I told Jerry, "Yes." I truthfully figured he probably had another one in him, but lived to regret it.

Sam showed up on a green Harley Hog with a white girl and three ounces of cocaine. Just what we needed. He was way too focused and chomping at the bit. The session was a nightmare. Sam's bullshit didn't go over with Dowd, and Wexler backed further away from the project. Duane Allman was called in to put more muscle in the session. With Sky Dog came the heroin. Duane and Charlie brought out the worst in each other.

First, we cut a single, a Tex-Mex version of Kris Kristofferson's "Me and Bobby McGee." I turned Charlie on to Kristofferson's first album with Donny Fritts, Billy Swan, and the guitarist from the Lovin' Spoonful. Charlie loved it. He said, "This is the best rock 'n' roll band in America."

"Charlie," I said. "They don't even have a drummer."

"They don't need a drummer."

Our Sam the Sham version of "Bobby McGee" came out only weeks before Janis Joplin's hit. Once again, a day late and a fucking dollar short.

The Dixie Flyers were on the downbound train. Added to the psycho-drama of this seemingly endless session from hell, we had other problems: two redheaded women. Claudia and her nothing-happening publishing company were bad, but McClure's wife was also a fiery redhead ready to boil over. She hated Miami. Tommy had a great job and was making more money than ever, but she was hell-bent on returning to Memphis and finally did. Tommy drove two thousand miles weekly to be with her until it finally exploded. One Friday night at Freeman's house, Tommy slammed his right fist into a cast iron drainpipe and shattered his knuckles.

Wife and I had enjoyed a little purple mescaline the night before, and were wrapped in Morpheus's sweet arms when Freeman and McClure's clatter arose on the lawn. T. Tommy McClure is a tall, thin, country-fried version of Victor Mature, replete with iron-gray hair, a youthful face, a serial killer's cold grey eyes, and is the best Fender bass player with whom it has ever been my privilege to work. He wept like a child and held his right hand, bandaged in a wet T-shirt. Charley said, "We've got to get Tommy to the emergency room. He broke his hand." I stood wrapped in a zebra-striped sheet.

"Shit," I replied, looking around for my jeans. McClure sobbed on the sectional couch. The bottled water deliveryman came to the door. Tommy pointed his broken hand at the man carrying the huge plastic watercooler bottle and screamed, "That's the only happy man in this house." Charlie restrained him one-handed. "The only God damned happy man!" Tommy bellowed. The water deliveryman disappeared. We never saw him again. He didn't even come back for the empty.

We put Tommy up in the yellow sled's back seat and headed for the hospital, whose whereabouts was vague if not unknown. I was still trip-ping. Our first stop was at the Veteran's Hospital. Tommy said, "I knew we were in trouble when I seen the footprints painted on the floor!"

When we arrived at Miami General Hospital's emergency room, we discovered a gateway to Hell from an Elmore Leonard novel: bright, in-candescent lighting, a human cattle call with bodies everywhere. Like my grandmother's butcher shop, you took a number and waited your turn. Snot-nosed babies crawled unattended around ancient retiree mummies huddled in inhuman positions on the plastic seats. People writhed in pain. A man on the telephone held a bloody towel to his throat, which was cut from ear to ear. We waited with the other lost souls. Tommy moaned, increasingly upset. Charlie sat silently, chewing on his mustache, his emotions a mystery behind his black sunglasses. I shivered in the air-conditioned, freezing cold, Miami fashion. I had dressed quickly in jeans, sandals, and a purple wife beater undershirt. We looked like hard cases, even here. We moved to a private space behind sliding curtains. Finally a nurse with a clipboard and stethoscope asked, "Which one is the patient?" A good question. We pointed to Tommy.

She took Tommy to the examination room. He returned with a white plaster cast halfway up his right arm and a big bottle of pain pills. His hypnotic, medicated daze was the calmest I had seen him in weeks. He must have felt a great need to be off the unending Sam the Sham session. Luckily, Butch Boehm and Freddy Hester, a jazz upright bass player, were visiting from Memphis. Freddy played out the date, and Sam the Sham finally split after an unfortunate incident with Dowd and a handgun in the studio. Typically, Sam had taken it too far and had to be treated like a child. He made himself scarce, leaving his Harley-Davidson with Charlie. Great idea.

Charlie wrecked Sam the Sham's Hog on a midnight run down the Keys. The incident involved an encounter with a homosexual truck driver, culminating in the unforgettable line, "If there's anything I like better than butt-fucking, it's bare knuckles man-to-man." Charlie escaped virtually intact. Sam's motorcycle lay in a heap in Freeman's driveway. He buried what was left of the cocaine in his backyard. His house had belonged to a rich Peruvian living in exile. Lavishly landscaped, with exotic fauna that had gone to seed, it looked like a haunted fairyland, a drug-induced dream world set apart from reality.

Adding to the chaos, Stanley Booth came to visit. Stanley was working on his Rolling Stones biography, as he would for the next decade. He wrote of his trip to Miami: "I've seen a wild man eat a snake, watched a monkey fuck a football. I've been on the road with the Rolling Stones, but I've never seen anything crazier than Charlie Freeman's house in Miami."

Wexler brought the Memphis Horns to do Sam the Sham overdubs. In Memphis, the Horns were Wayne Jackson and Andrew Love, with an occasional baritone sax. Dowd preferred to work with a four-piece section. Wayne added trombonist Jack Hale, an old-school jazz cat who played in Elvis's stage band, and Ed Logan, a redneck tenor sax man. Logan and Charlie hated each other. Ed called Charlie a communist, which he wasn't. Charlie called Logan a Nazi, which he was. The Horns were too much for Sam's low rent, Tex-Mex, beer joint music. Like a tuxedo on a hog, it just didn't fit.

The horn session gave us time to work on the McClure problem. Tommy's wife was back in Memphis, and Tommy was living in a codeine daze at Charlie's house. We called the old bass player from Cold Grits. He took one look, and wisely declined. We called Duck Dunn. We were desperate; the Hawk was coming. Ronnie Hawkins was a god to Freeman, who saw him with the Hawks when the great Fred Carter played guitar, before Robbie Robertson took over and they became The Band.

Hawkins showed up early, wisely giving himself time to acclimatize. Atlantic housed their artists at the Thunderbird Inn on the beach. Hawkins got a suite. I picked him up. On the way to Freeman's jungle house, Ronnie bought a cardboard crate full of booze, including a red-satin-boxed decanter of Metaxa brandy, his personal favorite. Charlie and Hawkins got on like gangbusters. Thus began one of my last adventures with the Dixie Flyers.

Ed Kollis and Donald Crews were in town. Don was Chips Moman's bean farming partner in American Studio, and Kollis, one of the greatest harmonica players I ever heard, was Chips's engineer on *Elvis in Memphis*. He truly transcended his instrument. His superbly musical phrases sounded like songs sung in Hell. I told Ed about the Hawkins session, and hired him without thinking to ask permission. Ed showed up at Charlie's that night. McClure was zoned out on pain pills, his gray eyes unfocused like a zombie from a forties B movie. He sat and stared.

For all his bravado, Hawkins was notorious for a no-drugs policy with his musicians. Even at Muscle Shoals, there was plenty of nightly drinking but substance abuse was strictly on the sly. Ronnie realized this was a different deal. When in Rome . . . We drank Metaxa brandy. Around midnight we were standing in Charlie's exotically landscaped backyard, using Sam the Sham's crippled motorcycle's headlights to look for the buried cocaine. I remember an illustration from Edgar Allen Poe's "The Gold Bug," wherein lanterns light the culprits digging beneath the sign of the skull. It was a great night.

Duane Allman showed up the next day. He was also at the Thunderbird. Charlie and I went to welcome him. Duane had the smack. I found cocaine boring. Heroin is a different story. It's like going to the moon with Jesus, at least the first time. Within minutes, Freeman and I were on our lunar journey. After I couldn't tell how much time, Hawkins knocked on the door. I was momentarily confused about his reaction to the dope: "Where is it? What is it? How do you do it?" Within seconds, Hawkins crossed the room, knelt at the nightstand, and inhaled heroin. We entered a warm and friendly realm of junkie brotherhood. Duane called room service and ordered Singapore Slings. He said, "Honey, I don't care how many it is. Just fill up the tray."

Hawkins realized this was his moment. His backup band, now working with Dylan, had gone into historic rock stardom. This was his last record for Atlantic. He was living larger than life in Canada, expatriated from the very thing that he represented.

We cut the session in studio A, where the Allman Brothers had recorded. Playing with Duck was different. He played fully in front of the beat, pulling the drums behind him. Duane was on fire. He loved playing with Charlie. They were kindred souls. Hawkins was a senior member of the old school. Duane had nothing but respect for him. Ed Kollis was brilliant as usual, playing a classic solo on "Lonely Weekends." We got an enormous piece of "Red Rooster Blues" at light speed. I hammered the eighth notes like a jackhammer. Freeman destroyed the solo back and forth with Duane. My favorite cut was "Treasure of Love," with Freeman on acoustic and Allman playing his best Lowman Pauling doowop fills. Hawkins sang like his heart was breaking.

On the way to the studio one afternoon, I picked up Charlie at the jungle house and Duane at the Thunderbird. We discussed the conflict Charlie and I created with our Led Zeppelin experiment, and how Miami sucked. Duane was behind me in my yellow muscle car. He leaned forward close, and said, "You know, man, you ought to go to Wexler. Do what I did when I was playing in Muscle Shoals. Go to Wexler and tell him you can't play with these rednecks anymore." Charlie sat silent behind his sunglasses. "Tell him you want your own band," he added.

"That's the trouble," I said. "This is my band."

Last night of the session, Hawkins told a great story. Ronnie described moving to Toronto: "I came to live in a rooming house and let me tell you, boys, it was rank. The landlady's old man was a wino. He'd go off on a binge, and stay gone for days. When he finally came back, they'd prop him up in a rocking chair in the front room. He'd sit there not rockin' or nothing. Just sat there with a shawl over his shoulders and shake. He had the D.T.'s so bad you had to watch what you said around him. Grease, for instance. The word 'grease.' If you said 'grease,' he'd commence to heave.

"On top of that, the old lady had a puking dog. Had to stay on the porch 'cause the old man couldn't stand the sight of him. So the dog is on the porch spitting up and the old man sitting in the front room, shaking and twitching. Finally I saved up enough money to move. I go down to the front room real quiet, the old man is sitting there, vibrating. I poured a jar of apple sauce on the rug where he couldn't see and said, 'Looky here, Henry, the dog has done puked up on the rug.' Henry looked around and started to heave. 'I believe I'll eat it,' and I fell down on my knees and start rubbing it in my beard."

As a child you read fairy tales about giants. Your parents and teachers tell you all of that is not real. If you are lucky, you meet a man who proves your parents and teachers wrong.

The scene was crazy. The drugs became more exotic. Charlie got some opium but was disappointed it didn't give him visions of tigers. He gave it to me. I liked it. Dowd had sent me to a doctor who gave me five hundred yellow jackets, Tuinal, perhaps my favorite sedative, always capable of getting forty-five minutes of hot guitar out of Charlie before he went into a coma. I would take a couple at night after the session, and sink to the bottom of our tide pool, the best escape from the goddamned no-see-ums, the tiny sandflies permeating the false turf of Miami Beach, a manmade landfill. I started to truly hate Miami, the elephants' graveyard where old Yankees came to die. Old people jumped into traffic trying to commit suicide at your expense. We lived so close to the 163rd Street mall that high crime lights illuminated our home with an unceasing orange glow. The seasons never changed. Spring? Nothing. The leaves didn't fall. All you had to look forward to was hurricane season, which I found hard to anticipate with great joy. The place sucked. Drugs and death surrounded us. Next to the studio, on the so-called Dixie Highway, was a funeral home, which emitted a faint foul aroma. Between the studio and my house was a huge cemetery with a section for dead circus performers who wintered in Miami. There were statues of elephants, giraffes, lions, and tigers standing as silent mourners. It gave me the creeps. I passed it every day.

Summer was a pressure cooker. The steamy nights sucked my soul. Going to Texas was a nightmare; Miami was a mistake. I longed to see the river, the bluffs, and the "negro streets at dawn." This was the most concentrated period of playing music in my life. I was chopped out like a racehorse, playing more and better than ever. Yet I had no control. It would erupt in the middle of a session. It scared me. I went to Tom. "You've got some time off coming," he said. "You and Charlie take your wives and go down to the Keys and do whatever you do. We'll talk when you get back."

That's what we did. Key West is sad. Like Coconut Grove, it must have been like paradise, with bars where Ernest Hemingway drank, when it was a sleepy fishing village. Commercialization and tourist traffic had consumed the community. When we returned to Miami Beach, the ship hit the sand. Carol Freeman told Mary Lindsay that Claudia Creason claimed the rhythm section's "problem" was that Tom Dowd hated me. As soon as Mary Lindsay told me, I phoned Wexler. "I hear there's a problem and it's me."

Band meeting. We would meet at Jerry's the next day. I called Dowd. I asked him to show up at the band meeting. He said, "I owe you that."

Apparently Sammy and good old Duck Dunn had been playing golf with Dowd. I am basically offended by musicians playing golf. It's a little too Nashville for me. During this alleged game, Sammy and Duck saw it fit to indulge in the old musician game of badmouth the band. Sammy is one thing. I can understand that from his point of view; I was a thorn in his flesh. God only knows what his wife said. But Duck Dunn? I never did anything to Duck Dunn but hire him. At Wexler's I stated, "If I am the problem, then let me offer the solution. I'm out."

Jerry jumped up, shook his head, and flapped his hands, "Baby, I refuse to talk about this."

We converted the remaining six months of my Dixie Flyer employment agreement to an artist contract entailing two separate projects: my solo project, to be recorded wherever I wanted, and the band's instrumental album as conceived by Sammy to be recorded at Criteria. The company would accept or reject either or both albums. I would be paid out as contracted, and Atlantic would pay for my sessions. I felt a great relief. There is an incredible feeling of freedom associated with quitting, a decision that cannot be undone. Life had changed. Mary Lindsay and I were going back to Memphis.

McClure said, "Let me get this straight. You're going home and they are paying you to make your own record, and I'm staying here and cutting sessions for the same money. I'd say you made a pretty good deal."

I played the Petula Clark session for *Warm and Tender* before I left. Everybody walked on eggshells. Dowd carefully avoided all conflict. Years later, I read it was Clark's favorite record.

We drove home. On a foggy night, we followed an eighteen-wheeler into Macon, Georgia. The back of the truck read, "Eternity Coffin Company—Satisfaction Guaranteed." It was good to be going home. Good to have the infighting and politics of the Dixie Flyers behind me, propelling me into an unknown future. Would I have to go to the end of the line? The Atlantic job had come from nowhere. I had no idea what awaited in Memphis. I had a guaranteed income for six months, and a budget for my own album. Before we left, Utley came to me, and tearfully asked me not to go. Sammy was man enough to say, "I don't know what happened, man. But I'm sorry." Only Charlie said nothing. I could never know to what extent the whole episode was Dowd "solving problems." His and mine.

We spent the night in Macon. Duane Allman had set up an appointment for me to meet Phil Walden at Capricorn Records in the morning. We sniffed armpits for a couple of hours and I hit the road. I liked Phil but it didn't feel right. I have never felt sorry. I had a job, a budget, and a grocery bag full of Colombian pot. Showtime!

Chapter 41

RETURN OF THE PHANTOM
(1970–71)

We stayed with my parents when we returned to Memphis. Memphis! Mary Lindsay trained horses, gave riding lessons on a horse ranch in the country, and we rented a cool old farmhouse behind the stable. After living on Miami Beach, we swore never to live in town again. The ranch had a manmade lake and tenant house, complete with an old black tenant, Chicks, who had stubs for fingers on his right hand and ran the local Saturday night craps game. Our old rental house had a screened-in porch. I strung a hammock and spent many happy hours in it. In Miami I wrote in my journal, "If you want to sing a country song, it would help to live in the country."

Here I was.

I struggled with the solo artist concept. I had forgotten what I wanted to do. Wexler expected to produce my record in Muscle Shoals. I wanted to record in Miami with Tom Dowd producing. I knew the Flyers would play their guts out.

In an early attempt to mix my ethnic roots, I recorded the blues song "Messing with the Kid," and a country ballad, "Louise," with the Flyers in Miami. One blues, one country song, but still no clear direction. Utley and I had written a New Orleans–sounding tune, "The Judgment," about Nixon and Armageddon. I'd cut it if I could get a handle on it. Jerry Jeff Walker had turned me onto "Louise," a song about a prostitute's death by Walker's teenage bandmate, Paul Siebel. To me it represented the recent suicide of Mike Alexander, the drug-map hustler who first told me about Duane Allman. Facing another stint in a Texas prison, he blew his brains out with a shotgun at the Alamo Plaza on Summer Avenue in Memphis. "Louise" still makes me think about Alexander.

Mary Lindsay and I tried to start a family, but she was having trouble. Her female plumbing reacted to withdrawal from birth control pills. She bled. She was brave. It scared the crap out of me. She bought a horse but was too sick to ride it. I was so worried I had furniture-throwing fits. Her body was attacking her. I felt helpless. Her moron doctor should have been parking cars. Finally, on a day I was scheduled to play a typical festival gig, Mary Lindsay was admitted to the Baptist hospital, where a ruptured cyst was removed along with her right ovary. She had been bleeding to death and had shrunk to little more than a skeleton. After the operation, life returned to her body, the mischievous magic light came back into her dark brown eyes.

In Memphis, performance artist Randall Lyon and Lee Baker, with his re-formed monster blues-rock band Moloch, had come up with a post-blues concept festival, the Dream Carnival. We performed at the Peabody Hotel's Plantation Ballroom, my first public appearance upon my return. Sid Selvidge and I each played solo. Randall put together a pantomime troupe to perform with Moloch and old bluesmen Furry Lewis and Bukka White. Jimmy Crosthwait performed his infamous puppet show, "Iom Dode," with the melting-face clown and the immolating monk, that he had done at the Electric Circus psychedelic nightclub in New York. After the Market Theatre, Jimmy went to New York, where he entertained Andy Warhol, the Rolling Stones, and Jimi Hendrix. Muddy Waters described the Electric Circus as a lot of "blinkin' blinkin' jivin' jivin' shit."

The show featured amoebas swimming in a petri dish, trying to find each other, create life, and erupt into three-dimensional reality. It had started long ago, that rainy night at the Shell when ex-slave children met fledgling flower children and both changed forever, for better or for worse.

After Mary Lindsay's health crisis, I dove into my album project. In desperation I drew on my Baylor Theatre exercises, and constructed an art object on our dining room table. The table had teeth marks on the legs from my boyhood companion, Doodles. Faint imprints of ancient homework and space cartoons were barely visible on the polished surface. My grandparents had bought it on their honeymoon, just after the turn of the century. At my parents' home it was my cave, playpen, place of refuge, as well as the scene of nightly conflict. Now, a ridiculous figure constructed from the dried-out stump and root of a long deceased, middle-sized tree sat on it, like one of my mother's seasonal centerpieces. The object consisted of the body and the neck of a Turkish hookah pipe from a Coral Gables head shop. A horned goat's skull perched atop the pipe's bowl, which was inverted on the stump. In front, like a medieval knight's shield, was a bumper medallion from the Chicago Motor Club. I stood before my nature object's hollow empty eyes during the long nights I nursed my wife.

I started to see a pattern, if not a prevailing theme, of my record. My working title, "So Ready from the Creeks," was a line from hipster philosopher-comedian Lord Buckley's treatment of Robert Service's "Shooting of Dan McGrew." His description of an avenging angel fit my impressions of Miami.

I was falling like a rock into our new country lifestyle. I took long walks in the pasture, stared at the sunset's reflection on our lake, and enjoyed long and fruitful naps in the clover and cool moss by the dam.

> Even though you may know that career burnout is real,
> You don't think it will happen to you until it already has.
> Fourteen albums in six months
> To the unending nightmare
> Of Sam the Sham.
> Psychodrama,
> Drugs,
> Betrayal,
> Divorce,
> Nameless outside presences
> Unknown and unknowable.
> A game of tug
> Of war
> With all the pull
> On the other side
> Of the rope. It's a simple
> Fact of life
> You don't get
> Hot without burning.
>
> I was charcoal.
>
> But ever so slowly
> The internal embers
> Started to smolder.

My chops were pumped. My edge was razor sharp. My creative instincts were at a peak. If I focused, flipped it over, and played the conflict's negative power to a climax in the studio, I would have a record. One night while my wife slept, fueled by a small handful of Mandrax, I "walked out" my rhythm. As I stumbled around the pasture, literally falling on my face, I saw tiny glowing objects in the grass. I lay on my stomach, and watched little glowing spots start to move; it's the first and last time I would see tiny glow worms. I watched the creatures crawl slowly through the dewy pasture turf. My brain opened up. I thought of a song I performed in high school, The Nightcaps' "Wine, Wine, Wine," a hard-rocking screamer that I could get my teeth into, that would showcase the band's strength, and give me a chance to use the power of personal style, like I had with Ronnie Hawkins. It was the beginning of a record. There is power in faith and I was a true believer. I had no question about the future. I was locked into the moment. I booked my album session at Criteria with the Dixie Flyers, Albhy, and Mac Rebennack, a.k.a. Dr. John, the Night Tripper (probably the funkiest of white men).

Back in Miami I had a beachside room at the Thunderbird. I ordered a Singapore Sling, kicked back on my private balcony, and watched the almost full moon over Biscayne Bay, anticipating my very own Monday with the Dixie Flyers.

It used to be my job to worry about the band on Monday mornings. I had to wonder if McClure had returned from Memphis and his melodramatic wife; if Charlie had been arrested and/or how hungover he would be; if Slamming Sammy was on a tourist fishing boat, as he had been when Aretha landed at the studio. It was no longer my job to worry about these things. I didn't give a shit whether the weekly checks were late again. I was the FUCKING ARTIST this time around and Bo Diddley is taking three breaks! I was ready for Freddy and loaded for bear. Move over, Elvis. Little Jimmy is coming through!!!

It was a typical Dixie Flyers Monday. Tom Dowd was super friendly, over the top in his overly optimistic way. Charlie never took his shades off. Mac Rebennack, in a beret and with a rag around his neck, played guitar and puked in a wastebasket. Naturally, McClure was right in the pocket. We tried to record "Sanctified," the tune Bob McDill and I had written and pitched to Wexler. We didn't get a cut. I told Dowd, "It's the full moon fucking with us. We'll be okay tomorrow."

Dowd shook his head, not accepting my lunar phase theory. I could not have been more pleased. I had the band on edge, where they were best. Mac Rebennack was a treasure trove of funk and groove. I got serious. "We are obviously vulnerable at sea level," I added.

Tuesday, in the full moon's glow over Miami, we cut "Wine, Wine, Wine" and "Strength of Love," the Elvis-like ballad John Hurley and Ronnie Wilkins had demoed at old Ardent. I stood in the vocal booth in true artist fashion and sang as Albhy played the biggest triads he could manage on Studio B's grand piano. "Aretha loves that piano, baby," Wexler said.

I hated that piano. It sucked, always tuned sharp, as if we were cutting orchestral classical music at European pitch. Barefooted, Albhy used his big toe to make the bottom C note after the bridge. In Memphis I replaced his piano (except for the foot note), as well as Utley's B3. I wanted the sound of Fry's Chickering baby grand and the Hammond A100 with console speakers Booker T. Jones used on "Green Onions." No Leslie speaker. Sam Phillips later said, "Listen to that organ talk."

We got the two cuts. Dowd was so pleased he pushed on, starting to arrange Dylan's "John Brown." We broke before recording it in order to keep it in our brains overnight. On a session like this, where tension was high, dream work was critical.

I wanted to cut "The Judgment," the song Utley and I had written about Nixon, but I could only barely play the song in the key of C, which was too high for me to sing. Showering at the Thunderbird, I wondered who I was kidding. Dr. John was capable of killing the song in B flat, making it considerably easier for me to sing. It was a decision beyond ego. Mac Rebennack chewed it up and spit it out, playing how the piano sounded in my dreams.

On the original demo, cut in the key of C, Charlie hit one single solitary note in the outro so sweet and so sad the band stopped playing. With the key lowered, Charlie missed the transposition, and bent the string in tune on every note. He never captured the magic note, but he made a valiant effort. Again Dowd was happy.

We recorded the Bob Dylan antiwar song "John Brown." McClure composed a truly remarkable bass pattern, sliding up and down. Dowd plugged him into a Leslie cabinet and mic-ed it in stereo. It was brilliant. Freeman played a swamp guitar pattern that sounded like Dr. John, forcing Mac to play something even farther out. I did the song as a recitation, like Tex Ritter's "The Phantom White Stallion of Skull Valley." Tom wanted me to recite across the bar lines. I didn't understand what he meant until years later.

Wednesday we cut "Wild Bill Jones," taken from traditional sources by Bob Frank, my old buddy at the Market Theatre. I really got a piece of it, giving it a Jerry Lee Lewis/Gene Autry feel. Charlie passed out in the booth with his acoustic guitar. Dr. John played electric. You can hear his amp in the process of dying. The next day it didn't turn on. I got my best piano performance on "John Brown," since I was following Mac on "The Judgment."

The next day we cut "Lady from Baltimore" and Blind Willie's "If I Had My Way," with another spectacular performance by T. Tommy at his best. I was done and more than happy. I gave the band Friday off, and returned to Memphis to finish up at Ardent.

Dowd was not crazy about my taking the master tapes to overdub unchaperoned, but gave in. I cut several experimental tracks at Ardent with Teddy Paige and Jimmy Crosthwait. "Oh, How She Dances" came from my old folk act. Finally, I cut Furry Lewis's "Casey Jones" with Tarp Tarrant on drums, the brilliant Travis picker Gimmer Nicholson on electric guitar, and a younger musician, Ken Woodley, playing Fender keyboard bass. Richard Rosebrough engineered. Several prominent drug dealers seldom seen in public were hanging out. As we finished the first and only cut, Ricky Ireland walked into the control room, hit the talkback, and said, "That's the closest thing to real music you've played in years." Compliments from Ricky are rare.

I returned to Miami for my vocal overdubs with Dowd, and to fill him in on the new tracks. I had done background vocals with Mary Unobsky, Ginger Holliday, and the one-of-a-kind Jeanie Green, girls who had sung on *Elvis in Memphis*. I love to overdub professional background vocals, male or female, black or white. It's like doing horn parts. Black males, white females, that's my favorite; Elvis's choir in reverse. The girls dress and get their hair done for the session. They gossip, pop bubble gum, and pretend to "really like" the songs, moving in and out on the microphone like they're making love. They hold out their vibrato, throbbing like Bo Diddley's tremolo, like angels in a strip joint. Mary wore a black lace brassiere under her see-through brown gauze shirt, one of the sexiest things I ever witnessed.

Terry Manning played Moog synthesizer gas bombs on "John Brown" and ghostly wind on "Wild Bill Jones." Terry turned me on to a steel player from Nashville. The fiddle player had played with Governor Jimmie Davis back in the day. Dowd liked the overdubs, and admitted I improved the record.

Eric Clapton showed up with Bobby Whitlock, Carl Radle, and Jim Gordon. They were in America for Jimi Hendrix's funeral. During my absence at Criteria they had recorded *Layla and Other Assorted Love*

Songs as Derek and the Dominoes, with Duane Allman on guitar and Tom Dowd producing. Clapton was unhappy with Dowd's mix of the record, and Dowd asked me to give up my studio time for the remix. I agreed and hung around. The rest of the band went to the funeral but Eric stayed. Soon Duane Allman showed up. It was hardcore. We did some heavy hanging out. After the second night, I careened from wall to wall, right to left, down the corridor from the elevator, trying to get back to my hotel room. I hid my gold tooth slide-over and my golden frog pinky ring from imaginary interlopers before passing out, unsure if I'd wake up. I woke, but never found my gold tooth or my ring.

The next morning at the studio, while Clapton was waiting for a limo to take him to the airport, we recorded a version of "Mean Old World," with Clapton and Duane playing double slide and me on piano. It appeared years later in a box set with my piano credited to someone else.

As payback for the unused studio time, Atlantic flew Mary Lindsay in and put us in Clapton's suite at the Thunderbird. We had a ball. The first afternoon in the studio, I stood at the mic ready to sing. Dowd said over the talkback, "Dickinson, there's somebody on the phone who wants to talk to you. Some friend of yours."

It seemed odd, but I walked into the control room, and took the telephone from Dowd, who grinned like a 'possum.

"Yeah?" I said.

"'Ello, Jim. This is Mick Jagger." He had called the studio, and Dowd didn't know what to do so he called in "The Kid!"

We made dinner plans for Wexler, Dr. John, Jagger, and his not-so-secret paramour, a South American goddess, Bianca. A limo picked up wife and me at the Thunderbird, and took us to the Marco Polo. We met Wexler and Dr. John in the lobby. Mick walked up, all smiles. I introduced him to Mary Lindsay. He bowed deeply and introduced his soon-to-be bride Bianca, exotic as a silent movie siren, thin to the point of being hollow-cheeked. Dark skin and raven hair, she looked like a gypsy princess or the Queen of the Nile. Her mouth was huge.

We walked toward the Hump Room's roped-off door, and heard blind Clarence Carter and his band doing "Dark End of the Street," the Dan Penn/Chips Moman song James Carr made famous. Jagger said, "Oooooh, that's my favorite song. Hope he does it second set."

We got celebrity seating down front. Bianca sat across from me with Mick next to her. We ordered margaritas and Singapore Slings. Clarence Carter was led to our table after his set. He genuflected and kowtowed to

Wexler and Dowd, displaying snowy white teeth in a blind man's insincere grin. Bianca ate a double order of French fries, on which she squeezed fresh lime juice. I tried it later. It's pretty good.

We stayed through the late show and left around two a.m. Jagger prowled the lobby like a kid looking for mischief. Two plump, overdressed, bejeweled, blue-haired women looked at us in disapproval. Jagger gave them the evil eye and commented, "These women look like hookers to me. Say, Dickinson, you want a couple of hookers?" I declined. As we passed the mortified matrons, Mick bowed and tipped an imaginary bonnet. We slipped into the Miami night.

Mary Lindsay wrote an account of the evening, which *Rolling Stone* published verbatim in "Random Notes." Wexler was pissed; the Stones deal with Atlantic was not official yet. I shifted the blame to Charlie Brown, who willingly took the heat. Wexler didn't buy it. He said, "Baby, you seem to be developing a flair for publicity." It was about to backfire.

I did an unforgettable interview in a local underground newspaper published by a friend from my creative writing class at Memphis State. I committed the unforgivable sin of talking money and telling a heretofore-unspoken story about Aretha Franklin and a bottle of pickled pigs' feet in the Fontainebleau Hotel's lobby. A local enemy or coward with an ancient ax to grind made it appear on Wexler's desk in New York.

Jerry went ballistic. "Baby," he screamed into the telephone like a furious Elmer Fudd. "Awetha will be vewy upset." It took time and Bob Dylan's intervention to get him over it. I limped along on the shit list. Things went downhill fast. At Atlantic I received the "Jessie Davis treatment," named after the guitar player I had met in Hollywood and with whom I later recorded on a never-released Taj Mahal session. He was the most hated artist at Atlantic. I was a close second. I had never dealt with anyone lower on the totem pole than vice presidents. Now I was talking to the maintenance man. I had dug a deep hole I needed to fill.

I enlisted Herbie O'Mell to straighten out my artist contract and legal situation with Atlantic. Herbie went to high school with Elvis, who had performed at sock-hop dance parties put on by Herbie and DJ Dewey Phillips, dispelling the longtime myth Dewey did not know who Elvis was the first time he played "That's All Right, Mama" on WHBQ. Herbie had been a nightclub entrepreneur and professional manager of Chips Moman and Jerry Lee Lewis. Now he ran TJ's, a popular nightclub and after-hours hangout, and ran gambling junkets for area high rollers, taking groups to Vegas, Monaco, and hot spots around the world. Herbie probably had the fullest knowledge of show business of anyone in Memphis. His hands were full with my situation.

Herbie shared a small office/demo studio with Dan Penn, the producer/songwriter from Muscle Shoals who moved to Memphis after successfully producing the Box Tops' "The Letter" at American Studio. Penn was fascinating. Born one day after I was snatched from the womb, we were nearly astrological twins. He had one of the best white-boy country soul voices around. I believe his second Box Tops album, *Cry Like a Baby*, was Memphis pop production at its best, on a par with the great *Dusty in Memphis*, recorded by the same cast of characters in the same time period. Those two records are as good as it gets.

Our friend, writer Lisa Robinson, set me up with a New York session so I could mend fences. Her then husband, Richard Robinson, produced a San Francisco group for Buddha Records. The Flamin' Groovies, a roots band with a little rockabilly and a little Detroit garage mixed in, wanted me to do keyboards. Lisa also booked interviews for me, including one with *Esquire* magazine. Mike Golden, my friend from a Nashville whorehouse, had moved to New York City and was driving a cab. I could crash with him.

I bought a white sheepskin rock-star knee-length coat at the local high-end hippie shop. With my "lizard king" black leather pants and steel-toed work boots, I went to New York to, in Jimmy Reed's immortal words, "try and rescue my wounded career." New York was in the middle of a garbage strike. Mountains of multi-substance frozen grunt lined every street. I thought of the spring thaw. I did damage control at Atlantic's New York office. Danny Fields gave me the best advice: "Spend as much money as you can. Don't turn the record in until you have to. Re-mix, re-master. The more expense the company puts forward, the more work the record gets at release. The deal you have is golden. Work it if for all you can get."

The Flamin' Groovies session entailed two parties, one in the control room with Richard Robinson, the producers, Lou Reed, a midget, and many other near-greats and ingrates hanging on and hanging out. I befriended the band, and we held our own party in the tracking space. I overdubbed on tracks that ended up on *Teenage Head*. But an interesting thing happened when everybody was too drunk to have an agenda. We jammed on fifties hot instrumentals like "Rawhide" and "Rumble." I think I sang "Red Hot." I'm not sure. At one point the guitarist (either Cyril Jordan or Tim Lynch), who had spoken not a word all night, rolled a studio mic out of the piano and delivered a sizzling version of "Ubangi Stomp" that would have tickled Warren Smith's black heart.

When the smoke cleared, I went to Michael's apartment and slept under the sink in my White Mountain goatskin coat and steel-tipped work boots. I did my best interview with *Esquire*'s Lenny Kaye, who went on to fame with Patti Smith. He liked the story of Dishrag and was musician enough to understand the genius of the codes. The story was never written. He was mugged on the way home. The mugger grabbed the tape recorder. Lenny chased the guy hollering, "Give me the tape!"

My Atlantic record was frozen in time. Dowd sent me an unbelievably bad mix. Atlantic refused to pay for a color photo of me on horseback in the pasture by the spirit pond in front of our place. I changed the name to *Dixie Fried*, after a track I cut on which Lee Baker and I played everything, and Memphis songbird Brenda Patterson did background vocals.

I put on my father's white linen wedding suit and took my grandfather's gold-tipped cane in hand. Jere Cunningham, my high school friend and now Stax's official photographer, shot a two-click black-and-white picture of me standing on my ancient family carriage stone, which read DICKINSON. I love the photo. It represents an idea from *Homer Price*, a children's book from my morbid past.

Out of money, I took the acetate of the mastered Dowd mix to John Fry. I had nothing left to count on but my fingers. I had done what I could do with what I had to do with, as Larry Raspberry once told me. Fry listened to my acetate. He avoided commenting on Dowd's miserable mix but got his point across: "I believe that's the worst tape-to-disc transfer I've ever heard."

John did his best. His mix captures perfectly the music's feeling and spirit, the image, the original concept twisted into a new and revealing shape. But *Dixie Fried* entered suspended animation.

Chapter 42

HOLLYWOOD BE THY NAME
(1972)

Donna Weiss, my buddy from the White Station High School talent show, was in L.A. trying to be a songwriter. She had been one of the four female background singers in the super big deal Mad Dogs and Englishmen Joe Cocker tour band, fronted by Leon Russell. Later, she would sing the haunting background on Bob Dylan's "Knockin' On Heaven's Door." She sent me a plane ticket to Hollywood to help her rehearse and record a vocal supergroup of the other girls from the tour: Donna Washburn and Claudia Lennear, "Brown Sugar" herself. Ironically, the Dixie Flyers were in L.A., rehearsing as backup band for Rita Coolidge, the fourth and final lady from Leon's traveling circus. I had cut Rita's demos at Ardent when she first came to Memphis, before she took up with Don Nix, and later, Leon. She hired the Dixie Flyers after Atlantic fired them.

I still wasn't crazy about air travel, but flew west. Donna had a ranch house in the Valley. My first night in town, the three girls and I crashed the Rita and Flyers rehearsal on A&M's back lot, the old Charlie Chaplin studio. When we walked in, time froze. Sammy Creason ran to the nearest telephone. He called his bitch wife and gleefully reported, "Jim Dickinson just walked in with three Hollywood hookers." She called Carol Freeman, who naturally called my wife, who told me about it the next day. I could see the smile on Mary Lindsay's face when she relayed the tale to me. "Some people never learn," she said.

We rehearsed the killer trio. It's impossible to describe the beauty of Claudia Lennear singing "Blue Kentucky Girl." The girls sang bluegrass harmony as Donna Weiss played acoustic guitar. Unfortunately, Claudia developed vocal nodes and a stupid white manager jammed it all up. We were close, but the group went south. Rita and the Dixie Flyers were jealous. Leon was pissed. My trip was cut short by a big earthquake. Donna had an abundance of sleeping pills and I slept through it. I returned to

Memphis. Later I cut Claudia Lennear's only solo record for Warner Brothers, but as they say, that's another story.

Dan Penn was producing an album on Ronnie Milsap, the blind phenomenon from Herbie O'Mell's nightclub in Midtown. Herbie was Milsap's manager and had made a sweet deal with Warner Brothers Hollywood rather than Nashville, making it a pop signing rather than country. We started in Nashville at Quadraphonic, a new studio owned by the rhythm section from what I considered Penn's high school band, Mark V., Jerry Carrigan, Norbert Putnam, and David Briggs were now Area Code 615, the hottest rhythm section in Nashville (named after Nashville's long-distance code). Penn hired Eddie Hinton from Muscle Shoals for rhythm guitar and James Burton, Elvis's sideman, on lead guitar. Briggs was on keyboard. Ronnie Milsap also was a remarkable piano player. I played xylophone in the hallway, like on the Ivory Joe Hunter session with Chips. Things were tense. Milsap was nervous as a horse before the race. He didn't like Hinton's vibe and fired him on the spot. I heard him ask Herbie who was playing vibes. I figured that was it. Herbie said, "That's Jim Dickinson."

Ronnie said, "Oh good! He's a musical genius."

Right on, Ronnie. I stuck to the session like glue.

Penn didn't like the restrictions of the union clock Nashville session. He especially didn't like cutting off at midnight. Penn, Eddie Hinton, and I stayed in the studio into the small hours. On the second night, as Penn ran two-inch tape onto the floor, protesting working in Nashville, someone knocked on the door. Two vagabond pilgrims in dusty hats and cowboy boots stepped in, looking like they had just gotten out of prison. The big one had two missing fingers and a greasy brown paper sack. Dan knew him: Billy Joe Shaver. He wanted to play the demos of a new song. Billy Joe pulled a tape out of the greasy sack. Dan put it on the reel-to-reel. We listened to song after song. It was killing me. The tunes were pure gold, as real as death and raw as chitterlings. Funny, sad slices of life, as they say in Nashville. Penn rewound the tape, and shook his head. "I don't know, Billy Joe. I just don't hear 'em." I couldn't believe it. Billy Joe was crushed. He and his little buddy stumbled into the night. Six months later every song Billy Joe played for us was on Waylon Jennings's *Honky Tonk Heroes*, by far the Outlaw movement's greatest album.

We left Nashville and headed for Muscle Shoals. Penn was pissed off. His old high school buddies had treated him badly.

The Muscle Shoals leg of the session was a safari. We took our female companions—Dan's wife, Linda, and Herbie's girlfriend, Baby Jane (with her obnoxious toy poodle)—and joined Mary Lindsay. Herbie hired a bodyguard, Campbell Kensinger, an East Memphis tough guy I knew from my days as a Toddle House cowboy, to care for the women while we worked. Kensinger, the firstborn son of a rich, socially prominent family, was one of Herbie's bouncers from TJ's. His mother collected dolls on an enormous scale; his father had trained him in seven martial arts from childhood, like Doc Savage, the pulp fiction hero of old. His father had taken him at age twelve to a New Orleans whorehouse, and gotten him his first tattoo, a cartoon buzzard on his upper left arm. Down the road Campbell made a wide left turn, and ended up facing prison time at age eighteen. He chose a Marines enlistment instead, and was a special training instructor in Hawaii to the Alpha 66 troops who had failed the Bay of Pigs invasion. Asked if he had been at the invasion, Campbell replied, "shooting women and children." I think we got along because he remembered me from his past.

Our safari was to meet Chris Ethridge, the Flying Burrito Brothers' legendary bass player, when we got to Muscle Shoals. Ethridge, whom Willie Nelson nicknamed Easter, was originally from Meridian, Mississippi, and as a teenager had gone to L.A. with Johnny Rivers. He played on Rivers's huge hit album *Live from the Whiskey A Go Go*, and many other Hollywood hits. He was a great guy. We hit it off instantly. Penn used the rest of the Muscle Shoals Swampers' current lineup. Tippy Armstrong and "Lightnin'" Wayne Perkins were on guitar; the superhuman Roger Hawkins was on drums. Penn's writing partner, the incomparable Spooner Oldham, played extra keyboard. Spooner is hard to describe: a soft-spoken southern gentleman who plays piano like no one else on Earth. My personal theory is that Spooner is an angel.

The session went much better in the old coffin warehouse where I recorded with the Stones. Penn felt at home and was treated like royalty. The girls were having a big time. Linda Penn was a pistol. She and Dan were high school sweethearts; she could match him blow for blow. She loved to drive her new Cadillac with a fifth of Wild Turkey between her legs (she has since cooled her act).

We went back and forth between Muscle Shoals and Memphis. Easter Ethridge and his wife, a waitress from the Troubadour in Hollywood, went with us. She taught Mary Lindsay and Kensinger to embroider. I vividly recall Campbell, tattooed and in motorcycle boots, with the girls in a Muscle Shoals laundromat embroidering blue jeans.

As the album session wound down, we did a couple of days at American with Chips Moman's rhythm section: Bobby Woods, Bobby Emmons, Gene Chrisman, the great Reggie Young, and my old buddy, bassist Tommy Cogbill. Penn cut "Sanctified," my song that McDill and I had pitched to Wexler. Dan wanted me to play piano. I was nervous. Bobby Woods outplayed me hands down. I managed to hold my own. The Thomas Street boys were courteous and friendly (believe me, they didn't have to be). I greatly appreciate professional courtesy.

We went to Muscle Shoals Sound for the mixdown. The local studios were holding the first Muscle Shoals music celebration, a self-promotional honors ceremony attended by locals and members of the industry nationwide. Of course Wexler was there; he was closely associated with Muscle Shoals Sounds and Rick Hall's Fame Studios, where he had first cut Aretha Franklin and Wilson Pickett. We had trouble getting hotel rooms, so Herbie and I doubled up.

Memphis songbird Brenda Patterson came to meet Wexler as a potential producer of her first album for Epic. I didn't know Brenda well, but greatly respected her vocal chops. She came from rural North Arkansas and, with the Coolidge sisters, Rita and Priscilla, had been a regular fixture at the Little Abner Roadhouse. Brenda had an odd request. She wanted me to attend the meeting with Wexler and sit between them. Brenda had good instincts. Jerry hit on her repeatedly and shamelessly. I helped Brenda ward off his advances; she later asked me to produce.

My first Hollywood session, and I got my new friend Chris Ethridge to book the musicians. Whenever anyone mentioned Duane Allman, Chris replied, "Man, you gotta hear Ry Cooder." It became a joke on the Milsap session. I told him, "Get me your Ry Cooder and Jim Keltner too." Chris complied gladly. I booked "Lightnin'" Wayne Perkins and Dr. John. We recorded in the world-famous Capitol Records studio and had rooms at the Continental Hyatt House.

I worked hard on the material. I had a tight arrangement of "Wallflower" by Etta James (commonly known as "Dance with Me, Henry"), a jacked up version of "Jesus on the Mainline," and "Big Party," an obscure Stax record produced by Chips Moman that featured the amazing Lowman Pauling–like guitar of my old American cohort, Clarence Nelson.

The first night went almost too well. Dr. John did not show up, so I played piano. We cut the Jerry Lee Lewis "B" side, "The End of the Road." Cooder was amazing. Tall and tanned from the sun, he claw-hammer finger-picked the guitar like a mountain banjo, suspending the 4 chord over the blues progression and adding the 5 of the 5 as an extension of the typical blues progression in ways I had never heard.

There are special people. You see it in their eyes. They shine. They sparkle. You see through to their souls. Some are politicians, some are religious leaders, and some are everyday people on the street. You can see it in the way a musician holds his instrument, the way he carries it into a room, and walks—what we called "their rhythm" at Baylor. Ry was special.

Ry asked me to join him for lunch the next day. He picked me up at the Riot House in a vintage woody station wagon, and we drove to an over-lit fern bar for a lunch of tuna and bean sprouts on hippie bread. He discussed music and stared over my shoulder. I couldn't figure it out. He seemed to be talking about working together. I thought he was discussing going on the road and playing live. It was like the Mar-Keys European tour goes Hollywood. I was trying to figure out how to turn him down and still be cool. Then I realized he was talking about production. He wanted me to produce him. What do you think I said? He had worked with Van Dyke Parks, but they were having creative differences. Cooder had to run it by A&R at Warner Brothers, but as far as he was concerned we were ready to rock.

I still had Brenda Patterson to finish. Epic vice president Larry "the Fed" Cohn—he had worked at the FBI—was in charge of the project. He wanted to do the producing and hung around too much. The Columbia engineer wouldn't smoke dope while Larry "The Fed" was present. He had gotten some killer blond hash from Andy Williams.

Second night I launched into "Wallflower (Dance with Me Henry)," with an elaborate rhythm guitar part based around open D tuning. Cooder, it turned out, played in open G, an old banjo tuning. He was happy to accommodate and eager to learn.

I had booked the mighty Jim Keltner, but he had cancelled at the last minute to play George Harrison's Concert for Bangladesh. What could I say? Ethridge made a good call: Johny Barbata, from the Turtles' road band. Johny was hard in the pocket and tried to do whatever I gave him.

"Wallflower" was a handful. I could see Cooder respond to the beat. I played acoustic guitar with a matchbook to get the Bill Black dumbstrum sound. I tried to get Barbata to skip eighth notes on the chorus. He said, "Let's get this fast. This is the beat that Muddy Waters was looking for for forty years. I'm just barely holding onto it."

As we played back the master take, I got the message Dr. John was at the door. The studio go-fers were afraid of him and wanted me to go get him.

Mac stood in the hall, draped in beads and chains and a long embroidered robe, full New Orleans voodoo regalia. He carried a long crooked walking stick and his gris gris bag. I tried to steer him into the studio, but he veered into the green room and sat at a table. He fished for something in his bag. "Want to show you my union card" he said, calling it his "onion card." In vain, I assured him such a formality wasn't necessary. As he fumbled thru God knows what in his bag, he asked "What do you want me to play?"

"Piano," I replied but he didn't seem to hear.

"I could play bass," he said.

"I've got Chris Ethridge playing bass."

He pulled out his passport and showed me it, shaking his head. "Naw, that ain't it," he said, "or I could play guitar-a." He added the extra "a" to guitar. Mac speaks his own mixture of New Orleans patois and hipster bop talk, not always easy to understand.

"No Mac, I've got Ry Cooder and Wayne Perkins on guitar."

"Well, what do you want me to play then?" he asked.

"I thought you could play piano, Mac. That's what I wanted," I said.

"Well, do you want me to play FULL piano?" he asked. "'Cause FULL piano, that's my thing. And I got to get double scale if you want me to do my thing."

It was a negotiation. "Sure, Mac," I said. "Whatever you want." He pulled a light green credit card–looking object, his New Orleans Musicians Union card with nothing on it but his name and the musical notes from the treble clef spelling out "Way down yonder in New Orleans" in musical notation.

Mac sat at the piano. I played the Stax recording of "Big Party" by Barbara and the Browns over the studio speakers. Cooder marveled at Clarence Nelson's unique guitar. Chris Ethridge made a chord chart. Brenda worked a handheld 57 microphone, which seemed to relax her. Studio tension was considerable. She sang her ass off. You could hear pain in every note, the pain of a poor Arkansas girl who had married a truck driver at fourteen to escape a life of picking cotton.

Then I did a stupid thing. I asked Mac to count off the tune and instantly realized the mistake I made: it was his intro to play and did not need a count-off. It was not cool. Mac paused for a minute. Then he did it. The song was in 12/8, so Mac counted "1-2-3, 4-5-6, 7-8-9, 10-11-12." He stopped a full count and began the intro, which was all him anyway and required no count. He ate the song up. Cooder converted the Clarence Nelson licks into bottleneck and tore thru them. Brenda delivered the song about seduction and betrayal beyond anything I had heard her do. When it was over, Dr. John disappeared before I could discuss another selection. I learned from Leland Rogers not to be greedy. Enough is enough. I called the session for the night.

The third night we recorded Memphis Minnie's "In My Girlish Days" and the hymn "Jesus on the Mainline." That was all I had. We returned to Memphis with hopes of finishing the record in a more familiar environment.

In Memphis, we cut "I Smell a Rat" with Lee Baker and Jerry Patterson, the drummer from the Pharaohs. Patterson was the best white boogaloo player I had heard. I overdubbed the Bar-Kays horn section on "Wallflower." It was my best horn chart ever, building to a syncopated horn breakdown into the last verse. Larry "The Fed" said the horns were out of tune and finagled the project away from me. I had done the heavy lifting. He ended up pulling the record from Epic, and using it to get a job at the brand new Playboy Records. He put the Tower of Power snow-white horns on "Wallflower," playing whole note pads where my Afro-Cuban syncopated dance pattern had been. He ruined the record. "Big Party," probably Brenda Patterson's best vocal performance, was never released. I lay up in my Collierville horse ranch and licked my wounds. Freeman and his wife, Carol, came out for a weekend of commiseration. Atlantic had rejected the Dixie Flyers' instrumental album and fired the band, which was talking to Rita Coolidge about touring.

Charlie and I took the remaining blue mescaline, four or five hits each. We were flying. Charlie pulled out a bag of coke he said Terry Johnson found in a deserted house down in the ghetto. Freeman often had some elaborate story regarding the source of drugs. In the grip of a psychedelic substance, we thought the cocaine crystals seemed alive, a cubist animation of maggots crawling on the old piano bench where Charlie dumped the drug. "That's the devil," Freeman stated. "That's a pile of dope," I replied. "Let's take it." We did.

We ran out of pot in the middle of the second night, and called Bobby Ray Watson, who grew his own. Bobby Ray showed up with a bale of Delta Delight, and we kicked back.

We sat on my screened porch. The Sunday sun rose over the neighbor's pasture. A thick fog drifted up over the spirit pond and started to glow pink. "You got to admit," I said, "this is pretty cool."

Charlie did not like admitting he was high. "It's pretty good," he replied. "What would make it better?"

"Well," he said, "Fred Ford could be standing in that pasture wearing a white tie and tails and a full Indian headdress, playing 'Green Dolphin Street.' That would be cool." I had to admit he was right.

Charlie didn't like primitive country blues. He said, "I just don't get your Furry Lewis. He's just a nice old black guy that can't play anymore. I don't get it." I told Bobby Ray to take Charlie to see Fred McDowell. They split. My wife was asleep. I sat there and vibrated.

We were broke. The Atlantic deal was sweet, but it ran out. Local work was sketchy, and Memphis music industry types were not used to me being home. Our telephone was broken and had not rung in weeks. In the middle of our mescaline weekend, with my head full of the coke from the deserted ghetto house and Bobby Ray's Delta Delight, out of nowhere the phone came to life. *Ring!* I was shocked and almost didn't answer. "Is this Jim Dickinson?" Affirmative. "This is Ry Cooder," the voice at the bottom of the well stated. "What's it going to take for you to come to Hollywood and finish up this damn record?" He had fired Van Dyke Parks. I tried to clear my mind. I said the only thing I could think of. "Fifteen-hundred dollars and a plane ticket." "Done," he replied.

A few hours later the phone rang again. It was Charlie Freeman. First thing he said was, "OK. I get it. This guy is the real thing. I understand the blues in a whole new way." I heard Fred McDowell playing guitar in the background. Charlie spent the better part of the day and night listening to the blues master.

I still feared flying, but sucked it up. Cooder met me at LAX. I settled into a bungalow at the Miramar Hotel in Santa Monica, walking distance from Cooder's minimalistic little house on Ocean Way. It was simple, filled with light, air, and a slightly oriental flavor. His wife was an artist. He had rented a spinet piano so we could work in his living room. We shared interest in more than a few obscure records, especially Joseph Spence and the collection *Sounds of the South*. I studied his books, his hanging art, and his speech. I wanted to think with his mind. We ran over various pieces before going into Warner Brothers' Amigo Studios. Cooder's co-producer was a short Jewish guy roughly my own age, Lenny Waronker, a vice president of Warner Brothers, head of the A&R department, and son of the infamous president of Liberty Records from the fifties. We worked with Lee Herschberg, a contemporary of Tom Dowd, with a light touch and an easy way.

The first order of business was overdubbing my piano on an existing track, replacing three tracks of Van Dyke piano. He had a unique con-voluted technique that sounded like turn-of-the-century light-classical parlor piano. Stephen Foster meets Jelly Roll Morton. Lenny instructed me to "play across" a dramatic stop in the middle of the brilliant Jim Keltner drum track. Ironically, the song was "Money Honey," my debut from the Blue Ridge talent show long ago. It was in B flat. I killed it, blast-ing across the drum stop like a runaway train. Lenny said, "That was the best save I've ever heard." The drum track sounded like it was exploding, like the drummer had kicked the drums down a long, winding stairway. I loved it. Keltner, the jazz drummer I had met at Leon Russell's home studio on my first trip to L.A., had taken a giant step into rock 'n' roll; it was like working with a drum god. Imagine Coltrane's drummer, Elvin Jones, playing with Muddy Waters in Sonny Boy Williamson's band with Chris Ethridge pumping the bass.

Milt Holland, the greatest white musician I've worked with in the stu-dio, played percussion. I'm reluctant to use racial differentiation but there's that magic difference, the light shuffle over a tight four on the floor that defines rock 'n' roll, that separates old-world Europe from swing funk of Mother Africa. I'd heard stories about Milt from Donna Weiss and Mary Unobsky, who had worked with him on a John Hurley session. Tiny, white-haired, and Jewish, he had been the fourth man in the otherwise black Nat King Cole trio in the forties and fifties. He traveled the world in search of master musicians from whom he could learn and obtain exotic percussion instruments. He laid down a groove like nothing and no one else.

My second task was tracking live from the floor. I figured I was still auditioning, which Charlie Freeman had taught me not to do. This was worth it. The song was an old New Lost City Ramblers regular, "Taxes on the Farmer Feeds Us All." I suggested a pump organ or harmonium. Cooder was delighted. We rented the antique instrument from the newly formed Studio Instrument Rental Company; it was delivered within the hour.

Probably the best rhythm track I ever produced was an old Wilson Pickett semi-ballad, "Teardrops Will Fall." It took me a day and a half to get the near-perfect basic form from Ry, Keltner, and Ethridge. After I overdubbed my own convoluted part, Milt played vibraphone on a huge African thumb piano, with a Communist Chinese gong at the end. I loved it. I put the female trio of Donna, Donna, and Claudia on background voices, though Ry much preferred male singers in the old quartet tradition. Ry and the girls' voices had a dramatic contrast. "Billy the Kid," a chestnut from my old Tex Ritter album from childhood, was another standout track on *Into the Purple Valley*. Throw in a little Joseph Spence, some Blind Willie and Woody Guthrie, and we had an album. Cooder was happy and that wasn't easy.

I was in. Lenny took me to the Warner Brothers A&R office, and introduced me to Teddy Templeman and Russ Titelman, Ry's brother-in-law.

I walked around Santa Monica, getting familiar with the territory. I found a health food store with a good tuna and sprouts sandwich, and a pretty good record store where I picked up a cassette copy of Miles Davis's *Sketches of Spain*, which became my traveling companion for the next thirty years.

I liked walking down the Santa Monica Pier at the end of Route 66, as far west as you can go without getting very wet. Cooder kindly gave me Raymond Chandler paperbacks, which I read for the second time with a new, more native viewpoint. My cabana cottage at the Miramar had a forties black-and-white film noir atmosphere, stronger than the reality of 1971.

After a few weeks the company flew Mary Lindsay out, and we enjoyed the full services of Warner Brothers' cordiality. While I worked, she toured the movie lot and wandered the mall. On the weekends we lay on the beach. The ocean was too vile to swim in, but we tried. We spent Thanksgiving with old friends John Hurley and Ronnie Wilkins, who had a Hollywood hill-hugger up on Mulholland Drive with the full-tilt Hollywood view. Thanksgiving is big in Nashville, and John and Ronnie, old-school Nashville cats, put on the big turkey dinner with a trash fire roaring in the gas log fireplace. Donna Weiss was there, and would soon pen "Betty Davis Eyes," changing her life.

Mary Lindsay returned home as we began the mixing process for *Into the Purple Valley*, Cooder's second album. The record company wanted Cooder to tour in support of the new release. He was to open for and back up Arlo Guthrie, Woody's son. It was several years after his monster antiwar hit "Alice's Restaurant." I surprised myself by agreeing to play piano in the touring band. Ry was delighted. I enlisted Gimmer Nicholson from home to play bass. He was friends with Arlo's sideman and sidekick, guitarist John Pilla. Ry hired the fabulous "Johnny C" Craviotto from Santa Cruz, the drummer who played with Cooder on the Jack Nitzsche–produced soundtrack for the Mick Jagger movie, *Performance.* He played on "Memo from Turner," a track most people assume is by the Stones. We rehearsed at Arlo's farm in upstate New York.

I sat at Guthrie's baby grand piano in his living room and looked out the window as snowflakes fluttered to the ground. This is the way to make a record, I thought. All we needed was a Scully eight-track with mic-in capability. Charlie Freeman often fantasized about building a studio at Jack's Boat Dock in the Ozark Mountains. Why endure the sterile environment of a modern recording studio when it would be easy to record in a scenic rural setting? I watched the snow; a single cow wandered past the window.

Arlo was managed by Harold Leventhal, the Godfather of fifties folk music. He had managed Arlo's father. His befuddled nephew, Bruce, was our tour manager. We were to travel like hippies in a VW van. I didn't see that working.

Sure enough, the first gig was a cluster fuck. The van was too crowded. Johnny "C" and I volunteered to ride with Bruce in the equipment rent-a-truck. The vehicle was equipped with a speed governor, which Leventhal blew out. The truck lunged down the highway, accelerating up to 45 mph and then shutting off. Bruce was losing it. Craviotto began speaking in leaping octaves, like Hylo Brown, the bass player for Flatt and Scruggs. Johnny sounded like a man doing two voices in a ventriloquist act. "Oh, Jimmy, what are we gonna do?" the "Fabulous Johnny C" octavated. When we arrived at the gig, Arlo, Cooder, Pilla, and Gimmer were faking it with half the equipment and PA. We finished the gig, and retreated to Troy, New York, where we had motel reservations.

After a restless sleep, I stumbled downstairs in the morning, headed for the coffee shop for a universal motel breakfast. As I walked into the restaurant, someone called out "Hey, Memphis!" Blues legends Bukka White and Mississippi Fred McDowell were sitting behind platters of fried eggs and hash brown potatoes.

"What are you doing here, Little Muddy?"

"Same as you, Bukka. Playing my gig."

The men laughed. I walked over to Cooder. "Goddam!!" he stammered. "That's fucking Fred McDowell!" "And Bukka White," I added. He grumbled something I didn't get. He seemed pissed they knew me.

The tour went into high gear. We abandoned the VW van, and per Arlo's request, flew long hauls and traveled short runs in limos. Arlo sensed my reservations about flying. He told me, "Don't worry as long as you're with me. I know I won't die in a plane." Silly as it seems, that did it. I overcame my fear of flying.

We had a Halloween show at the Main Point in Philadelphia, one of the route's famous venues. We would do two sets with a crowd change. We were in the basement when Dickey Betts and a couple of guys from the Allman Brothers road crew came in. I could see something was wrong. Dickey said, "Duane is dead." Killed in a motorcycle accident. He loved to ride his cycle naked, high on LSD. "Just like Captain America," he used to say. One more rounder gone.

We toured down the East Coast to Miami, where we had three days off. It was the middle of nowhere and my thirtieth birthday. I made a deal with Charlie Brown for his little cottage in Coconut Grove and flew my wife down for the layover. We were trying to get pregnant, with no luck.

We worked our way westward. Our tour manager, whom we lovingly referred to as "Loose Bruce," had two solutions to any problem. If it couldn't be fixed with duct tape, he had a gallon-sized bottle of Quaaludes. Cooder, otherwise drug free, didn't count Quaaludes as drugs. Gimmer and I saved our doled out Qs, and gave them to Ry. One night in Austin at the Armadillo World Headquarters Auditorium Ballroom, Ry took a few too many. Thank God we played the show sitting down. I doubt he could have stood. He played up to six solo verses instead of one in a very loose, freewheeling set. After that, no more Qs for Mr. Cooder. He told me later he was hallucinating, watching a railroad train plow thru the venue. It was a great show, the run's highlight.

Warner Brothers had an Arlo session scheduled with Lenny Waronker producing. The session featured Cooder, Keltner, R&B master Wilton Felder on bass, Spooner Oldham on B3, and me. We cut "The City of New Orleans" in three takes. Everyone knew if we went to cut seven or eight, we would have something special. Arlo wouldn't go. He had what he wanted on the third take. It was his biggest record since "Alice's Restaurant."

After a hiatus in Hollywood, I flew to Palm Beach, Florida, to play what would be the best gig of my life. Alan Pariser, Bonnie and Delaney's manager and the possessor of the best pot I ever smoked, specially grown for him in Mexico, was marrying the Dixie Cup heiress (some kind of minor English royalty). On the *Tonight Show* Johnny Carson referred to it as "the wedding of the season." Pariser booked a lineup of blue-eyed soul musicians, most of whom knew each other by reputation only. The band was Chris Ethridge, Jesse "Ed" Davis on guitar, Dan Penn on vocal and acoustic, Jimmy Karstein from J.J. Cale on drums, Jimmy "Junior" Markham on harmonica and vocal, and me. Markham was the notorious "Jimmy" from Leon's famous song "Shootout on the Plantation" and a front man bandleader of the old school.

We converged at the Breakers, a super classy hotel resort on the ocean, where the waves broke against the walls. An upscale joint not used to the likes of us. We all looked pretty bad. Chris and I arrived together. Dan and Herbie O'Mell showed up in motorcycle jackets and cowboy hats. Herbie sported a Mickey Mouse T-shirt from Disneyland. Jesse "Ed" had the sleeves torn off his blue jean jacket and looked like he was ready for the ghost dance.

We hauled in our gear and set up in the ballroom. Jesse was thirsty. He walked to the long mahogany bar and asked a bartender doing nothing for a highball. The bartender didn't respond. Jesse reached across the bar, picked him up by his white starched jacket front, and said "I want a fucking drink!" The tone for the evening was set.

We didn't make a set list, and played songs everybody knew. After "Hold On, I'm Comin'," Jesse said, "I get it. The old frat party songs." Sure. Dan, Jesse, and I alternated singing leads and harmony. The crowd, classy upper-crusters unaccustomed to the world of rock 'n' roll, loved it. They wanted to know who we were. Herbie told somebody we were Crosby, Stills, and Nash. They didn't know any better. He told somebody else we were the Doobie Brothers. The Duchess of somewhere was there in a sequined silver evening gown and diamond tiara in her silver-blue lacquered hair. At one point, I saw the Duchess doing the dirty bop with a twelve-year-old boy in a tuxedo. She was smoking a huge cigar and having the time of her life. Jerry Wexler, the only industry type in attendance, stood on a chair, holding up a microphone to capture the event for posterity. After the gig Alan Pariser gave us each a plane ticket to wherever. I returned to L.A. to rejoin Cooder and Arlo for the remainder of the tour.

We broke for the holidays. Thanks to pressure on Wexler from Sam Phillips, Atlantic finally released *Dixie Fried*. By this time I was so immersed in Cooder's career that I hardly noticed. I did some press but played no gigs in support. There was talk of another Arlo/Cooder tour in the spring. We were booked into the Troubadour in Hollywood. Ethridge was back in the band. I was always glad to work with him. Chris and his wife lived in a camper-back pickup truck in the parking lot of the Troubadour, where she worked as a waitress. We split the bill with Todd Rundgren, "the Duke of Puke," opening one night and closing the next. *Purple Valley* was well received and reviewed. *Billboard* said, "Waronker and Dickinson have created a timeless masterpiece." But it was a musical enigma, a modernized history of American roots music painted in broad strokes and basic colors.

The Stones' *Sticky Fingers* finally came out with my credited performance on "Wild Horses" and Cooder's classic slide on "Sister Morphine." Also there I was in *Gimme Shelter*, the Maysles brothers' documentary of the Altamont concert. I was creeping up the ladder of my fifteen minutes of rock stardom.

Part II

EPILOGUE AND THE
BIBLICAL CHAPTERS

EPILOGUE

The South is haunted. The air hangs heavy with ghosts. Graveyard angels guard the burial of dead warriors immortal in defeat. There is something in the land that fights back the invasion of crawling civilization, something in the nature of time itself that resists thieving hands of greed and self-serving morality.

Modern Mississippi reverberates with human history. Shotgun shacks and silver metal cotton gins go the way of the lowly mule, sexless beast of burden replaced by soulless progress tractor, strip mining the black dirt in parallel lines of row crop conformity, bending the rhythm of the land to the stubborn will of corporate agriculture, evil grandchild of the plantation.

The music comes up out of the dirt-peyote drum circle to slave son in sharecropper shape note harmony from the minstrel past—Pentecostal plow boy and hillbilly blues on the midnight radio from Memphis, Mecca of the new religion and its liberating freedom.

Sing the phantom song. Let the music become a magic current, a path from the holy past to the unknowable future. Honeysuckle sweet with the mule kick of moonshine lightning, original sin to Sunday salvation. Sons and daughters of Mississippi sing out. The world listens.

The blues changed color in the fifties, became rock 'n' roll, and was re-discovered by a new generation in the sixties and infused with a jolt of fresh life energy from the international youth culture. Although diluted, defused, and sometimes misdirected, the blues have survived.

The first Memphis Country Blues Festival in 1965 created a symbiotic community of the remaining first-generation blues musicians of the Mid-South and the Memphis music underground bohemians. From the Insect Trust and the Electric Blue Watermelon to Panther Burns and Mudboy and the Neutrons, hipsters, hippies, and punk rockers have been interacting with Delta and Hill Country masters and the flow has gone in both directions. As surely as R. L. Burnside and Junior Kimbrough can be heard in Tav Falco and Jon Spencer Blues Explosion, the chaos of the "crazy white boys" has crept into the sound of every artist on Fat Possum. I perceive this to be a miracle.

There has always been racial spillover, the two-culture collision of black-white co-fusion like Paul Burlison from the Rock 'n' Roll Trio playing with Howlin' Wolf on West Memphis radio. Charlie Feathers and Junior Kimbrough.

Hank Williams Senior learned guitar from Tee Tot, a street musician. In the fifties I learned from Butterfly Washington and Dishrag. Furry Lewis taught Lee Baker. As Mississippi Joe Callicott taught young Kenny Brown, as Otha Turner taught my sons, the tradition transcends color lines and generational boundaries. It's a complicated process of push and pull from both sides of an ever-changing line in the sand. Each time it is crossed the line blurs and becomes less important. This mutant musical form traces the history of one of the most significant changes in the social fabric of the Western world in the twentieth century.

The blues roll on—father to son, hand to hand. My sons, Luther and Cody, spent their early childhood in Fayette County, Tennessee. Our farmhouse was next door to a honky tonk juke joint named Parks's Spot and an African American Missionary Baptist Church. My boys heard the music in the night. They witnessed baptismal services held in our neighbor's stock pond. The other end of our gravel road was in Marshall County, Mississippi.

As civilization and suburban squalor closed in on our home-school hideaway, our family moved to north Mississippi. The first time our two family bands played the Southern Heritage Music Festival, my sons met Otha Turner. Luther had focused on the slide guitar of Mississippi Fred McDowell, Otha's neighbor who used to pump gas at Stuckey's. They developed an amazing relationship. It wasn't long until Luther and Cody found R. L. Burnside, Junior Kimbrough's Juke Joint, and the younger generation of Hill Country musical families. The North Mississippi Allstars were the result. After family friend Kenny Brown took Luther as third guitarist on tour with R. L. Burnside, the boys hit the road. The North Mississippi Allstars make no claim to being a blues band. Something happens when white boys play the blues. Rock 'n' roll. Whether it's Elvis, the Beastie Boys, or Mudboy.

This music has come to symbolize freedom the world over and to illustrate the interracial brotherhood of man.

POSSILUTELY BONNAROO

We met the Allstars' tour bus at dawn, Dickinsons, Burnsides, Turners, stage crew, film crew, and a Mississippi lawyer on the road to Bonnaroo Music Festival. We were two races and three generations met in brotherhood to rob the train. R. L. Burnside, godfather of the Hill Country blues, was in good spirits, wearing a ball cap that stated "Retired" instead of his usual "Burnside Style" slogan. His wife, "Big Mama," was ready to party. Across the state of Tennessee our Silver Eagle flew the backroads, avoiding the traffic of 95,000 souls descending on the little hillbilly community to celebrate life and music.

Mid-afternoon the bus parked at Motel 6, and we shuttled to the festival grounds, parting a sea of humanity, and chilled backstage until showtime. In the hospitality tent a retro-hippie girl came up and asked Mary Lindsay if she was really Mountain Girl. Mary Lindsay thanked the girl for the compliment as her stunning white curls blew in the Tennessee breeze. We were treated like royalty. The festival promoters had constructed a wooden throne with a red velvet seat and and padding for R. L. Burnside to sit on stage as we played. My sons' band, the North Mississippi Allstars, joined by R. L. Burnside, his son Duwayne on guitar, three other Burnsides, four surviving members of Otha Turner's Rising Star Fife and Drum Band, keyboardist Jo Jo Herman from jam band giants Widespread Panic, and myself on keyboard. We stomped ass. We rocked like a La-Z-Boy recliner on the back porch of some backwoods double-wide. This was my son Luther's vision realized. A traveling Dream Carnival of Southern culture and lifestyle evolved from the Memphis Country Blues Festival of the sixties, the punk rock/blues fusion of the nineties, Otha Turner's goat Bar-B-Q picnics, and Sunday nights at Junior Kimbrough's Juke Joint, joined on stage by Chris Robinson of the Black Crowes as a shadow of things to come.

Chainsaw guitars scream in the night and church organs moan like a fat country girl in love. Drums thunder-roll like the circus from Hell is coming to town. Sounds echo like two freight trains trapped in the same tunnel, running head-on for Doom's Day. Phantom riders patrol the darkness, sabers drawn. Trembling in their ancient graves, the Confederate dead lie restless for Revelation's final conflict.

The set was like Mudboy on steroids. Field drummers and Hill Country rappers mixed in gumbo jam of Jujuka warriors at the rise of the full moon. The audience snake-danced in full-trance bond—like a huge, sweating reptile god, undulating to the magic of the cumulative song of the South—beyond time and space. Song from my own musical past handed down father to son in the way of all true knowledge in culture.

Later I was told the temperature reached 140 degrees on stage. I hid behind Cody's drum riser on one of the trio songs and smoked a joint, trying to hang on. I made it through the insanity of "Snake Drive," the encore, and staggered off stage like a drunken sailor on sea legs. I stumbled into one of the courtesy tents and that's when the lights went out. As Philip Marlowe once said, "A black hole opened up at my feet and I fell in. There was no bottom."

When I semi-woke up, Luther and some of the Turner crew were dumping me into the back of a pickup truck. Luther knew not to take me to the festival medical tent, which was full of brown acid and ecstasy O.D. victims. Thank God.

"I've been carried out of better places than this," I told my son. They took me back to the motel room. I drifted in and out of so-called consciousness. A bottle of water and a fat joint later I thought I might live. I lay there with my wife watching me like a mother hawk protecting her nest. We were supposed to meet Bob Dylan at his stage after our set. Sorry, Bob. Not today.

Ghosts floated around the bed. Time shifted and swirled together in a milieu of past memories. Laughing phantoms circled me like the trinity of Christmas spirits that haunted Scrooge, both Ebenezer and McDuck. Alec Teal was there dressed up for a funeral or a Saturday night craps game. My mother and father joined together in the eternal night of death. Randy Moore danced by singing, "Once in Love with Amy." The organ grinder and his tireless monkey with Two Ton Baker playing a piano on bicycle wheels. Froggie the Gremlin, "Li'l music box is running down. KERPLUNK!" Captain Midnight trying in vain to decode the chaos of my gradual return to so-called reality. "What's the matter, Dickinson? Can't you take it anymore?" They chanted in unison. "Getting old?" Charlie Freeman drifted by wearing his sunglasses, headed for the vocal booth to pass out. Time passes and people change. Junior's Juke Joint has burned to the ground. The world of Otha Turner is passing away, but it will not be gone. Like images scratched on the back wall of some prehistoric cave, the reverberations communicate with the future—immortality—an act of communion. I have stared into the void of the pit, like Knox Phillips at Mark Unobsky's funeral, looking down into the empty grave. What if anything waits on the other side of the closed door?

As the Allstars' tour bus rolled back to Mississippi on what seemed like an endless journey, I was afraid to sleep. Afraid of not waking up. It seemed to take forever to skirt the perimeter of Memphis, the ancient City of the Dead.

Finally at dawn my wife and I walked up the driveway too narrow for the Silver Eagle, up the gravel path to our two-trailer home in front of the red barn studio compound. I felt the weight of my history pressing down on my aching body. Our basset hound greeted us with tail wagging and huge ears flapping, asking, "Where have you been?" Where indeed? Glad to be alive and home, I slept.

> Blind Lemon and the Hook Man
> stand face to face and fight it out
> face to eyeless face
> misty formless ghosts of the early greats.
> The campfire flickers spinning shadows into the dark.
> Ghosts whisper.
> Too briefly trapped in the moment, we struggle to understand
> In Faith we sing
> play your song forever
> no surrender–no defeat
> As surely as the dawn there comes another night
> Reach out in the darkness

In the Coldwater bottoms, prowling panthers scream like a woman. Secret bones of ancient outlaw phantoms stir in the thick, red mud of the riverbed, as grandfather catfish circle silent in the green water. Evening rain has left the air thick and steam rises from the dark, mossy earth, bubbling up from what unknown caverns. The sun bobbles like a fishing cork, as it sinks into the cypress trees along the levee and finally slips below the horizon. It's showtime.

Time, the River, and Death—

The river moves in mystery, carrying unknown substance beneath the surface, under the level of perception. Perfectly as the patterned maze of night sky moves, destruction, creation, and infinity, ordered to filter out never too much or too little, retaining the balance like the river secrets deep in the mud, order is kept below the currents. Meaning moves noiselessly, slowly without wave. Time is around us, singing, and behind us pushing, the past urging us on.

Deep down in the earth in each place the old has lost its battle to the invader change. Every tribe builds its monuments to fall; its fortress for the fight each has lost in turn. Graves remain where the new stand on the old. Each old thing not gone, built on another's foundation, deep down in the earth. Change is slow.

Time passes like the river, moving and flowing the same muddy way. Out across the night, there is no past. Everything is still. The ghost of time walks infinitely and settles in the about-to-happen. The same unending path. No one can tell when the present slips into the past. Each man is alone within himself for a brief life, as every father before him. Each holding a piece and passing it on. Each the possessor of time, only that long within his soul-skin. Coming to the end, stained and broken, he will wring out the life with his own hands, with no answers given. The heart breaks from the not-knowing.

Below the stream of all that time, I was carried along slowly, barely moving, time swirling all around. There under the shift, order carries us, not too fast or too slow, until death comes on wings of crepe and performs its endless ritual duty.

The body feels the pain, but it is the soul that cries out. What I have tried to express—the output—music, painting, theater, written experiences . . . ? Has it all in the long run only added to the frustration? Still looking for the outlet. The point of departure. There have been moments. Long passages with Mudboy or with Cooder and Keltner. Nights on stage with the phony Mar-Keys or Sleepy John Estes. Recording with Dylan or the Stones. Shouldn't they add up? Or do they subtract? Is there less every time rather than more? Where does the payback come from? What recharges the battery? Is rebirth the miracle of nature or just another trick to keep you going until you finish the game? Winning? Nobody wins. It's not a race. Things you accomplish fade out into the horizon, to a point in space that becomes unperceivable, nothing. Fate, Karma, God's plan, dumb luck. Call it yo' ol' Mama if you want to. It's like looking for meaning in the stars. Surely it's there, but no one understands it. Chinatown. To read the secret message you must know the code, have a decoder badge. Three up and four down. Major triad over an octave. That's the only place I know to start.

It's not that I know; it is that I no longer wonder.

Long is the road to the true Negro bebop. Unending is the search for Blind Lemon. Out there somewhere some sad kid pours his broken life into a three-chord pattern. Some white kid discovers Howlin' Wolf. Some black kid finds the Doobie Brothers. Keith Richards goes to Switzerland to change his blood and snort the ashes of his father up his nose. You got to finish the set. If it comes down to it, what better way to go than the Country Dick Montana exit? Teenage Steve saved the bass sax for his last note. I have taught many a young musician—my sons included—to play every note like it's your last one because one of them will be.

> Life and love are short and sweet with a long reflection
> Pour some on the floor for fallen friends and heroes—
> Soldiers of the Cross. +
> Chariots a comin' to carry us home
> or is it the hoodoo wagon
> the drinks are on the house

I still dream about music. Every morning I wake up with a different song in my head. I used to relive my gigs in dreams the night after the job. My dreams have become more abstract. I have a recurring ending that fits into always changing dreams about a Mar-Keys gig. It takes place downtown on what is now South Bluff. It is in the early sixties and Charlie Freeman and I are walking across the old Red Ball Truck lot toward Hopie Brooks's orange "A" frame by the Illinois Central train tracks down by the river. Sometimes Packy is with us. We are looking for something. We are distracted by a fat gypsy man with a bullwhip who is chasing two runaway elephants. The gypsy has a black handlebar moustache and looks like one of the Mario Brothers. The elephants look like Dumbo's mama. The gypsy chases the elephants to the railroad bridge north of the Harahan. He is yelling curses and laughing. The fleeing elephants climb up into the steel girders of the old bridge, wild-eyed and trembling in fear. I wake up hearing "I Remember You" by Charlie Parker.

Message from the last of the great barbarians:
The world of Otha Turner will pass away but it will not be gone. Like the scratches on the rock wall of some prehistoric cave, the recordings we leave behind are our immortality, our means of communicating with the future. This is an act of communion between you and us. Though we are separated by time and space as you listen, we are together.

"I will lift up mine eyes unto the Hills . . ."
Psalm 121

INDEX